3

2

4

14

12

15

16

300 m

THE DOUBLE LIFE
OF FIDEL CASTRO

THE DOUBLE LIFE OF FIDEL CASTRO

MY 17 YEARS AS PERSONAL BODYGUARD TO EL LÍDER MÁXIMO

JUAN REINALDO SÁNCHEZ

WITH AXEL GYLDÉN

ST. MARTIN'S PRESS 🏵 NEW YORK

www.stmartins.com

Endpaper map of Cayo Piedra courtesy of DigitalGlobe.

Designed by Steven Seighman

Library of Congress Cataloging-in-Publication Data is available upon request.

ISBN 978-1-250-06876-7 (hardcover)
ISBN 978-1-4668-8828-9 (e-book)

St. Martin's Press books may be purchased for educational, business, or promotional use. For information on bulk purchases, please contact the Macmillan Corporate and Premium Sales Department at 1-800-221-7945, extension 5442, or write to specialmarkets@macmillan.com.

First published in France under the title *La vie cachée de Fidel Castro* by Editions Michel Lafon.

First U.S. Edition: May 2015

10 9 8 7 6 5 4 3 2 1

To my mother, the light of my life, shining example of humility and devotion. To my children Aliette and Ernesto. To their mother, who so often played the role of father in my absence. To my uncle Manuel, that "dad" who passed on extraordinary ethical values to me. To my grandparents Ángela and Crespo, guardian angels whose presence I still feel. To my grandchildren and to my brother. And to all those who supported me in difficult times. May God bless you all.

CONTENTS

1.   Cayo Piedra, the Castros' Paradise Island   1

2.   Juan Sánchez, Fidel's Bodyguard   19

3.   The Castro Dynasty   42

4.   The Escort: His Real Family   67

5.   Guerrilla Fighters of the World, Unite   93

6.   Nicaragua, Fidel's Other Revolution   114

7.   Fidel in Moscow, Sánchez in Stockholm   129

8.   Raúl's Clan   139

9.   A Mania for Recording   152

10.   The Venezuelan Obsession   170

11.   Fidel and the Tin-Pot Tyrants   180

12.   A King's Ransom   193

13.   At Death's Door   205

14.   Fidel, Angola, and the Art of War   217

15.   The Ochoa Affair   228

16.   Prison and . . . Freedom!   245

Index   265

THE DOUBLE LIFE
OF FIDEL CASTRO

CAYO PIEDRA, THE CASTROS' PARADISE ISLAND

Fidel Castro's yacht was sailing in the Caribbean Sea, on the azure waters off the southern coast of Cuba. We had weighed anchor just ten minutes earlier, and already white dolphins had come to join us. A school of nine or ten of them were patrolling on the starboard side, right next to the hull, while another group streamed along in our wake, thirty yards or so behind the rear port side, looking for all the world like the motorized escort of a head of state on an official visit.

"The reinforcements are here—you can go and relax," I said to Gabriel Gallegos, pointing to the multitudes of dorsal swimmers cleaving through the water at high speed.

My colleague smiled at my quip. Three minutes later, however, the unpredictable creatures changed direction and moved off, disappearing into the horizon.

"No sooner do they get here than they leave! What lack of professionalism . . . ," Gabriel joked in his turn.

Neither of us were strangers to professionalism. We had both joined the personal security team of the Commander thirteen years earlier, in 1977—and in Cuba, nothing is more "professional," more developed, or more important, than the protection of the head of state. Fidel had only to make the smallest excursion out to sea on a simple fishing or underwater hunting trip for an impressive apparatus of military defense to come into operation. And so *Aquarama II*—Fidel Castro's yacht—was unfailingly escorted by *Pioniera I* and *Pioniera II*, two powerful, virtually identical fifty-five-foot-long speed-boats, one of which was kitted out with every form of medical care to deal with the slightest health problem that might arise.

The ten members of Fidel's personal guard, the elite corps to which I belonged, were divided among these three vessels—just as, on land, we were divided among three cars. The boats were all equipped with heavy machine guns and stocks of gre-nades, Kalashnikov AK-47 rifles, and ammunition to prepare us for any eventuality. Since the start of the Cuban Revolu-tion, Fidel Castro had lived under the threat of attack: the CIA admitted it had planned hundreds of assassination attempts, involving poison or booby-trapped pens and cigars.

A bit farther out to sea, a lifeguard patroller was also deployed, providing maritime and air radar surveillance of the zone and with instructions to intercept any boat coming within at least three sea miles of *Aquarama II*. The Cuban air force was also in-volved: at the Santa Clara air base, sixty or so miles away, a fighter pilot in combat gear was kept on red alert, ready at any moment to jump into his Russian-made MiG-29 to take off in less than two minutes and reach *Aquarama II* at supersonic speed.

It was a sunny day. Nothing surprising about that: it was the middle of summer, 1990, the thirty-second year of the reign of Fidel Alejandro Castro Ruz, then sixty-three years old. The Berlin wall had come down the previous autumn; the American president George W. Bush was getting ready to launch Operation Desert Storm; and, for his part, Fidel Castro was sailing toward his private, top-secret island, Cayo Piedra, on board the only luxury yacht in the republic of Cuba.

Put into service in the early 1970s, *Aquarama II* was an elegant vessel with a ninety-foot white hull, a larger replica of *Aquarama I*, the racing yacht that had been confiscated from someone involved in the regime of Fulgencio Batista—overturned on January 1, 1959, by the Cuban Revolution that had begun two and a half years earlier in the jungle of the Sierra Maestra by Fidel and sixty or so *barbudos*. In addition to the two double cabins—one of which, Fidel's, was equipped with a private bathroom—the vessel could sleep twelve other people. The six armchairs in the main sitting room could be converted into beds, and there were two berths in the radio communication room and four more in the cabin reserved for the crew, at the bow. Like all self-respecting yachts, *Aquarama II* had all mod cons: air-conditioning, two bathrooms, a toilet, television, and a bar.

Compared with the playthings of contemporary Russian and Saudi Arabian nouveaux riches who cruise across the Caribbean or the Mediterranean, *Aquarama II*, however handsomely done up in its "vintage" style, would probably seem outdated. But in the 1970s, 1980s, and 1990s, this luxury yacht, entirely decorated in exotic wood imported from Angola, could hold its own against any of those moored in the marinas of the Bahamas or Saint-Tropez. Indeed, it was even clearly superior, because of its power. Its four engines, given to Fidel Castro by Soviet leader Leonid Brezhnev, were identical to those fitted on Soviet navy patrollers. At full throttle, they propelled *Aquarama II* at the phenomenal, unbeatable speed of forty-two knots, or about forty-eight miles an hour.

Hardly anyone in Cuba knew of the existence of this yacht, its principal mooring a private creek invisible and inaccessible to ordinary mortals on the eastern side of the famous Bay of Pigs, around ninety miles southeast of Havana. Since the 1960s, Fidel's private marina had been hidden here, in the middle of a military zone and under close surveillance. The site, named La Caleta del Rosario, also housed one of his numerous vacation homes and, in an extension, a small personal museum devoted to Fidel's fishing trophies.

It was a journey of forty-five minutes from this marina to Cayo Piedra, the paradise island—a trip I made hundreds of times. Each time I was struck by the vivid blue of the sky, the purity of the water, and the beauty of the marine depths. As often as not, dolphins would come to greet us, swimming at our side and then leaving again as their fancy took them.

We often used to play a game of seeing who could spot them first: as soon as somebody shouted *¡Aquí están!*, there they were. Pelicans would often follow us from the Cuban coast as far as Cayo Piedra, and I loved watching their heavy, rather clumsy flight. For other members of this Cuban military elite, that crossing of three-quarters of an hour constituted a welcome break; protecting someone as demanding as Fidel required constant vigilance and afforded no opportunity for letup.

El Jefe (the chief), as we privately called him, generally stayed in the plush atmosphere of the main sitting room, usually in his large black CEO chair, in which no other human being had ever sat. A glass of his favorite drink of whisky on the rocks in one hand, he would immerse himself in the summarized reports from the intelligence services, go through the review of the international press prepared by his cabinet, or scour the telegrams from Agence France-Presse, Associated Press, and Reuters.

El Jefe would also take the opportunity to discuss current affairs with José Naranjo, the faithful aide-de-camp known as Pepín, who shared almost every moment of his boss's professional life until his death from cancer in 1995.* Dalia was also there, of course. Mother of five of Fidel's children, Dalia Soto del Valle was the woman who had secretly shared his life since 1961—although Cubans did not learn of her existence until the 2000s. Finally there was Professor Eugenio Selman, Fidel's personal doctor until 2010, whose professional competence and political conversation were highly valued by *El Comandante*. The primary function of this elegant, considerate, and universally respected man was obviously to look after the chief's health—but Fidel's personal doctor also ministered to the whole of his entourage.

Guests—company directors or heads of state—rarely came on board. On the few occasions when that occurred, *El Comandante* would invite his guest to accompany him onto the upper deck from where the panorama of the Cuban coast, particularly the famous Bay of Pigs from which we had just set sail, could be admired. As *Aquarama II* moved off, Fidel—an incomparable raconteur—would regale his guest with an account of the

---

*He was replaced by Carlos Lage, who ultimately became vice president of the Council of Ministers and executive secretary of the Council of State, before being dismissed in 2009.

tragic landing on that now celebrated bay. We would watch him from the rear deck, launching into great explanations and pointing to different parts of that swampy, mosquito-infested area, a teacher dispensing an open-air history lesson to his erstwhile student.

"You see down there at the bottom of the bay—that's Playa Larga! And there, at the eastern entrance to the bay is Playa Girón! It was there that at exactly 1:15 a.m. on April 17, 1961, the contingent of fourteen hundred CIA-trained Cuban exiles landed in an attempted invasion aimed at overthrowing the nation. But nobody here surrenders! The people resisted heroically, and after three days the invaders had to withdraw to Playa Girón and hand over their weapons."

Planned by Dwight Eisenhower and launched at the beginning of John F. Kennedy's presidency, the operation was a complete fiasco: 1,400 members of the expeditionary unit were taken prisoner and 118 killed. On Castro's side there were 176 deaths and several hundred injured. It was a total humiliation for Washington. For the first time in history, "American imperialism" suffered a crushing military defeat, and Fidel Castro established himself on the international stage as the undisputed leader of the developing world. Now openly allied with the USSR, he could deal with the great powers on an equal footing.

Fidel was without question a participant in History with a capital H, and his captive guest, standing on the top deck in the scorching heat, would be hanging on to his every word, enthralled. It was almost as though he, too, were now experiencing history firsthand; he would doubtless treasure for the rest of his life the memory of those few hours of holiday spent on Fidel Castro's yacht. Afterward, the two men would return to the sitting room to join Dalia and Professor Eugenio Selman. That is when the captain of *Aquarama II* slowed down and the water began to turn emerald green: we were approaching Cayo Piedra.

Few people know that, in an irony of history, Fidel Castro indirectly owed the discovery of this vacation home to the American invasion launched by JFK.

In the days following the failed Bay of Pigs landing in April 1961, Fidel was exploring the region when he encountered a local fisherman with a wrinkled face whom everyone called *El Viejo* Finalé. He asked Old Finalé to give him a tour of the area and the fisherman immediately took him on board his fishing boat to Cayo Piedra, a little "jewel" situated ten miles from the coast and known only to the local inhabitants. Fidel instantly fell in love with this place of wild beauty worthy of Robinson Crusoe and decided to have it for his own. The lighthouse keeper was asked to leave the premises and the lighthouse was put out of action, and later taken down.

In Cuba, a *cayo*—the Spanish word for key—is a flat, sandy island, often thin and narrow. There are thousands of them off the Cuban coast, and many are today visited by tourists and deep-sea diving enthusiasts. Fidel's island stretched over a mile and was slightly curved in shape, oriented north to south. On the eastern side, the rocky coast faced the deep blue sea. To the west, sheltered from the wind, was a fine, sandy coastline and turquoise water. It was a paradise surrounded by glorious ocean, all as virtually untouched as it had been in the time of the great European explorers. Pirates might once have broken their journey, or buried treasure, there.

To be precise, Cayo Piedra consists of not one island but two, a passing cyclone having split it in half. Fidel had, however, rectified this by building a seven-hundred-foot-long bridge between the two parts, calling on the talents of the architect Osmany Cienfuegos, brother of the Castrist revolutionary Camilo Cienfuegos. The southern island was slightly larger than its northern counterpart, and it was here, on the site of the former lighthouse, that the Castro couple had built their house: a cement-built, L-shaped bungalow arranged around a terrace that looked out to the east, onto the open sea. The house was functional and devoid of any showy luxury. Other than Fidel and Dalia's bedroom, it comprised a dormitory bedroom for the children, a kitchen, and a dining-cum-sitting room that looked out onto the sea-facing terrace with its simple wooden furniture; most of the pictures, drawings, and photos on the walls represented fishing or underwater scenes.

From the French windows of this room, to the right, one could see the heliport and about three hundred feet or so further on, the house reserved for us, Fidel's bodyguards. Opposite that was the garrison building that accommodated the rest of the staff—cooks, mechanics, electricians, radio officers, and the dozen armed soldiers permanently stationed on Cayo Piedra. A hangar adjoining the garrison housed a gas storage depot, supplies of drinking water (brought from the mainland by boat), and a miniature generating station.

On the west side of the island, facing the setting sun, the Castros had built a two-hundred-foot-long landing stage. It was situated below the house on the little beach of fine sand that lined the arc-shaped interior coastline of the *cayo*. To allow *Aquarama II* and the *Pioniera I* and *II* to dock, Fidel and Dalia had also had a half-mile-long channel dug; without this, their flotilla would not have been able to reach the island, surrounded by sand shoals.

The jetty formed the epicenter of social life on Cayo Piedra. A floating pontoon, twenty-three feet long, had been annexed to it, and on the pontoon stood a straw hut with a bar and barbecue grill. This was where the family ate most of their meals—when they were not served on board the yacht. From this floating bar and restaurant, everyone could admire the sea enclosure in which, to the delight of adults and children alike, turtles (some three feet long) were kept. On the other side of the landing stage was a dolphinarium containing two tame dolphins that livened up our daily routines with their pranks and jumps.

The other island, to the north, was practically deserted, housing only the guest quarters. Larger than the master's house, this one had four bedrooms and a large sitting room; it also had an outdoor swimming pool as well as a natural whirlpool carved out of the rocks and fed with seawater via a sort of aqueduct cut into the stone that would fill with water with each new wave. The two houses were connected by a telephone line. We would travel the five hundred yards between them in one of Cayo Piedra's two convertible Volkswagen Beetles; a Soviet-manufactured army vehicle was used for the transport of equipment and goods.

All his life, Fidel has repeated that he owns no property other than a modest "fisherman's hut" somewhere on the coast. As we have seen, the fisherman's hut was really a luxury vacation home that involved considerable logistics in terms of its surveillance and upkeep. In addition, there were twenty or so other properties, including Punto Cero, his huge property in Havana near the embassy quarter; La Caleta del Rosario, which also houses his private marina in the Bay of Pigs; and La Deseada, a chalet in the middle of a swampy area in Pinar del Río province, where Fidel went fishing and duck hunting every winter. Not to mention all the other properties reserved, in every administrative department of Cuba, for his exclusive use.

Fidel Castro also let it be understood, and sometimes directly stated, that the Revolution left him no possibility for respite or leisure and that he knew nothing about, and even despised, the bourgeois concept of vacation. Nothing could have been further from the truth. From 1977 to 1994, I accompanied him many hundreds of times to the little paradise of Cayo Piedra, where I took part in as many fishing or underwater hunting expeditions.

In the high season, from June to September, Fidel and Dalia went to Cayo Piedra every weekend. In the rainy season, on the other hand, Fidel preferred the house in La Deseada, where he hunted duck. The Castros would spend the month of August on their dream island. When duty called or a foreign VIP obliged the Commander of the Revolution to go to Havana, no problem—he would climb into the helicopter that was always ready and waiting at Cayo Piedra when he was there and make the return trip, sometimes in one day if need be!

It is extraordinary that I am the first person to reveal Cayo Piedra's existence or describe it. Other than the Google Earth satellite images (in which Fidel's house and the guesthouse, the jetty, the channel, and the bridge connecting the two islands can all be clearly seen), no other photo of this millionaire's paradise exists. Some people might wonder why I didn't film the place myself. The answer is simple: a lieutenant colonel in the security service charged with the protection of an important figure walks around with an automatic pistol in his belt, not a camera slung over his shoulder! What is more, the only person authorized to immortalize Cayo Piedra was Fidel's official photographer, Pablo Caballero—but he was naturally more concerned with photographing the Commander's activities than the landscapes around him. That is why, as far as I know, there are no images of Cayo Piedra or *Aquarama II*.

The private life of the *Comandante* was the best-kept secret in Cuba. Fidel Castro has always made sure that information concerning his family is kept private, so that over the course of six decades we have learned almost nothing about the seven brothers and sisters of the Castro family. This separation between public and private life, a legacy of the period when he lived in hiding, reached unimaginable proportions. None of his siblings was ever invited to or set foot on Cayo Piedra. Raúl, to whom Fidel was closest, might have gone there in his absence, although personally I never encountered him. Other than the closest family circle, in other words Dalia and the five children she had with Fidel Castro, those who can pride themselves on having seen the mysterious island with their own eyes are few and far between. Fidelito, the oldest of Fidel's children from a first marriage, went there at least five times; Alina, Fidel's only daughter born from an extramarital relationship (who today lives in Miami, Florida), never set foot there.

Other than several foreign businessmen whose names I have forgotten and several handpicked Cuban ministers, the only visitors to the island I can recall were the Colombian president Alfonso López Michelsen (1974–1978), who came to spend a weekend there with his wife, Cecilia, around 1977 or 1978; the French businessman Gérard Bourgoin, aka the Chicken King, who came to visit in around 1990 at the time he was exporting his poultry producing know-how to the whole world; the owner of CNN Ted Turner; the superstar presenter of the American channel ABC Barbara Walters; and Erich Honecker, communist leader of the German Democratic Republic (GDR) from 1976 to 1989. I will never forget the latter's twenty-four-hour visit to Cayo Piedra in 1980. Eight years earlier, in 1972, Fidel Castro had rechristened Cayo Blanco del Sur island Ernst Thälmann Island. Even better: in a show of symbolic friendship between the two "brother nations," he had offered the GDR this morsel of uninhabited land, nine miles long and five hundred yards wide, situated an hour's sailing from his private island.

Ernst Thälmann was a historic leader of the German communist party under the Weimar republic, ultimately executed by the Nazis in 1944. In 1980, during an official visit by Honecker to Cuba, the leader of East Berlin gave Fidel a statue of Thälmann. Very logically, Fidel decided to put the work of art on the island of the same name—which is how I came to be present at that incredible scene in which two heads of state turned up on *Aquarama II* and disembarked in the middle of nowhere to inaugurate the statue of a forgotten figure on a deserted island, witnessed only by iguanas and pelicans. The last I heard, the immense statue of Thälmann, six and a half feet high, had been toppled from its pedestal by Hurricane Mitch in 1998.

In fact, the only two really frequent visitors to Cayo Piedra other than the family were Gabriel García Márquez and Antonio

Núñez Jiménez. The former, who spent a good part of his life in Cuba, was doubtless the greatest Colombian writer, awarded the Nobel Prize in Literature in 1982. The second, who died in 1998, was a historic figure of the Cuban Revolution, in which he participated with the rank of captain and in remembrance of which he sported a bushy beard all his life. A respected intellectual figure, anthropologist and geographer, he also belonged to the very limited circle of Fidel's close friends. These two were the main users of the guesthouse on Cayo Piedra.

On Cayo Piedra, wealth did not consist of big houses or yachts in the moorings. The real treasure of the island was its fabulous underwater life. Totally free from tourism and fishing, the waters that stretched out around the island constituted an incomparable ecological sanctuary. Fidel Castro had a personal aquarium of more than 125 square miles right in front of his house! It was an underwater playground unknown to millions of Cubans, as well as to millions of tourists who came every year to take part in deep-sea diving around the *cayos* run by the Ministry of Tourism.

Other than the famous French commander Jacques-Yves Cousteau, who came on a special mission on board the *Calypso* with Fidel's express authorization, nobody else was ever able to marvel at the incredible animal and vegetable treasure house to which he enjoyed sole rights. Moonfish, squirrelfish, catfish, butterfly fish, boxfish, flute fish, trumpet fish, hamlet fish, cardinal fish, striped surgeonfish, pumpkinseed sunfish, tuna, sea bream, lobster—every imaginable variety of yellow, orange, blue, or green fish swam in and out of the red and white coral and the green, black, and red algae. Dolphins, tiger sharks, hammerhead sharks, swordfish, barracudas, and turtles completed the enchanted scene in this silent world.

Fidel Castro was an excellent diver. I am in a good position to know: throughout the years I spent in his service, it was my job to assist him during underwater fishing expeditions—in order, principally, to protect him against attacks by sharks, barracudas, and swordfish. I am sure that many envied me this aquatic mission, much more than my other duties such as keeping his diary or organizing security during his trips abroad. There was no greater privilege for one of Fidel's escorts than accompanying him on his underwater expeditions and I went on many of them. . . . Though he liked basketball and hunting duck, deep-sea diving was his real passion. Fidel, six-foot-three and weighing 209 pounds, had an impressive lung capacity, able to free dive thirty feet below the sea without the least difficulty.

He also had a very particular way of practicing deep-sea fishing. The only thing I can compare it to is Louis XV's royal hunts in the forests around Versailles. At dawn, when the sovereign was still asleep, a search party of fishermen led by Old Finalé would go out to find the places richest in fish in order to satisfy the monarch's expectations. Mission accomplished, the team would return to Cayo Piedra during the morning—Old Finalé still in attendance—where they would wait for Fidel, who rarely got to bed before three in the morning, to wake up.

"So what have we got today?" Fidel would ask before climbing on board *Aquarama II*.

"*Comandante*, skipjacks and dorados should be around. And if we're in luck, lobsters will also show up."

The *Aquarama II* would cast anchor. On board, it was preparation time, and we would get the masks and snorkels ready while Fidel sat, legs astride, waiting for somebody to kneel in front of him to put on his flippers and gloves. When I was equipped, I would go down the staircase first, followed by *El Comandante*. Underwater, I swam at his side or just above him. My working tool was a pneumatic rifle shooting round-tipped arrows that bounced back from their target, acting like punches to the head; they would see off any sharks or barracudas that came dangerously close to Fidel.

I also carried the chief's hunting rifle so that he did not have to weigh himself down with it; when Fidel caught sight of prey and wanted to use the rifle, he would hold out his arm in my direction without looking at me. I knew what I had to do: immediately place the weapon in his hand, ready in shooting position. Fidel would shoot his harpoon and then immediately give it back to me. Whether he hit his target or not, I had to reload the rifle or go back up to the surface to place Fidel's catch in the dinghy floating above us.

When the monarch decreed, we would return to Cayo Piedra. The ritual on our return was immutable. Fidel's numerous catches would be lined up on the jetty and sorted into species: breams together, lobster together, and so on. The fish caught by Dalia, who hunted separately under the protection of two combat divers, were arranged next to them, she and Fidel then reviewing the ensuing feast to the admiring, amused commentaries of their entourage.

"*Comandante, ies otra una pesca milgrosa!* [another miraculous catch!]," I would say, certain that my comment would win me the smiles of the main party concerned as well as of all those present.

Then, the barbecue coals already glowing bright red, Fidel would indicate which fish he wanted grilled immediately; those he was magnanimously giving to the garrison; and those, finally, that he wanted to take in iceboxes to Havana to eat at home within forty-eight hours. Then the Castros would sit down to eat in the shade of the family beach restaurant.

This dolce vita represented enormous privilege compared with the lifestyle of ordinary Cubans, whose already Spartan way of life had gotten considerably harder since the fall of the Berlin wall and the collapse of the Soviet Union. Subsidies from Moscow, which had maintained a certain level of prosperity, had dried up. The Cuban economy, which derived almost 80 percent of its external trade from the Eastern Bloc, was collapsing like a house of cards and households were surviving on the breadline while the GNP had decreased by 35 percent and electricity supplies were seriously inadequate. In 1992, in an attempt to tackle the dramatic decline in exports and imports, Fidel decreed the start of the Special Period in Time of Peace that marked the official beginning of the era of shortages and of mass international tourism.

Until the turning point of the 1990s, I never asked myself too many questions about the way the system operated. That is one of the flaws of military men. . . . As a good soldier, I carried out my mission to the best of my ability, and that was enough for me. What is more, my service record was impeccable: I was a judo black belt, a karate black belt, and a tae kwon do black belt, and also one of the best elite marksmen in Cuba. In 1990 I was declared sniper champion on fixed and mobile targets at twenty-five meters (about twenty-seven yards) in a two-day competition organized by the Cuban Ministry of the Interior. I was even the very first person to be awarded the honorific title of gun expert. At the same time I had earned my master's degree in law and climbed every rung of the hierarchy to the rank of lieutenant colonel. I was given more and more onerous duties—organizing, for example, the security arrangements during the head of state's international trips. Fidel himself was happy with me. More than once during these trips abroad, I heard him say as he walked down from the airplane to the runway, "Ah, Sánchez is here! Everything is in order. . . ." I could say that professionally I had succeeded. Socially also, come to that: in Cuba, there was virtually no more prestigious or enviable job than that of devoting one's life to the physical protection of the *Líder Máximo*.

However, it was at that time that a crack began to appear in my convictions. It must be pointed out that in Cubans' collective memory, 1989 corresponded less to the year in which the Berlin wall fell than it did to that of the so-called Ochoa Affair. This Castrist Dreyfus Affair will always remain an indelible stain on the history of the Cuban Revolution. At the end of a televised Stalinist trial that still haunts all our memories, Arnaldo Ochoa, national hero and the most respected general in the country, was sentenced to death and executed as an example for the crime of drug trafficking, along with three other members of the highest military echelons. Now, from my privileged position of intimacy with the country's figurehead, I was well placed to know that this trafficking, designed to rake in funds to finance the Revolution, had been organized with the express approval of the *Comandante*, who was therefore directly mixed up in "the affair." To divert attention from himself, Fidel Castro had not hesitated to sacrifice the most valiant and faithful of his generals, Arnaldo Ochoa, hero of the Bay of Pigs, of the Sandinista revolution in Nicaragua, and of the Angolan war against South Africa.

A little later I realized that Fidel would use people for as long as they were useful to him, and then dispose of them without the slightest qualms.

In 1994, a tad disenchanted with all I had seen, heard, and experienced, I wanted to retire. Nothing more than that: simply retire two years early and withdraw peacefully into the background—while obviously remaining faithful to the oath I had sworn to keep secret all the information to which I had been party over the seventeen years spent in the private circle of the *Líder Máximo*. For the capital crime of having dared say I wished to stop serving the Commander of the Revolution, I was thrown into a cockroach-infested prison cell like a dog. I was tortured. They even tried to poison me. For a time, I thought I would die there. But I come from a tough breed. During my imprisonment from 1994 to 1996, I swore to myself that the day I managed to escape Cuba (as I did in 2008, after ten unsuccessful attempts), I would write a book revealing what I knew, what I had seen, and what I had heard—telling the story of the "real" Fidel Castro as nobody had ever dared to do. From the inside.

JUAN SÁNCHEZ,
FIDEL'S BODYGUARD

For as far back as I can remember, I've been passionate about firearms. It was not altogether a coincidence when, at the peak of my career in 1992, I won the rank of best pistol shooter in Cuba in a contest that brought together the cream of the crop: my New Year's gift when I was six was my first cowboy set with a magnificent silver cap gun. Over the following years I regularly received a new outfit and, above all, a new gun. My childhood was thus dedicated to putting imaginary Indians and fearful bandits out of action. But instead of just playing "Bang, bang, you're dead!," I took my mission very seriously, applying myself to getting my moving targets precisely in my sights, my arm stretched out and my right eye focusing.

When I was a teenager, I moved on to air rifles with lead pellets, ideal for shooting cardboard boxes from ten yards away. Which was why I later became the best trigger in Fidel's escort team. Today, in my sixties, I train at least once a week at a shooting range in Florida, where I have lived in exile since 2008—and, of course, I don't set foot outside the house without my shooter: in the eventuality of the many Cuban agents in Florida trying to stop me speaking out, the welcoming committee is ready! But let's go back to my childhood. . . .

I was born on January 31, 1949, in Lisa, a poor quarter in west Havana, almost exactly ten years to the day before the Castrist Triumph of the Revolution. When I was two years old, my father, a worker in a poultry factory, separated from my mother, a cleaning lady. As she was too poor to bring me up by herself and my father didn't see himself taking on the task in her place, he decided to entrust me to my paternal grandmother and uncle who lived in the same house. Such an arrangement is not unusual in Cuba: as elsewhere in the Caribbean, family is a fluid concept.

I was the apple of my grandmother's eye, becoming like her own son to her. My uncle quickly became a substitute father and I called him "Dad." My mother lived in the neighborhood and I saw her from time to time. I lacked for nothing, for my uncle had a good job as head accountant at the large abattoirs in Havana. The happy owner of a white 1955 Buick equipped with an air-conditioning system—an unheard-of piece of modern technology—he would drive us around in his fantastic car on weekends, sometimes as far as Varadero, the famous coastal resort less than a hundred miles from the capital.

It was the 1950s, Cuba's golden age—above all, in Cuban music: rumba, mambo, cha-cha. The stars of the period were Benny Moré, Orlando Vallejo, Celia Cruz; they performed in the fashionable nightclubs (the Tropicana and the Montmartre), the luxury hotels (the Nacional, the Riviera), or else in the casinos run by Lucky Luciano or other Italian-American gang leaders.

Although we did not realize it at the time, it was also a golden age economically speaking. Distinctly wealthier than General Franco's Spain, Cuba at that time produced sugar, bananas, and nickel. It was one of the most modern countries of Latin America, as proved by the Organisation for Economic Co-operation and Development figures: with gas-producing Venezuela and meat-producing Argentina, Cuba was one of the countries with the least inequality and the best record of human development (literacy, life expectancy, and so on) in the region. The wealth of the middle class was measured by the number of cars "made in the USA," the boom in electrical goods (such as televisions and refrigerators), regular people's ability to eat at restaurants and shop at the always-full small shops. Havana radiated the atmosphere of a consumer society. At Christmas, market stalls in the capital proffered apples and pears imported from Europe and garish neon discotheque lights flashed in the night, but people gave little thought to the problems of rural life, where illiterate workers were exploited with rock-bottom wages by American multinationals such as the United Fruit Company. Anyway, who cared about social inequalities, apart from a handful of idealist students dreaming of revolution?

It was a troubled decade, a swirling mix of political turbulence, corruption, and student agitation. An explosive cocktail. In August 1951, the leader of the Orthodox Party, Eduardo Chibás, a great polemicist and leading political figure, committed suicide live on the radio after an umpteenth tirade against the rampant corruption and gangsterism of the Ramón Grau and Carlos Prior governments. There was widespread shock. The following year in 1952, Fulgencio Batista took back the reins of power after a coup d'etat, a month before the elections planned for March that he had been certain to lose.* A year went by, and then on July 26, 1953, a young lawyer named Fidel Castro, who had already made a name for himself during the student demonstrations, burst spectacularly onto the scene by carrying out an armed assault against the barracks of Moncada in Santiago de Cuba, in the east of the country. Most of the conspirators were killed in action or arrested, and many were executed. It was a bitter failure. Arrested, tried, and imprisoned, Fidel Castro was amnestied two years later.

It was, however, only the beginning of the story. Fidel Castro went into exile in Mexico, where his brother Raúl introduced him to an Argentinian named Ernesto Guevara, known to everybody by his nickname of Che. After several months of preparation, a group of eighty-two men led by Fidel landed on the southern coast of Cuba on board the *Granma*, a yacht bought secondhand, and from there the guerrillas took to the bush. So in 1956, here was Fidel Castro in the Sierra Maestra mountains at the head of a guerrilla group, the July 26 Movement or M26, so called in reference to the date of the attack on the Moncada.

In 1958, the story accelerated: Washington withdrew its sup-

---

*Rubén Fulgencio Batista (1901–1973) had been president of Cuba from 1940 to 1944 after democratic elections. His government included communist ministers.

port from Batista's corrupt and increasingly discredited regime. In February of the same year, the M26 carried out one of its most memorable feats: two masked men went into the Lincoln Hotel in Havana and kidnapped one of its VIP guests, the Argentinian race car driver Juan Manuel Fangio. The police set up roadblocks and checkpoints everywhere, but Fangio could not be found. His kidnappers installed him in a comfortable Havanan house where they tried to win the sportsman over to their revolutionary plans—with limited success, since the Argentine driver was apolitical. Nonetheless, well treated by the young rebels and freed after twenty-nine hours of capture, he had had time to forge friendships with these idealists. The publicity stunt by Fidel's men had been a total success. They had got people talking about them and they had tarnished the government's image a little further by disrupting the big occasion of the Cuba grand prix. The victory may have been psychological, but it was undeniable: after the Fangio affair, more and more Cubans sensed that Batista's power was toppling. Ten months later, it fell like overripe fruit. On January 1, 1959, with the dictator having fled to Portugal, the exultant population filled the streets, which were decked with the red and black colors of the M26. It was ninety degrees in the shade; the crowd sang, danced, and shouted *¡Viva la revolución!* Fidel, with his unparalleled sense of suspense, made people wait for him for no less than eight days—and then, like a Roman emperor, he made his triumphal entry into Havana. For a week, he and his *barbudos* had traveled the country from east to west, covering over six hundred miles, and all along the way they were greeted like heroes. The band of guerrillas finally arrived in the capital on January 8, Fidel standing in a jeep like Caesar raised up on a float.

I watched the event from a ringside seat: the balcony of my biological father's apartment, on the first floor of the avenue Vía Blanca, had a view straight out onto History. That day we saw for the first time "in real life" the faces of those demigods named Fidel Castro, Camilo Cienfuegos, Huber Matos, and Raúl Castro. They were young, relaxed, charismatic, and handsome: veritable Latin lovers.

I remember my father's exact words when Fidel passed by. He turned to me and said, "You'll see, that *hombre* is going to get Cuba back on its feet. Everything is going to be alright now." Little did I imagine that fifteen years later I would join the personal bodyguard team of the *Comandante*.

In middle school and then high school I was good at literature, history, and, above all, sports: baseball, basketball, boxing, and karate, in which I earned a black belt. Despite my average size, I was something of a fighter. Nothing and nobody frightened me. Because I had the reputation of defending my friends, I was also very popular. One Saturday evening when I was seventeen I was at a dance in the Havana district of Cano. A young, quite well-known boxer, Jorge Luis Romero, was also there, and he started chatting up my girlfriend with great insistence, at which point I asked him what he was doing. The explanation degenerated into fisticuffs, with neither of us coming out on top. The security staff fired shots into the air to disperse the crowd that had formed and the police swarmed in to arrest us, but the crafty boxer managed to slip away. At the police station, I refused to reveal his name—a question of honor. Three days later he rang my doorbell. I was certain he had come looking for trouble. "Wait for me at the corner of the street, I'll be there in two minutes," I told him, ready to do battle. But outside he explained he had come to thank me for not having given him up to the cops. From that day on, the hope of Cuban boxing became one of my best friends.

In 1967, my family was split up in a way experienced by many other Cubans. My uncle and my grandmother, disappointed by the Revolution, managed to settle in the United States. I did not see the people who had brought me up for another forty years. A chapter had closed and I went back to live with my mother, who, unlike my uncle and grandmother, remained a convinced revolutionary, although she was still as poor as ever. Through a friend, I got a job in a construction unit called the Special Works Program. Its function? Building houses for the leaders of the Revolution. So there I was, a construction worker, carrying bags of cement, pushing wheelbarrows of sand, and placing bricks on top of each other. A year later, however, the Special Works Program had accomplished its mission and all its workers were transferred to the sugarcane fields in the municipality of Güines, about eighteen miles from the capital. Here I now was as a machete-wielding cane cutter! A diabolical task, and dangerous, too. There was a permanent risk of getting injured in the sun-scorched fields, both because of the way the cutter was swung and because of the leaves, as sharp as razor blades. Fortunately, after thirty days in the suffocating heat of the cane fields, I learned that I had been called for military service, which, on the initiative of the minister of the Cuban Revolutionary Armed Forces (essentially, defense minister), Raúl Castro, had become compulsory in 1965.

When I went back to Havana, a recruiting officer explained

to me that I had not been called for national service but for something much more serious: I had been chosen by the minister of the interior (the MININT, a then-current abbreviation) to follow a special program. Unknown to me, the intelligence services of MININT had followed and observed me for several months. They had questioned my entourage, drawn up my psychological profile, realized that all the members of my family who had stayed in Cuba were real "Fidelists," and concluded that my "revolutionary profile" was above suspicion. The MININT therefore proposed that I embark on my military career without further ado.

"If you agree to sign, your salary will increase to one hundred and twenty pesos instead of the seven pesos given to ordinary soldiers," explained the recruiting officer. "And you'll have three leave permits a week."

I agreed, of course, becoming the first (and last) soldier in our family. The very next week, I entered the squaddie's life: being woken up at five in the morning, marching, making a bed with hospital corners, and carrying out cleaning tasks. Not to mention more noble pursuits such as exercise and shooting practice, quickly distinguishing myself as one of the best shooters in our contingent of 300 students. I aimed true, I shot true, and I hit the bull's-eye every time. After three months of classes, there was another selection: 250 were sent to the national police school while I and the 49 others who remained were assigned to Department no. 1 of Personal Security, which oversaw all the services dedicated to Fidel Castro's personal security.

It was an immense honor: in the praetorian Cuban mentality, there was nothing more important than Department no. 1, responsible for protecting Fidel, and Department no. 2, responsible for the personal security of the defense minister, Raúl Castro. As for Department no. 3, it ensured the protection of the other members of the Communist party politburo.

Fidel's *seguridad personal* was organized in three concentric *anillos* (rings). The third ring consisted of the thousands of soldiers assigned to all the tasks, including logistics, related to the security of the *Comandante*; the second ring, the "operational group," was made up of eighty to a hundred soldiers; the first ring, the *escolta*, was composed of two teams of fifteen handpicked elite soldiers who worked in relays, one day on, one day off, ensuring close protection of Fidel twenty-four hours a day.

As a member of the third ring, my first assignment was *El Once* (The Eleven). This was a block of houses situated in *la calle Once* (Eleventh Street), in the very pleasant quarter of Vedado, five streets from the seafront. This assignment was in no way routine because *El Once* was above all the building where Celia Sánchez, a notable figure of the Revolution in general and of Fidel's private life in particular, lived. Until her death from lung cancer in 1980, Celia participated closely in all the historic events of the Revolution; back in 1952, she was one of the first women to oppose Batista's dictatorship, and then to join Castro's subversive movement, the M26. In the Sierra Maestra she had worked as a courier, carrying telegrams in bouquets of flowers to get past the police. Celia also coordinated actions between the resistance fighters and clandestine urban cells; after the Triumph of the Revolution, she was rewarded with various official posts, including that of secretary of the Council of State, presided over by Fidel. Above all, this thin woman with an expression as dark as her hair was Fidel's mistress and, even more important, his confidante—a remarkable feat since the

Comandante confided in a tiny group of people: just his brother Raúl and the few "women in his life," who could be counted on the fingers of one hand. The love between them was also political; in return, Celia enjoyed a considerable influence, particularly in terms of appointments to the top. Fidel loved Celia so much that he waited until her death to marry Dalia, the woman who had, in the greatest secrecy, shared his life since 1961.

A part of Celia Sánchez's apartment on the fourth and last floor of the *Once* building, including a bathroom, was for Fidel's private use; unknown to Dalia, he went there almost every day before returning to the presidential palace. It was at the bottom of the *Once* building that I saw Fidel at close hand for the first time.

I was on guard duty at the entrance to the building one day when he and his bodyguard screeched up in the three burgundy-colored Alfa Romeos used by the escorts at the time—they would later be replaced by Mercedes 500s. The vehicles came to a stop several yards away from the entrance and the escort divided up according to the usual procedure: one soldier going ahead into the building to ensure the access was safe and then coming out to give the green light to the others, the following two taking up position on the pavement and, their backs to the building, observing the road, while six others took up position around Fidel, who was accompanied to the entrance by the head of the escort.

It was at that moment that *El Comandante* made his way directly toward me, placed his hand on my shoulder, and stared straight into my eyes. Petrified, I clung to my rifle so as to keep my composure. Then Fidel disappeared into the building. It had all lasted no more than two seconds, but I was overwhelmed at having met Fidel Castro in the flesh, the man I admired most in the world and for whom I was ready to give my life, no matter what.

The *Once* occupied a special place in the geography of Castrism. At the time it was a secret place that Fidel visited almost daily without anyone, or almost anyone, knowing anything about it. In order to guarantee its security, the entire block of houses was made private, and public access to that section of the street was blocked by checkpoints at both ends. All the rooftop terraces were connected, creating a vast open-air communication network. Over the years, other improvements were brought in. An elevator and a fitness room were installed—and even an ornately decorated bowling alley, two lanes of polished wood edged with clumps of ferns and rocks transported from the slopes of the Sierra Maestra. It was magnificent.

But the most astonishing feature was undoubtedly the stable that Fidel had built on the fourth floor of *Once*, in the very heart of the capital! At the beginning of 1969 *El Comandante* had four cows winched up from the street to the roof terraces with the help of a construction site crane so that he could indulge his great fad of the time: breeding European Holstein (black-and-white) cows with Cuban zebus in the hope of creating a new race of cattle that would modernize farming and improve milk yields.

The existence of this stable at the top of a residential building in the middle of a city might seem implausible to a reader unfamiliar with the history of Castrism, but it will not surprise the more knowledgeable because Fidel's passion for bovine genetics is a well-established historical fact. In December 1966, the Commander in Chief gave his first speech on this subject in the Santa Clara stadium. In the 1970s and 1980s, this crackpot passion turned into an obsession. In 1982, Fidel made Ubre Blanca, a cow famous for her prodigious production of milk, into a celebrity, using her as propaganda tool. The whole of Cuba watched on television as she set a world record for the Guinness World Records, producing 109.5 liters (about 29 gallons) of milk in a single day, irrefutable proof of the *Comandante's* agronomic genius! The subject of numerous television reports, the cow was elevated to the status of national symbol—a stamp showing her effigy was even produced. When she died in 1985, the national daily *Granma* gave her an obituary, and a marble statue still holds pride of place in her native city Nueva Gerona, on the Isla de la Juventud.

Finally, I cannot talk about the *Once* building without mentioning the private basketball court, reserved for the exclusive use of Fidel Castro. In 1982, two years after the death of Celia Sánchez, a Canadian company modernized the athletics track at the Pedro Marrero stadium in Havana by turning it into a synthetic track in preparation for the fourteenth Central American and Caribbean games later that year. In order to foster relations with their client, the company proposed to give Cuba a sporting terrain of Fidel's choice. Instead of seizing the opportunity to equip a school or sports facility in a locality that needed it, the *Comandante* asked them to construct an indoor basketball court for his sole use.

Basketball was always one of his favorite sports. Fidel never hesitated to take a break whenever he could in a school or a professional court to perform a few free throws or organize a game with his escort. The players would then divide into two teams: the reds and the blues. Obviously everyone played "for" Fidel—it was out of the question for him to lose a game. What is more, he chose the teams so as to keep for himself the best players, of which I had the honor to be one. Naturally, the *Comandante* played center—in basketball, this position is the mainstay of the game through whom all the balls pass. I remember him giving me a filthy look on one occasion because instead of passing him the ball I had thrown it to make a basket.

"*Coño*, why did you shoot, Sánchez?" he shouted at me, considerably irritated.

Fortunately, at almost that precise moment, the end of the game was declared. It was the last second of the match; Fidel realized I would not have had time to pass him the ball in order for him to score, so I was saved by the bell.

Also in 1982, toward the end of the year, *El Comandante* broke his big toe when he landed badly, trying to defend his ground. Vexed and irritated, he was forced to wear very unmanly slippers. Above all, he wanted his injury to remain secret, and so when he received a visitor at the presidential palace, he would slip on a pair of army boots (without doing up the zip) and stay seated behind his desk for the duration of the meeting without accompanying his guest to the door, as was his custom. For Fidel, orthopedic problems were state secrets.

But let's go back to 1970. After eighteen months in the service of the *madrina*, the godmother (as the members of the personal security guard called Celia Sánchez, who was always attentive toward us), I was transferred six miles away, to Unit 160, situated in the Havana quarter of Siboney at the other end of the city. Stretched over five acres and hidden behind high walls, the 160 was vital to the good functioning of Fidel's personal security corps, for it was the logistical unit that ran everything: transportation, fuel, telecommunication, food. There, car mechanics repaired Fidel's Mercedes and technicians mended walkie-talkies and radio receivers; gunsmiths looked after the store of Kalashnikovs, Makarovs, and Brownings; and launderers washed and ironed the soldiers' uniforms.

At 160 there were also the larders and refrigerated room where the stores of the Castro family and its escort were kept. To these were added laying hens and a flock of geese; during the festive season, Fidel would present a few specimens of the latter to his chosen recipients. There were also several bulls as well as zebus (domesticated oxen with humps) and Holstein cows, subjects of the lord of the manor's genetic experiments. This "town within a town" also included a miniature ice cream factory for the delight of all the highest leaders of the Revolution—ministers, generals, and members of the politburo—with the notable exception of Fidel and Raúl. So as to minimize any risk of poisoning, their sorbets were prepared separately in a little workshop elsewhere in Unit 160.

Leisure pursuits were not forgotten. Other than a museum of gifts housing the collection of all the presents received by the head of state (with the exception of the most expensive, which he kept in his own possession), a private cinema run by a projectionist from the Ministry of the Interior was placed at the disposition of the *Comandante* and his family, and it was here that Fidel, obsessive by nature, enjoyed countless viewings of his favorite film: the interminable and soporific Soviet version of *War and Peace* adapted from Tolstoy's novel that lasts at least five hours.

I was rapidly promoted to team leader at 160, my work consisting of assigning soldiers' tasks and coordinating our movements with the presidential palace as well as Fidel's private residence. In this post, I was soon in the know about everything—and as Dalia often called on our services, for a delivery of milk or to come and watch a film in the cinema, I soon learned of the existence of this "first lady," totally unknown to the general public.

Dalia did not know it, but she was not the only woman to frequent 160. Behind the gift museum was a detached house, the House of Carbonell, where my boss engaged in extraconjugal visits with the greatest discretion. And so I would regularly receive phone calls from Pepín, Fidel's aide-de-camp warning me in a laconic tone, "Be ready today, at such and such a time. A visit to the Carbonell House is planned."

I would create a diversion at the stated time by summoning the soldiers on duty into my office so that they did not witness the arrival of the Commander in Chief or his lady visitor, who always arrived separately.

After four years of good and loyal service at Unit 160, my career took a new turn. In 1974 I was promoted to the *grupo operativo*, the operational group composed of eighty to a hundred men that formed the second ring around Fidel. Its main function was to offer extra support to the first-ring escort during the

Commander in Chief's public movements, whether in a pro-
vincial factory or in Revolution Square in Havana. The operational group was also deployed when Raúl or the leading
members of the Cuban Communist Party politburo, such as
Ramiro Valdés or Juan Almeida Bosque, traveled around.

Barely had I integrated into the *grupo operativo* when, a
month later, I along with thirty colleagues were sent to the *escuela de especialistas*, a training school for elite security agents. It
had just opened and, attending from 1974 to the end of 1976,
we were the first graduates in its history. The training left us
barely any free time, the mornings devoted to physical education (race walking, martial arts, shooting practice) and the
afternoons to theory. There I learned how explosives worked
and, with a group of ten other students, mastered French. Another group of ten students learned Russian and a third English.
We also familiarized ourselves with basic intelligence techniques
and psychological motivation and studied in depth famous
historical attacks—that against General de Gaulle in Petit-
Clamart in 1962 and the assassination of John F. Kennedy in
Dallas in 1963—so as to learn lessons that could help in our
protection of the *Líder Máximo*.

When a foreign head of state or high-ranking official made
an official visit to Cuba, it was the students of the specialist
school who undertook their protection—this was how I met
certain great world figures, such as the Jamaican president
Michael Manley and prime ministers of Vietnam (Pham Van
Dong), Sweden (Olof Palme), and Trinidad and Tobago (Eric
Williams).

During those years, I really had the feeling that my career
was taking a serious direction. There were increasing reasons for

satisfaction. Very well graded by my superiors, I was promoted to sub-lieutenant, thereby joining the officers' ranks, and I also won two more black belts, one in judo and another in a close-combat technique called Protection and Attack developed by the Cuban army. These were added to my karate black belt, which I had held for years. The icing on the cake was taking my first foreign trip, in 1976. Of the thirty students in my year, I was the only one chosen to join the escort of high-ranking leader Juan Almeida Bosque to Guyana.

I had never yet left my native island and was impatient and excited at the idea of seeing the world, beginning with that exotic Amazonian country bordering Brazil, Venezuela, and Suriname. I remember that I was particularly struck by the social inequalities that I saw on arriving in Georgetown, the capital; ten years after the former British Guyana had achieved independence, the white elite still lived in a very colonial comfort while the black population, crammed into ghettos and wearing rags, struggled in deplorable conditions. What a shock! In comparison, Cuba was El Dorado.

In my private life, too, I was lucky. At that period, I had already been sharing my life with Mayda for eight years. We had met at the beginning of 1968 at one of those dances that took place every Sunday evening in what we call in Cuba a "social circle"—it was basically a dance hall. When I turned up that evening at the Patrice Lumumba social circle in the district of Marianao and saw Mayda, I was immediately smitten. As the salsa crackled out from the PA system in the Havanan night, I first caught sight of that gorgeous little face, unable to tear my gaze from her smile. To my eyes, she was the most beautiful woman I had ever seen. After exchanging several meaningful glances, I crossed the dance floor, victorious. As Mayda was accompanied by her mother, I turned toward the latter: "Please allow me to ask your daughter for a dance, Madam. . . ."

I led Mayda off toward the dance floor; seeing her mother's surprise, I shouted out to her, "Have no fear: we'll be married before the end of the year!"

I kept my promise. On December 21 that same year, we became a young married couple leaving for a week's honeymoon at the Hotel Riviera, one of the famous Havanan seafront establishments that were formerly owned by the notorious American gangster Meyer Lansky. Our daughter was born the following year and our son in 1971. For the first few years we lived with my mother in the district of Lisa, where I had grown up, but in 1980, at the age of thirty-one, MININT granted me an apartment right in the center of the city not far from the Palace of the Revolution where Fidel had his office. This was where I lived the rest of my time in Cuba, until I escaped to the United States in 2008. Mayda was the perfect wife and mother: hardworking, she looked after everything, oversaw the children's upbringing, and ran our household while I, consumed by my career, was always on the go.

It seemed as though the gods were with me: the good news kept on coming. At the end of 1976, back from Guyana, I was resting in the dormitory of the *escuela de especialistas* when an officer came in to tell me that I was to go immediately to see Eloy Pérez, the man who oversaw all the personal security arrangements for Commander in Chief Fidel Castro and on whom our school relied. Very surprised (and slightly worried), I spent the whole of the journey to the city center, where I had my appointment, wondering why I had been summoned. What could I have done wrong?

When I got there, I had not even had time to sit down when Eloy Pérez said to me, "Sánchez, the Commander in Chief has personally selected you to join his personal escort. From now on, nobody other than me or, obviously, *El Jefe* himself can give you orders or send you on a mission for any reason. Not even a minister, understood? From tomorrow, you will present yourself here every day at 8 a.m. And if at 5 p.m. you have not been given an assignment, you can go quietly back home to your wife and children."

The joy I felt at that moment was, I imagine, comparable to that of a Hollywood actor who has just been told he's won an Oscar. Several hours later I joined the crème de la crème of the Cuban army, its most prestigious, admired, and envied body of men: the group of twenty to thirty handpicked soldiers in charge of Fidel Castro's around-the-clock protection. I did not realize it yet but I would spend the next seventeen years of my life in the wake of the man who had launched one of the most famous people's revolutions of the twentieth century, after those in Mexico, China, and Russia.

However, I had to wait a little longer before I could take up a place beside the great man because from January to April our superiors were selecting the five other students of the Specialists' School who would swell the ranks of Fidel's escort. Finally, on May 1, 1977, after the traditional parade for the international celebration of International Labor Day on Revolution Square, our young group of six was introduced to the *Comandante* and joined the "holy of holies," *el primer anillo*, the first ring of protection.

The general public often confuses the work of a guard with that of a bodyguard. They imagine that our job consists of doing wrestling tackles and moving at the speed of light. However, the work of a "personal security specialist" or "VIP protection specialist" demands many qualities other than simple brute force. They must coordinate the escort's movements, anticipate potential threats, secure telecommunication, check foodstuffs to thwart any poisoning attempts, carry out spying and counterespionage assignments, uncover microphones hidden in hotel rooms abroad, examine all sorts of data with a fine-tooth comb, and draw up analysis reports. In addition, Fidel demanded that his escort attain a certain intellectual and cultural level.

In 1981, outside my career as one of Fidel's escort—that is during my free time—I therefore embarked on a penal law degree at the MININT Higher Institute as well as another course entitled "counterintelligence operational investigation," otherwise known as counterespionage, thanks to which I know how to carry out a police inquiry, examine a crime scene, take fingerprints, and so on. In 1985 I was awarded my master's degree in law as well as an equivalent diploma in counterespionage. Much later, the penal law degree would come in handy, when I was put on trial myself. . . .

When I reflect on it now, Cuban education at that time was insanely immersed in the climate of the cold war and Marxist thinking. One has only to reread the titles of some of the subjects we studied: dialectical materialism, historical materialism, the history of the Cuban workers' movement, enemy subversive action, counterespionage, or else the critique of contemporary bourgeois trends. However, it was the courses on psychology and applied counterespionage psychology that most helped me in understanding the personality of Fidel Castro.

After the MININT college course, I put what I had learned to practical use by drawing up Fidel's psychological profile, identifying certain of his personality traits. My conclusion was that he was egocentric and loved to be at the center of the conversation, grabbing the attention of all those around him. What is more, like many gifted people, he gave no importance to his clothing, hence his penchant for combat uniform. I often heard him say, "I gave up the constraint of a suit and tie long ago." In fact, the main reason he had a beard was because it meant he did not have to shave every day. Another of his personality traits: it was absolutely impossible to contradict him on any subject whatsoever. Anyone who attempted to convince him he was wrong, that he was going down a blind alley or that one of his projects could be improved, even slightly, by making some alteration to it, was making a fatal error. From that moment on, Fidel viewed the poor unfortunate as an idiot. The best way of living with him was to accept all he said and did, even during a basketball game or a fishing expedition.

During the Angola war in the 1980s, General Arnaldo Ochoa was on the ground when he dared contradict the military directives of the *Jefe*—6,800 miles away in Havana—by suggesting other options that seemed to him better. Fidel never accepted this crime of lese majesty, and I believed it played a significant part in Ochoa's death sentence in 1989.

In contradiction to what he always said, Fidel had in no way renounced capitalist comfort or chosen to live in austerity. On the contrary, his way of life resembled that of a capitalist, without any kind of limit. He never believed that his speeches required him to live the austere life of all self-respecting revolutionaries; neither he nor Raúl ever practiced the precepts they preached to their compatriots. Which leads one to the conclusion that Fidel was extremely manipulative; with his formidable intelligence, he was capable of manipulating a person or a group of people without difficulty or scruple—in addition to which, he was repetitive and obsessive. In discussions with his foreign counterparts, Fidel would repeat the same things as often as was necessary to convince them he was right.

It might indeed seem surprising that I did not question things earlier, given my understanding of Fidel's psychological profile and the luxurious lifestyle I soon began to witness. But one has to take into account my youth and the real hero worship we all felt for the victorious leader of the Cuban Revolution. His authoritarianism? A quality in a fighter. The comfortable lifestyle he enjoyed? Did he not deserve it? And then, as I have said, I was a soldier. Soldiers are trained to act and obey . . . not criticize.

The Cuban authorities will of course do all they can to discredit my words and this book: that is their job. However, the difference between these officials who are blindly obeying orders and me is that I know what I am talking about. I devoted seventeen years of my life to Fidel, in addition to those years when I was not yet a member of his personal escort. If I add it all up, I have spent more time, more weekends and holidays, with him than with my own children and wife. At the presidential palace, on trips within Cuba and abroad, during official ceremonies, in his plane, on board his yacht, on the paradise island of Cayo Piedra or his other private properties, I was often no more than a few feet behind him. He trusted me totally. I was able to observe all his activities. What is more, until now nobody has been in a position to talk about the "private Fidel," his women, his mistresses, his siblings, or his numerous offspring (he has at least nine children, products of various liaisons; almost all are boys). It is high time the veil is lifted on what Fidel Castro and the Cuban government have always treated as one of the country's greatest state secrets: the Commander in Chief's family.

THE CASTRO DYNASTY

There is nothing ordinary about Fidel Castro. He is unique, special, and different. One thing in particular, among all the others, marks him out from all his compatriots: he cannot dance the salsa! It holds no interest or attraction for him. Another thing that distinguishes *El Comandante* from "normal" Cubans is that he does not listen to music, neither Cuban nor classical—and certainly not American. His predilection for marital infidelity, on the other hand, is typically Cuban: it is a veritable national sport. Without being a woman chaser or a compulsive lover, like so many politicians all over the world, he still belied his name (*fidel* is Spanish for "faithful"). In games of love and seduction, he never encountered the least difficulty, resistance, or frustration. True, Fidel was not one of those all-powerful dictators who organized orgies—but he was no saint, either.

Married first to the upper-middle-class Mirta Díaz-Balart and then to the teacher Dalia Soto del Valle, he cheated on the first with the very beautiful Havanan Natalia Revuelta and on the second with "comrade" Celia Sánchez, his private secretary, confidante, and guard dog for thirty or so years. Other mistresses must be added to the tally: Juana Vera, aka Juanita, his official English-speaking interpreter and intelligence service colonel (she now works for Raúl); Gladys, the Cuban airline flight attendant who was present on foreign trips; and Pilar, aka Pili, another interpreter, this time French-speaking. He had doubtless had other relationships that I did not know about, before I took up my post.

Cubans had virtually no idea about any of this. For decades, the private life of the *Líder Máximo* was one of the best-kept secrets in Cuba and the public knew about only a tiny part of it. For, unlike his brother Raúl, the number-one Cuban has always been almost pathologically careful to hide almost all facets of his private life. Why? He thinks it is pointless, even potentially dangerous, to expose his life or display it to all and sundry in the full light of day. That was why, except in the early years, he separated his private life from his public life. This cult of secrecy doubtless originated in his clandestine years when, as with the resistance movements during the Second World War, compartmentalizing information was a question of survival.

As incredible as it seems, Cubans therefore did not see or even know of the existence of Dalia Soto del Valle, the woman with whom he had shared his life since 1961, until after 2006, when a seriously weakened Fidel was hospitalized and decided to hand over the reins of power to Raúl. For four decades, Fidel was always accompanied by a symbolic "first lady" who was not his spouse. During great occasions such as a national holiday or the visit of a foreign head of state and so on, it was actually Vilma Espín (1930–2007), Raúl's wife and president of the Federation of Cuban Women, who appeared on stage in public beside Fidel, thereby filling the subliminal role of *la primera dama*.

Similarly, for almost as long, virtually nobody knew that in the 1960s and 1970s, Dalia had given no fewer than five sons to the *Líder Máximo*! Incredible but true: even the four children of Raúl Castro, who were kept out of the limelight, were not lucky enough to meet their first cousins before they reached adulthood! For almost twenty years, these close relatives lived just a few miles away from each other without ever meeting. As for the general public, they learned of the existence of Fidel's five boys only after 2000, and even then they were given no information concerning their professional activities or personalities.

I, however, knew them all well. Having frequented the family for seventeen years, I can not only draw up a detailed family tree of the dynasty and set out each member's qualities and flaws but also reveal several secrets and describe Fidel as a not very good father. This might all seem no more than gossip, but it sheds new light on the personality of one of the most influential public figures of the second half of the twentieth century.

Everything begins with the birth of the son who was "officially" the oldest of the Castros: Fidelito ("little Fidel"—named Fidel like his father, he was called Fidelito from the beginning to distinguish him from his illustrious genitor). Their physical similarity was striking: the same nose, the same Greek profile, the same hairline, the same beard . . . but such different lives.

Born in 1949, Fidelito is the only son of Mirta Díaz-Balart, a beautiful Havanan whom Fidel Castro had married the year before when he was still a simple law student—but already a committed political activist. In one of those strange quirks of history, Mirta's family had been intimately linked to the Batista regime when the latter became dictator in 1952: her father, a lawyer, defended the American companies that reigned over the banana industry while her brother was no less than the reviled president's minister of the interior! Mirta's brother also formed part of the first wave of Cubans to choose exile in Florida at the time of the Triumph of the Revolution in January 1959. Another irony of history was that Lincoln and Mario, the sons of Mirta's brother, forged careers within the American Republican party: elected as members of the House of Representatives, the Díaz-Balart brothers even became, for decades, the loudest spokespersons against Castrism. And all this while having Fidelito as their first cousin and Fidel as an uncle by marriage!

After their honeymoon in New York, Fidel—more in the grip of his political passion than of his relationship—rapidly lost interest in the elegant Mirta, whom he divorced in 1955. However, he won custody of little Fidelito despite being devoid, as we will later see, of the slightest paternal feeling. Long deprived of her son's company, in 1959 Mirta settled in Spain, where she still lives today; for several years now she has been allowed to visit Fidelito, who remains in Cuba.

Early on, "little Fidel" took on the heavy mantle of potential heir, thus becoming the only one of the many Castro children to be introduced to the media. In 1959, in a memorable moment of television—which can be seen on YouTube—the little boy appeared in his pajamas next to his father, also wearing pajamas, in a program broadcast by the American channel CBS. In this somewhat ridiculous setting, the guerrilla fighter who had just triumphed in Cuba managed to reassure American viewers: for ten minutes, he ingeniously explained that he was not a dangerous communist but a good family man, like any other American. And it worked—at least for the time being.

A decade later, we find Fidelito in the USSR. Thanks to a favor to Fidel by the Soviet number one, Leonid Brezhnev, his son went there under a false identity to study at an ultrasecret nuclear research institute. His pseudonym was José Raúl and none of his fellow students had the faintest idea of his real identity, apart from a pretty Russian girl, Natalia Smirnova, whom he married and with whom he had three children named Mirta, Fidel, and José Raúl. His nuclear physics qualification in hand, Fidelito went back to Havana in the 1970s, staying with his uncle Raúl rather than his father, who in fact had little interest in him. For among the Castros, it is Raúl and not Fidel who has a sense of family and who is the pivotal member of the clan.

However, Fidel did appoint this brilliant scientist to the head of the Cuban Atomic Energy Commission (CEAC) when it was created in 1980. Over the years, Fidelito has shown himself to be his father's son. Drunk on the trappings of power, he walks around the streets of Havana, for example, accompanied by bodyguards when that is theoretically a privilege exclusively reserved for the members of the politburo of the Cuban Communist Party (PCC). Such arrogance ends up annoying people; what is more, Fidelito took to embezzlement. In 1992, he was sacked from the CEAC because of his bad management. "He did not resign, he was sacked: Cuba is not a monarchy!" Fidel publicly thundered, particularly critical of his son's "incomprehensible thirst for power," apparently not realizing that this character flaw might have been hereditary.

Overnight, Fidelito was demoted to the rank of an ordinary official, an adviser on energy questions for the PCC Central Committee. The eldest of Castro's legitimate children thereby became part of the "pajama plan," the humorous Cuban expression for being sidelined. The uncompromising Fidel did not speak to him for several years after that; around the year 2000, Fidelito returned to favor, although he did not rejoin the circle of power. In March 2013, he even made a televised comeback at the age of sixty-five—without pajamas, this time. On the occasion of a trip to Moscow, he answered at length the questions of a journalist from the Russian channel Russia Today. The scientist praised the government of his uncle Raúl but was more reticent about the legacy left by his father, whom he never named, calling him instead by the rather distant term of "historical leader."

Who knows, perhaps Fidelito's career is not over? Intelligent, very well educated, and gifted with charisma, he is perfectly capable of exercising high office, all the more easily since he has remained close to his uncle Raúl and his physical resemblance to Fidel symbolically favors his return to the corridors of power.

Whereas Fidelito is the most famous of Fidel's descendants, his half-brother Jorge Ángel, also born in 1949, is on the contrary the least well known. He was the fruit of a three-day passing encounter with Maria Laborde, an admirer from the province of Camagüey whom nobody has ever seen and who is today deceased. The Commander in Chief has always given a wide berth to this unplanned son. If Fidel barely concerned himself with Fidelito, he was even less interested in Jorge Ángel: he could go for months without asking for news of his sons, each of them taking refuge in turn with their uncle.

I later found out Jorge Ángel's exact date of birth, thanks to the database of the Cuban civil identity service, which I managed to pirate and copy, with inside help, before leaving Cuba. I recently met a Cuban exile who had just arrived in Miami; having worked for State Security (the secret police), he personally knew Jorge Ángel and he confirmed the information I already had: Jorge Ángel was born on March 23, 1940, six months before Fidelito, who was born at the end of September that same year. Not only had no one ever known that Fidel had a hidden son, but, even more surprising, we now know that the "bastard" is in fact the real eldest of the Castros.

The relationship between the rather starchy middle-class Mirta and the feverish Fidel had never been one of consuming passion, to put it mildly—unlike his love for Natalia Revuelta, or "Naty," with whom he had blithely cheated on Mirta. With her green eyes, her perfect face, and her natural charm, this Havanan was considered in her day the most beautiful woman in the capital. Married to a doctor, Orlando Fernández, Naty sympathized with the ideas of the revolutionary movement, frequenting Fidel first as a friend and then as a mistress. From 1953 to 1955, when the budding *guerrillero* was imprisoned in the penitentiary on Isla de Pinos (today Isla de la Juventud) after the failed attack on La Moncada barracks, she regularly went to visit him.

After two years of imprisonment, Fidel and his comrades

were amnestied by Batista—whom they would overthrow three and a half years later. Fidel was then able to demonstrate all the gratitude he felt to his friend. . . .

In 1956, Naty gave birth to Alina. Fidel's only daughter, this child was also the only one who dared to stand up to him. After his accession to power on January 1, 1959, Fidel Castro was still seeing the very beautiful Naty, whom he visited at her home, generally in the evening. One day when Alina was ten, Fidel told her that her real father was not Dr. Fernández, who had gone to live in the United States after the Triumph of the Revolution.

Being the daddy of an adorable little girl did not awaken paternal feelings in the *Comandante*: in the 1960s, the new leader of the third world had other fish to fry. When she was twelve, Alina and her mother were sent to Paris for a year, on Fidel's orders. The little girl was sent to a boarding school in Saint-Germain-en-Laye, where she learned French—which she still speaks fluently. Back in Havana, the teenager asserted her personality: as she recounts in her autobiography, at the age of fourteen this budding rebel announced her intention of leaving Cuba.* At the time, Fidel paid no attention, but Alina—who always does things her own way—persisted in the idea when she was an adult.

Her relationship with her genitor, whom she saw sporadically, became stormy. I remember her in the 1980s, a pretty young woman who had become a model. One day when I was in Fidel's anteroom, Pepín Naranjo, the Commander in Chief's

*Alina Fernández, *Fidel, mon père, confessions de la fille de Castro* [Fidel, My Father: Confessions of Castro's Daughter] (Paris: Plon, 1998).

aide-de-camp, showed up with a copy of the magazine *Cuba*. Spread across its second page, Alina could be admired posing on a sailboat in a bikini, alongside two other superb models, in an advertisement for Havana Club rum.

"What on earth is this?" fulminated Fidel. "Call Alina, at once!"

Two hours later, Alina strode into his office, not in the least intimidated. The ensuing argument was the most memorable of them all: shouting reverberated all over the room, shaking the walls of the presidential office.

"Everybody knows you are my daughter! Posing in a bikini like that is unseemly!"

"Oh, so you're interested in what I'm doing now?" replied Alina, screaming even louder. "I don't care about your aesthetic considerations—I want to live!"

It was truly *la fiesta del Guatao*, a Cuban expression referring to that village where, according to legend, festivals often degenerate into general free-for-alls. Alina eventually tore out of the office like a rocket, Fidel and Pepín standing there speechless.

Several years went by and then, in 1993, Fidel learned via the secret services that Alina was making serious plans to flee Cuba. Fidel immediately summoned the head of the escort, Col. José Delgado Castro, my boss at that time: "I am warning you: Alina must not leave Cuba under any pretext or in any way. You've been warned!"

But two months later, the dramatic news fell: on Christmas Eve we found out that Alina had succeeded in secretly leaving her native land, wearing a wig, equipped with a false Spanish passport, with the help of a network of international accomplices. She went first to Madrid, where she gave numerous press conferences denouncing Castrist totalitarianism, then to Miami, where she settled permanently. The announcement of the defection of Fidel Castro's daughter was as scandalous as that of Juanita, one of Fidel's four sisters, had once been; in 1964, she had left Cuba via Mexico for Miami. She never saw her six brothers and sisters again.

One rarely sees the *Comandante* allowing his anger to explode. In seventeen years, I saw it only twice. Generally his anger was cold and withdrawn. But when Pepín broke the unpleasant news to him that day, Fidel went mad with rage. In these situations, his gestures resembled those of a capricious child in the middle of a tantrum: standing up, he stamped his feet on the ground while pointing his two index fingers down to his toes and waving them around.

"What a band of incompetent fools!" he cried, foaming at the mouth. "I want those responsible! I demand a report! I want to know how all this could have happened!"

When Fidel got himself into such a state, you could hear a pin drop. Everybody scampered, pretending to go about their business while they waited for the tropical storm to pass.

Fifteen years later, I saw Alina again in Miami, where she lives modestly, never having set foot in Cuba again. When I reminded her of that episode, she smiled, with that touch of sadness that can be seen in the eyes of every exile in the world.

After Mirta and Naty, there was Dalia Soto del Valle, the most important but also the least known of Fidel's women. She met him in 1961—the year of the Bay of Pigs landing—during a public event in the province of Villa Clara related to his government's big national literacy campaign. As he was giving a speech in the open air, Fidel spotted in the first row a gorgeous girl with whom he rapidly started exchanging furtive and meaningful glances. Like Mirta and Naty, this stranger was a blue-eyed blonde who also possessed another quality essential in the Commander in Chief's eyes: she was thin, as slight as a ballet dancer. Thinness, much more than blondeness, was an essential criterion in Fidel's romantic choices.

It was love at first sight. Later that day, Pepín, the aide-de-camp, introduced the beauty to him and Fidel discovered she was a teacher. After three meetings, and above all after the customary checks carried out by Pepín (to make sure she was not a counter-revolutionary and that her family had not been linked to Batista's regime), Fidel proposed that she move to Havana, where he lodged her very discreetly in a house situated on the outskirts of the capital, in Punta Brava. Some time afterward, they set up home together for good. From the beginning, their relationship was carried out under the greatest secrecy, both as a security measure in terms of the United States, who Fidel knew wanted to assassinate him, and from concern to keep the relationship from Celia Sánchez, with whom he was simultaneously involved.

Fidel and Dalia would have five children, all sons, all bearing a first name beginning with the letter A: Alexis, Alex, Alejandro, Antonio, Angelito. The first three names were all variations of Alexander, the pseudonym adopted by Fidel when he was a guerrilla fighter, in homage to his admired Alexander the Great. The five A's grew up far from the seat of power, from other Cubans, and even from their relatives. As I have said, before they reached adulthood, they never met Raúl's children, even though they lived nearby. The very family-minded Raúl leaped for joy the day his son, already an adult, met two of his first cousins, encountered by chance at a party. The government's second-in-command and minister of defense had asked his aides-de-camp for bottles of vodka to raise a toast to the occasion.

During seventeen years in Fidel's service, I encountered the five A's almost daily. They were all intelligent but without, for the most part, any particular brilliance. They all went to the Esteban Hernández primary school that their mother had set up especially for them in 202nd Street in the Coronela district, not far from the family home. Dalia quickly became the de facto principal of this made-to-measure establishment, personally choosing the teachers in collaboration with the Ministry of Education and selecting the students who would be admitted to it, according to the solidity of their parents' revolutionary convictions. A total of fifty or so children were enrolled, from establishment families or those of the escort. I was happy that mine did not go there: I never took advantage of the system. It was much better that way.

There was something else Fidel's children all had in common: none of the five A's ever did any military training or took part in any international aid mission to assist "brother countries," contrary to what Fidel recommended for or imposed on all young Cubans. Similarly, those who were of an age to do so did not fight in the Angolan Civil War (1975–1992), even though the Commander in Chief had sent hundreds of thousands of their compatriots there, to be killed at the front.

As with all groups of siblings, the five A's defined themselves by their differences, their personalities, and their career paths.

Alexis, the tall and thin eldest child, born in 1962, was an introverted loner with no real friends who rarely socialized or flirted with women, whereas Alex, born the following year, was affable and outgoing. The eldest, trained in computer science, had the habit of wanting to impose his views on his brothers—though he did not meet with much success. The second, more well-padded, had always won people's affection without even thinking about it. Naturally chubby, his nickname was El Buenachón, in other words a "good egg," which suited him perfectly: placid by nature, he was incapable of getting into conflict with anybody, not even his ungracious elder brother, to whom he had always in fact been close. A bon viveur, he was also called El Gordito (the Little Fat One), which did not annoy him at all. Alex was also the one to give Fidel and Dalia their first grandson, increasing his popularity ratings within the family even further. Initially an engineer, he soon branched off to follow a career as cameraman for TV Cubana before becoming a photographer in 1998. In 2012, this official photographer of his father exhibited a series of twenty-seven large-format images entitled "Fidel Castro: Intimate Portraits" in a chic gallery in Mexico.

Then came the third in line, Alejandro, born in 1969. Like his older brothers, he studied computer science, but unlike them he was passionate about programming. Today he is what could be called a geek. Around 1990, El Brother—the nickname he had acquired at university—developed software that enabled Russian computer systems to be adapted for Japanese ones; he subsequently sold it to a Japanese company, earning the congratulations of his father as well as the gift of a Lada car. A party animal, his favorite pursuits were frequenting discotheques, women, and prominent artists, much like Antonio, the fourth A.

The latter, nicknamed Tony, was born in 1971 and he is the sibling I knew best. I spent much time teaching him to swim, dive, and use an underwater spear gun on Cayo Piedra. Naturally, we bonded through these experiences. I was the sole member of the escort to be invited to the party for his fifteenth birthday along with a group of his teenage classmates; I imagine this provoked a little jealousy among my colleagues. On this occasion, Fidel had asked me to accompany his son to Unit 160, where the presents received by the president were kept, to choose a watch for Tony, who had set his sights on a quartz Seiko. I remember the teenager's radiant smile as he put it on his wrist.

Tony studied at the Lenin High School in Havana, where all his brothers had gone. I remember asking him one evening when I was on duty in the family property: "What are you going to do after high school?"

"My father wants me to study medicine, but I want to be a baseball coach. . . ."

Tony had always been mad about sports and played baseball and football whenever he could. Fidel's desires were, however, not up for discussion.

"In that case," I suggested to him, "choose sports medicine! That way you can have a career in the sports world while keeping on the right side of your father."

Years later, after my time in prison, I found out that Antonio had become an orthopedic surgeon. I don't know whether I had anything to do with it, but I have not forgotten our dialogue.

At any rate, of the five A's, Antonio was the only one to carve out a real life for himself. An accomplished athlete (he is a talented baseball batter, an experienced underwater diver, and an excellent golfer), he is head of the orthopedic surgery unit at the Frank País Orthopedic Hospital in Havana, doctor to the national baseball team, president of the Cuban federation, and vice president of the international federation of the same sport. In short, fortune has smiled on this brilliant, handsome "ideal son-in-law" who has twice been married to beautiful women and who has become known as a sort of Prince of Havana.

Last there is Angelito (Little Angel), about whom the same cannot be said. The youngest son, born in 1974, was the only one not to have gone on to earn a higher education. I remember him as a kid who was ultra-spoiled by his mother. Going to Varadero one weekend, for example, he demanded that he be picked up from there in a Mercedes-Benz. Dalia gave in to all his whims. Mad about cars since early childhood, Angelito was always getting in our hair; in the workshop, he lifted car hoods without asking permission, sat himself in the driving seat of parked cars, and touched tools without putting them back in their place. He was so exasperating that one of the Castro family domestics christened him *El Comandantico*, the little commander. Long after I had left Fidel's escort, I learned that he had become a senior executive at Mercedes-Benz in Cuba. Given all the talented people our country contains, I imagine that he essentially owes his position to the fact that his name is Castro. . . .

The five A's grew up and most of them still live in the immense family property of Punto Cero in the Havanan quarter of Siboney, in conditions that are starkly different to the revolutionary austerity advocated by their father.

Punto Cero is a vast terrain of about 75 acres situated to the west of Havana, not far from the sea: to be precise, 0.8 miles south of the Hemingway marina and 6 kilometers from the presidential palace. Four gardeners look after the upkeep of this leafy estate, which, in addition to the L-shaped, two-story family mansion with a 600-square-yard footprint, included a 50-foot-long swimming pool, six greenhouses for the cultivation of fruit and vegetables, and a huge lawn for the children to play on. There was also a second two-story residential building (with a 420-square-yard footprint) situated 550 yards from the principal residence where the bodyguards of the escort as well as the whole of the domestic staff for the house were lodged.

With its orange, lemon, mandarin, grapefruit, and banana trees, the estate resembled a veritable garden of Eden— especially if one compared it with the notorious ration book that all Cubans, including members of Fidel Castro's bodyguard, had to use to buy food: Per month, they were entitled to five eggs per person, a pound of chicken, half a pound of fish, 8 ounces of oil, black beans, powdered milk (reserved for children under seven), and a loaf of bread a day. It was impossible to keep going for more than two weeks on such a restricted diet, forcing the unfortunate Cubans to dream up all sorts of schemes to be able to satisfy their appetites.

The Castros' huge home was tastefully decorated, in the classical style of Caribbean family homes: shutters on the windows, furniture made of wicker and tropical wood, watercolors and porcelain plates hanging on the walls. To which were added a profusion of books on bookshelves and coffee tables. One of the domestic staff, Zoraida, ensured the smooth running of daily life, keeping tidy the private apartment of Fidel and Dalia on the first floor, as well as the communal areas of living room, small living room, and dining room on the ground floor, and looking after the laundry of the whole family, apart from that of Fidel.

Particular treatment was reserved for Fidel's clothes and underclothes. While the dirty clothes of Dalia and the children were washed by the domestics of Punto Cero, who ironed it in the laundry room, his was dealt with by the laundry in the presidential palace. Every day a chauffeur from Unit 160 went to Punto Cero to collect it and take it to the cleaners at the *palacio*. After washing and ironing, each shirt and pair of socks, boxer shorts, or trousers were subjected to a radioactivity test so as to make sure that the clothes of the *Líder Máximo* were free of any contamination. After all that, the same chauffeur did the same journey in reverse and delivered the impeccable clothes to Punto Cero, where the domestics tidied them carefully away in their place.

Two cooks, Pedro Moreno Copul (previously chef at the Habana Libre hotel) and Nicolas Mons del Llana, prepared the meals that were served at table by a liveried butler named Orestes Díaz. The Castros ate as if they were in a restaurant—in other words, à la carte. Each evening before going to bed, Dalia would draw up individual menus for the three meals of the following day for each of the family members according to his or her tastes, habits, and desires.

Fidel, who woke late—rarely before ten or eleven a.m.—and started his working day around noon, usually had just a tea or a fish or chicken bouillon for breakfast. He might sometimes drink a glass of milk like his children. It was home-produced milk, for it emerged directly from the udders of cows that grazed on the property. In a supreme touch of refinement, each member of the family possessed his or her own cow, so as to satisfy each one's individual taste, since the acidity and creaminess of fresh milk varies from one cow to another. And so the milk would arrive on the table, each bottle bearing a number, a little bit of paper scotch-taped onto the bottle, corresponding to each person's cow. Antonio's was number 8, Angelito's number 3, and Fidel's number 5, which was also the number he wore on his basketball shirt. There was no question of deceiving him: Fidel possessed an excellent palate that could immediately detect if the taste of the milk did not correspond to that of the previous bottle.

Fidel's lunches were frugal, often consisting solely of a fish or seafood soup, made with fresh produce. If the supplies of fish or crustaceans were running low, someone was sent to harvest the tide at La Caleta del Rosario, the coastal property where *Aquarama II* and the other boats in Fidel's private marina were kept.

Dinner was the Commander in Chief's main meal, consisting in turn of grilled fish, seafood, chicken, sometimes mutton, or even *pata negra* ham—never beef, which his dietician had outlawed—accompanied by moderate quantities of rice, red beans, and root vegetables (sweet potatoes, parsnips, potatoes). On the other hand, he ate large amounts of green vegetables, cooked or raw, which formed the base of his diet. Thanks to the greenhouse cultivation in the garden, the head of state never lacked fresh fruit and vegetables and ate organically in every season. Another advantage of that local production was that it enabled absolute traceability of products, minimizing the risk of intoxication or poisoning. In the same way, Fidel Castro only drank water drawn from the well that was tucked away in the garden.

The Commander in Chief would willingly wash his meals down with a little white, red, or rosé wine, mainly Algerian since President Houari Boumediene was in the habit of providing his Cuban counterpart with entire cases, a tradition that was continued after his death. As for President Saddam Hussein, he regularly sent pots of jam made from Iraqi figs to his dear Fidel. Careful about his diet and on his doctor's recommendation, the latter never drank coffee, although he sometimes allowed himself a digestive of Napoleon cognac. In Punto Cero, Dalia governed everything: the meals, the domestics' schedules, and even the relationship with the head of the family and his children. When one of the five A's wanted to talk with the patriarch, he had to go through Dalia, who would then approach her husband; he would grant a meeting at his convenience. Nobody, not even his offspring, was permitted to disturb *El Comandante* on the spur of the moment. Fidel Castro was the opposite of a doting father: in seventeen years, I never once saw him make a gesture of tenderness toward any of his children, although apparently after his convalescence in 2006, he grew a little closer to them.

Dalia was not exactly warm herself. She was rather a brittle, authoritarian, almost unpleasant woman. When Fidel was in the house, she eclipsed herself before *El Jefe*, "the Boss" (as she called Fidel in his absence, while he talked about her as *La Compañera,* "the Partner"). No sooner had he left, however, than she implemented a reign of strict discipline among the staff. Neither the domestic staff nor the bodyguards really liked her, which brings to mind an amusing anecdote.

At the Castros' estate, numerous chickens wandered at liberty around their laying nests scattered in the grass. Now, these birds with their excruciating cackling generally laid their eggs at sunrise, and so when we were on duty at night in one of the two surveillance posts situated in front of and behind the house, we would discreetly go on an egg hunt. Certain nests contained seven or eight eggs! We would slip them into our pockets and take them to our respective spouses, who would then make tortillas for the whole family. Then, one day, a very irate Dalia suddenly declared to all and sundry, "My goodness, these hens don't lay! I wonder if they're ill. . . . Or else there's a problem with the quality of grain I'm giving them. I'm going to call the vet just to make sure."

At that very moment, my fridge was full of fresh eggs. Funniest of all, everyone was in on the scheme, even the faithful aide-de-camp Pepín Naranjo, who was usually in the habit of reporting everything to the *Comandante.* For once, it was Fidel and Dalia who were the butt of the joke!

As I have said, Dalia turned into a protective she-wolf with her children. Egotistically, she considered her five boys Fidel's sole legitimate heirs. Fidelito, for example, only came once to the property of Punto Cero, and he had never been welcome on the island of Cayo Piedra.

On one of the few times he went there, his five half-brothers were also present. I don't know why, but it had been decided that family ties would be strengthened. After everyone had gone to welcome Fidelito and his wife, Natalia Smirnova, at the landing stage, Dalia felt obliged to murmur to me as an aside: "Ah, the family need to get to know each other a little." But it was obvious her heart wasn't really in it. As the awkwardness was palpable, Pepín suggested to Fidel that Fidelito be sent to Cayo Largo del Sur to supervise the worksite under way on that fifteen-mile-long island of fine sand that had been designated a future tourist site (which it has indeed now become).

So Fidelito, his wife, Pepín, and I took off in a helicopter for the tourist island, situated thirty miles southwest of Cayo Piedra. After a thirty-minute flight over the blue seas, we landed on Cayo Largo del Sur. We settled into the only existing hotel, where I rapidly noticed that Natalia, Fidelito's Russian wife, was a nuisance incarnate: at the restaurant, she sent her chicken back three times, on the pretext that, according to her, it smelled bad. Pepín, who knew her well, was unsurprised. "She's always in a foul mood," he told me.

At the time, Cayo Largo del Sur was still almost untouched, and it was impossible not to notice the presence of a rather luxurious forty-foot white yacht moored at the sole landing stage. From the intelligence officer posted on the island, I learned that it belonged to "the American." The American in question was Robert Vesco, the famous fugitive who had duped the U.S. tax authorities out of more than two hundred million dollars, and who was known by Washington to be in Cuba, despite Fidel's denials. The resulting Ameri-Cuban imbroglio lasted for years until, one fine day, *El Comandante* was forced to acknowledge the obvious: yes, it was true, Robert Vesco was indeed in Cuba. (I imagine that Fidel extorted a pretty sum of money from him in return for the Cuban hospitality. . . .) Later, when this criminal had become too burdensome to him, Fidel got rid of him by sentencing him to thirteen years in prison, where he died in 2007 without the American fiscal services ever being able to get hold of him.

After this rather strange episode, we took off again the following day to Cayo Piedra, and, to Dalia's obvious relief, Fidelito rapidly took his leave. Fidelito never again returned to the Castros' private island.

As with all couples, the relationship of the "boss" had its ups and downs. Nobody knew anything about it at the time, but the low point was reached in 1984 when Fidel found out that Dalia was cheating on him with Jorge, a member of the escort. . . . The official chauffeur of *La Compañera* at that time was René Besteiro; one day, Dalia sent him out to buy something and, taking advantage of his absence, asked Jorge to take her to her mother's, who lived on Seventh Street in the Playa quarter, not far from Punto Cero. Between ourselves, we nicknamed Dalia's mother La Abuela, the Grandmother. Fidel's mother-in-law was a rather unrefined, party-loving, heavily made up and very flirtatious lady who, despite the age difference, did not hesitate to hit on us young men.

In short, when Besteiro, Dalia's chauffeur, returned to Punto Cero and learned that his boss had gone to see La Abuela, his professional conscience obliged him to go there at once; when the Grandmother opened the door, a stupefied Besteiro glimpsed Dalia dancing in the sitting room with our colleague Jorge.

Instinctively drawing back, he said to the Grandmother,

"Tell Dalia I'm here." A moment later, Mrs. Castro appeared on the doorstep: "What are you doing here? Nobody asked you to come."

So René Besteiro left. Back in Punto Cero, he immediately went to confide in the head of the escort Domingo Mainet. In order to cover himself, Besteiro told him what he had seen and said he was worried about finding himself on the wrong side of Dalia. The head of the escort was flabbergasted. As he and I got on extremely well, he decided to talk to me about it and ask my opinion.

"It's simple, you have two options," I explained to him. "The first, which I do not recommend, is to say nothing. But the day Fidel finds out about it, you won't last very long. The second is to repeat Besteiro's account word for word to Fidel, as every military subordinate is supposed to do with his superiors."

We immediately set off for the palace, where the head of the escort had a private meeting with Fidel lasting half an hour. When he emerged, Mainet declared to me that from then on and until new orders were received, all communication with Dalia would cease. For a month, Fidel and his escort did not set foot in Punto Cero. Fidel traveled all over the country, sleeping in several of the twenty or so houses he owned, in the province of Las Villas, in Camagüey, or else on the island of Cayo Piedra. We all thought the relationship with Dalia was over at that point, but we were wrong. After four weeks, we returned to Punto Cero without warning Dalia of our arrival—and married life resumed its course as if nothing had happened.

As for the bodyguard Jorge, he disappeared from circulation overnight and we never heard of him again. I don't know whether he was transferred to the province of Oriente, far from

Havana, or whether he died. I didn't ask and above all I didn't want to know: at the time, what was uppermost in my mind was that Fidel should not find out that the head of the escort, Domingo Mainet, had taken me into his confidence. If he did, I ran the risk of the same fate happening to me. The official chauffeur of *La Campañera*, who had uncovered what was going on, was also effectively ousted, being demoted, I believe, to chauffeuring for the Fishing Industry Ministry. Which all goes to show that it is never good to be the bearer of bad news.

The Dalia affair had another victim of collateral damage: La Abuela. Fidel had already been unable to stand her for some years. Constantly at her daughter's in Punto Cero, she had the bad habit of drinking too much and *El Jefe* had more than once found her at his home in a state of manifest drunkenness, which made him mad with fury. A veritable Mrs. Do-As-You-Please, this inveterate drinker felt no qualms about plundering her son-in-law's cellar when he wasn't there. One day when he came back from Punto Cero—this was at the beginning of the 1980s, several years before Dalia's adultery—Fidel opened the bar and found *his* bottle of whisky empty! He exploded, stamping the ground with his feet and pointing downward with his two index fingers: "*¡Esto es ya el colmo!* [That's the limit!] Not only does your mother turn up here without warning, but she ransacks my things! I-do-not-want-to-see-her-here-anymore!"

The mother-in-law cleared off on the spot and her visits to Punto Cero became less frequent, although for two or three years she continued to put in an appearance. Dalia's infidelity (about which her mother was fully in the know, as she provided the setting for her daughter's secret meetings) was the final straw. From then on, La Abuela was no longer seen at Punto Cero.

At any rate, one thing can be retained from this marital crisis: Dalia Soto del Valle was the only person in the world who ever psychologically got the better of Fidel Castro Ruz. All-powerful macho, the Commander of the Cuban Revolution, had a single Achilles' heel: *La Campañera*.

THE ESCORT: HIS REAL FAMILY

Fifty-five years after the Triumph of the Revolution, the Castro family was a well-established dynasty: seven brothers and sisters (including Fidel), ten or so children, grandchildren, and even several very young great grandchildren. Not to mention nephews, nieces, and cousins. However, the real family of the *Comandante* has always been the guards that make up his escort. It was understandable: the *Líder Máximo* has certainly spent far more time in the company of the soldiers devoted, 365 days a year, to his personal protection than with his wife and children. A soldier to the core, Fidel had more affinity with his men in battle dress than with his own children, who had never known anything other than the comfortable status of "son of" and who had no personal experience of combat.

It was, for example, with his bodyguards and chauffeurs, not Dalia or his children, that the *Comandante* celebrated January 1, July 26, and August 13, the three key dates in Castrist historiography. January 1 commemorated the Triumph of the Revolution that took place on New Year's Day 1959. August 13 was

Fidel Castro's birthday (he was born in 1926). Finally, July 26 was the date on which the anti-Batista revolutionary era began in 1953, with the "heroic attack" (that ultimately failed) on the Moncada barracks in Santiago de Cuba. To ensure that everyone realized the historic importance of this event, Fidel even made July 26 the Cuban national holiday. The message was clear: it was on this date that everything in Cuba had begun, like some political big bang.

The Commander liked to be surrounded by his personal guard on his birthday. The tradition was that he and his escort would meet in the house at the heart of Unit 160—the same one where, unknown to Dalia, Fidel held his secret trysts. A whole sheep would be roasted and the guests would eat with their hands, in the Arab tradition, and wash it all down with Algerian wine. Also in attendance would be José Pepín Naranjo, the aide-de-camp who never left Fidel's side; Antonio Núñez Jiménez, the Commander's geographer friend who was one of the few people to visit the island of Cayo Piedra; and Manuel Piñeiro, otherwise known as Barbarroja (Redbeard), the head of the American department of the Cuban espionage service, one of the key figures of the administration. Once, I also ran into Gen. Humberto Ortega: President Daniel Ortega's brother was at that time the defense minister in the Nicaraguan revolutionary Sandinista government.

On his birthday, Fidel would unfailingly visit his brother Raúl and his friend the Colombian writer Gabriel García Márquez, who sometimes came to join our feast at Unit 160. The celebration would generally go on for three or four hours and was always immortalized by a photo session, usually after

Fidel had been given his presents. A lot of time was needed to open all these gifts, sent by Fidel Castro's foreign counterparts or admirers. There would be hundreds, among them the cases of wine sent by the Algerian president, the cartons of figs from the Iraqi head of state Saddam Hussein, or the *pata negra* hams given by a group of Spanish admirers who knew the Commander's penchant for the delicacy.

This moment of relaxation was always the opportunity for Fidel to recount several anecdotes and childhood memories to a captive audience that he knew would let him talk without interruption. *El Jefe* would also launch into such asides during our trips into the provinces or abroad, after dinner with a few select guests. From my continual presence at his side I was able to garner a detailed knowledge of his biography, including the period before I joined the escort in 1977.

Fidel Castro was an unrivaled raconteur. But repetitiousness was also one of his dominant characteristics; something of an obsessive, he would repeat the same stories year after year, which meant I got to know some of them as well as if I had experienced them myself. In retrospect, I can see that some of these recitals revealed aspects of his character, such as wiliness, absolute stubbornness, and his solidly anchored belief that the ends justified all and any means, including lying.

I don't know how many times he told us the "two notebooks story," but it must have been dozens. It occurred during the period when Fidel had left his family home and his native village of Birán (in the region of Holguín, in eastern Cuba) for the big town of Santiago de Cuba, about seventy-five miles away, where he attended the Jesuit Dolores school. The young

Castro boarded with one Luis Hippolite Hibbert, who was his godfather and a friend of his father's but also the Haitian consul in that town, the second largest in Cuba. The diplomat was a strict sort who, taking his role as godfather and guardian seriously, demanded that the boy earned his twenty centavos a week of pocket money—with which he went to the cinema or bought himself treats such as comics—by getting excellent grades at school.

One fine day, Fidel claimed to have lost the notebook in which grades were recorded so that the school would give him another one. From then on, he kept a duplicate set of accounts, presenting his guardian with a fake notebook in which he was top of the class with 10 out of 10 for every subject while also forging his guardian's signature in the real notebook so that he could give it back to his grade teacher, duly initialed. It was a fail-safe system. The only snag—this was the key to the story, which a mocking Fidel loved to recount—was that at the end of the school year, Luis Hippolite Hibbert was determined to attend the prize-giving ceremony. Here was how *El Jefe* gave us the end of the story:

And so we put on our Sunday best and set off for the Dolores school, my godfather of course convinced that I was going to bag all the prizes. Imagine his astonishment, sitting on the bench beside me, when the school principal began summoning streams of pupils to the stage—everybody but me. And so it was, "History . . . So-and-so! Biology. . . . Such-and-such! Mathematics. . . . Thingamajig! Congratulations, well done, etc." Throughout the whole ceremony, my godfather was bubbling over with impatience, determined to tear a strip off the principal there and then. He was livid and I had no idea how I was going to get out of the situation, feeling more and more ill at ease as the ceremony progressed. Suddenly, however, Eureka! I saw the solution. As I had missed a large chunk of the first term because of a minor operation on my appendix, I explained to him that it had been impossible to include me in the rankings because the first three months of my schooling could not be included in the calculations. This pirouette saved me in the nick of time—he believed me. But talk about a close shave!

Another favorite anecdote of Fidel's related to his youthful years in Havana. Now a university student, he had found a prospective furnished room to rent with the money that his father, a rich landowner, sent him. So Fidel duly put on his best suit to go and meet his future landlords and then, to demonstrate his good intentions and his solvency, he made the lordly gesture of giving them two months' rent in advance, on the spot. Having thus sweet-talked the landlords, he lived with them for four months without giving them another centavo, then did a disappearing act, only to repeat the whole thing somewhere else! Fidel would end his recount with a burst of laughter: "There must be people in Havana who are still looking for me. . . ."

The history of Fidel's escort is as old as the Revolution. From 1956, when the guerrilla fighter took to the bush in the Sierra Maestra, a small group formed of members of the revolutionary army was assigned to his personal protection. After the Triumph of the Revolution, in other words once he had come down from the mountains and had arrived in Havana, Fidel replaced his guerrilla corps with militants of the Communist Popular Socialist Party (PSP) and socialist youth movement. That was when Alfredo Gamonal and José Abrantes came on the scene; the former died in a car accident not long afterward, in 1963, but the latter quickly made a name for himself as one of Fidel's right-hand men. Fidel duly appointed him head of his escort and then, after the Bay of Pigs Affair in 1961, propelled him to the head of the *Departamento de Seguridad del Estado*, the State Security Department, otherwise known as G2, which oversaw all the branches of the secret police.

Abrantes was eventually replaced as head of the escort by Captain Chicho (real name Bienvenido Pérez), an old Sierra Maestra fighter. In the 1970s, Captain Chicho was himself replaced by Ricardo Leyva Castro, then by Pedro Rodríguez Vargas, and finally by Domingo Mainet, who headed Fidel's praetorian guard when I joined it in 1977.

At that time, Fidel Castro's personal protection unit was already a highly developed, perfectly trained organization. The "first ring" of protection was composed of a troop of thirty to forty elite soldiers, some of whom were also chauffeurs, who accompanied *El Comandante* night and day, wherever he may be: at home in Punto Cero, at the *Palacio de la Revolución* (where his office was), on his island of Cayo Piedra, in one of his other private residences outside the capital, or else during his official trips abroad.

The escort was divided into two teams (*grupo 1* and *grupo 2*) who worked alternate twenty-four-hour shifts every other day, taking over from each other at noon. To this program was added a half day of physical training, so that a typical week would consist of the following: physical training on Monday morning, then resumption of service at noon until the following day at noon, then a half day of rest until another physical training on Wednesday morning, before resuming service at noon, and so on. When Fidel went out into the country or overseas, the escort was obviously deployed twenty-four hours a day.

Fidel always traveled with a minimum of fourteen guards, spread over four vehicles, three of which were black automatic Mercedes. In vehicle 1: Fidel, his aide-de-camp Pepín Naranjo, one of his three personal chauffeurs (Jesús Castellanos Benítez, Ángel Figueroa Peraza, René Vizcaino), and the head of the escort Colonel Mainet or sometimes his personal doctor Eugenio Selman. Two other vehicles each carried a chauffeur and three bodyguards, all in military attire. The fourth car also had a chauffeur and three bodyguards, but these men were in civilian dress and riding in a manual Soviet Lada with a souped-up engine to increase its power. This vehicle followed about a hundred yards behind the three Mercedes so that the military presence around Fidel was not too overwhelming. When *El Comandante* left the capital to go out to the provinces or for a weekend on his Cayo Piedra island, a fifth Mercedes would complete the procession, carrying the personal doctor Eugenio Selman, the nurse Wilder Fernández, the official photographer Pablo Caballero, and the butler Orestes Díaz, all considered full members of the escort.

When Fidel traveled within Cuba or to take part in a particular event, the operational group or "second ring" was deployed as reinforcement to cover the positions of the escort, at a greater distance from Fidel. If the latter visited a factory, school, village, neighborhood, or ministry, counterespionage officers were also present. They put themselves at the escort's disposition, deploying all the intelligence agents inside and around the premises visited, while the air force took care of monitoring the air space with the aid of radars. When Fidel was on the coast or embarking onto a boat, the coast guards were also on red alert.

But let us return to the escort proper. Certain among this praetorian guard had not been chosen merely for their shooting skill or reflexes in one-to-one combat. Two of them, Andrés Arronte Martínez and Ambrosio Reyes Betancourt, had been selected because of their blood group. Their group of A negative, one of the rarest in humans (6 percent of the world population), was also shared by Fidel Castro. And so, in an emergency, their presence would allow an immediate, arm-to-arm transfusion of fresh blood to save *El Jefe*.

Fidel's escort also included a double. Clean-shaven and smaller than the *Comandante*, Silvino Álvarez was not, strictly speaking, his true double. However, sitting at the back of a car wearing a false beard, he could easily be mistaken at a distance for the *Líder Máximo* (their forehead and nose formed the same oblique shape, slightly bent where they joined).

This means of disinformation had been used on various occasions, notably in 1983 and 1992, when Fidel Castro fell seriously ill without anyone knowing about it, as I will recount in greater detail in chapter 13. *El Comandante* took to his bed for several weeks amid the greatest secrecy while the fake Fidel was installed at the back of the presidential limousine, which drove around Havana, taking care to go through numerous populated areas such as the port, the Malecón (the seafront avenue), Prado Avenue, Fifth Avenue, and in front of the embassies of capitalist countries such as France and the United Kingdom. Silvino Álvarez would then lower the car window and, from a distance, greet passersby with gestures similar to those used by Fidel. The people were completely taken in, as the police informers stationed in the town would subsequently tell us.

Few could surpass Fidel Castro in matters of disinformation. As the history books record, when American journalists secretly went to interview him in the mountains of the Sierra Maestra, the guerrilla fighter would mastermind a perfectly staged scene: this master of the art of illusion would make his soldiers move around every which way and that in the background so as to create the impression of a mass of people, making his interlocutors believe that his rebel troops were far more numerous than they really were.

Information manipulation techniques are at the heart of the work of protecting every prominent figure, but nowhere as systematically as in Cuba. There, each of Fidel's movements was planned with the aim of deceiving the public about the time, place, and means of transport used. When the Commander in Chief spoke in public, his arrival was announced at a precise time but, in reality, he always came before or after. Similarly, it would commonly be announced that he was arriving in a helicopter when in fact he was being driven to the destination by car. Another example: during his trips abroad, we would make provision for two or three different places to stay (for example two hotel reservations and the residence of the Cuban ambassador) before choosing one at the last moment so as to wrong-foot anyone who, for whatever reason, wanted to know in advance where Fidel planned to spend the night.

Even in Havana, when he made his daily journey to the presidential palace from his property of Punto Cero (a journey of around 7.5 miles), the route to be taken would change at the last minute so that even his own guards would not know what route the head of the escort would choose. In addition, the three cars driving in procession constantly changed position so that nobody ever knew whether the *Líder Máximo* was in the one in front, in the middle, or at the back.

But, until 1979 Fidel's car was easily identifiable: he drove around in a heavy black Soviet ZIL limousine, identical to those reserved for dignitaries in the USSR, that had been given to him by the Kremlin leader Leonid Brezhnev. We members of the escort would drive in burgundy-colored Alfa Romeo 1750s and 2000s—light, nervy, easily handled cars.

However, two years after I joined Fidel's service, the car fleet was totally replaced. On leaving the sixth Non-Aligned Movement summit,* which took place at the beginning of September 1979 in Havana, the Iraqi president, Saddam Hussein, gave his Cuban counterpart an armored Mercedes-Benz 560 SEL, which he had brought with him from Baghdad. Subsequently, Fidel ordered two mechanics from garage no. 1 of the personal security department, two fellows by the names of Socarras and Álvarez, to go to West Germany to buy some secondhand Mercedes-Benz 500s to replace the now obsolete Alfa Romeos.

---

*Formed in Belgrade in 1961, the Non-Aligned Movement is an international organization that groups together countries that define themselves as being allied to neither the Eastern nor the Western blocs.

In conformity with the security procedure applied to all official vehicles repatriated to Cuba after a stay abroad, the Mercedes were sent to the garage of Unit 160 to be thoroughly checked out. They were systematically and completely taken apart, down to the last bolt, in order to make sure that no microphone or explosive device had been slipped behind a door lining, inside a seat, in the dashboard, under the chassis, or in the engine. After the explosive detection specialists gave the all-clear, the Mercedes could finally be reassembled, then put into service.

The escort's weaponry was also not negligible. When Fidel Castro was driven in his armored limousine, he always had a 7.62 mm Soviet Kalashnikov assault rifle placed between his feet along with five cartridges, each loaded with thirty bullets. This weapon never left him. It stayed there even when Fidel invited a foreign guest to get into his car—never failing to greatly impress the latter.

Fidel always sat on the rear seat, to the right. Just behind him, level with his right shoulder, was a 9mm Browning pistol as well as three clips of thirteen bullets. There was also a second 5.45mm Kalashnikov and five clips of thirty cartridges placed at the feet of the head of the escort, Domingo Mainet, who sat in the front passenger seat. To this were added all the guards' weapons: each carried a Browning pistol at his belt and, situation depending, a Kalashnikov slung across the shoulder.

In addition, at that period, the presidential trunk always held a black suitcase containing a 7.62mm Kalashnikov AKM with a wooden butt as well as five clips of forty cartridges. This assault rifle was Fidel's personal weapon, the one he used during the shooting exercises he regularly imposed on himself; it was also the one he took home with him every night. Dalia, warned of our arrival by radio, would be waiting for him on the doorstep of the family home like a devoted wife. In an immutable ritual, Fidel would kiss her on the mouth and then give her his weapon, which she would religiously go and put away in their bedroom on the first floor. At Punto Cero or while traveling, the head of state always slept with his Kalashnikov right next to his bed, within reach.

The trunk of Fidel's Mercedes also held a first aid kit (under the responsibility of his doctor or his nurse), a spare pair of boots, a civilian suit, two or three combat uniforms, ties, military caps, and three spare sets of underwear—not to mention a complete basketball outfit, at least until Fidel decided to stop playing the game because of the injury to his toe in 1982.

Finally, one of the vehicles carried a cooler containing sodas, beers, and bottles of water as well as two pints of goat's milk and natural or lemon yogurts, Fidel's favorite flavors.

To conclude this description of the escort's vehicles, it needs to be pointed out that—despite what I have heard in Miami, from the mouths of so-called Castrist specialists—it is totally false that the presidential limousine carried grenades within arm's reach of Fidel. Like so much of the nonsense one hears about him, this is a case of wild imaginings, tall stories, and fantasies.

———

I occupied a particular, privileged place in the security system of the Cuban head of state, principally because of my three black belts (judo, karate, and close combat), my skill as a marksman, and my total devotion to the Revolution. Very quickly I was assigned the duty of Fidel's personal guard, the supreme honor. Of the thirty to forty escort members, I was called "first" guard, as though I played the first violin in an orchestra. As soon as we got out of the car, it was my duty to position myself right beside or just behind Fidel, to parry any unexpected eventuality and to be his ultimate shield. For seventeen years, I was in the forefront.

A zealous bodyguard, I soon realized that we could improve the personal protection of the "boss" still more. I talked about it with the head of the escort, Domingo Mainet, and we proceeded to make adjustments. For example, at the Ministry of the Interior training school, I had learned that one had to pay attention to people's eyes—do they not reflect everyone's soul and intentions? However, on the ground I discovered that danger came from hands, not eyes. Now, while a well-trained enemy agent could easily mask his facial expressions, it was more difficult for him to disguise the movements of his hands—indeed, he often didn't even think about it. This factor was soon included in the general training of Cuban guards who have since been taught to pay attention to the hands of the people within a crowd.

It was also I who was responsible for changing our shooting postures. Originally we drew our pistols, legs bent, because that gave greater stability. During training, I commented to Fidel that by bending down like that, we lost several precious inches that would have enabled us to screen him better. Fidel agreed. From then on, his bodyguards have been trained to stand up straight on both legs during shooting practice.

It is worth pointing out that it was always Fidel who had the final say in matters concerning his guard, from choosing its members to the weapons it used. Nobody, not the Minister of the Interior, the head of personal security, or the head of the escort, could take an initiative without his approval. In many cases, the head of the escort was no more than the driving belt for the will of the *Comandante*. Dalia made several attempts to get involved in the internal business of the escort, but Fidel did not allow her to do so, and it was much better like that.

Having become the "first" guard, it was logical that I should also become head of the car. As the name indicates, the *jefe de carro* occupied the highest position in the hierarchy of the car in which he found himself. In particular, it was he who liaised with the other heads of the car to coordinate the movement of the motorized cavalcade.

I had also been given another responsibility: the escort's physical training. In short, I was the one who devised the sports training program: a minimum of four hours spent jogging, weight training, and close combat, from eight a.m. to noon. I also naturally carved out a position for myself as a shooting instructor. Every morning we would go to the firing range to practice shooting at fixed or mobile targets while standing, crouching, lying down, or even running, with all sorts of weapons: pistols, rifles, machine guns.

Some training took place at the *Ciudadela* (the Citadel), a ghost town near Mariel, between the Pan-American route and the sea, around twelve miles away from Havana. Still used by the soldiers of the *tropas de choque*, the Cuban shock troops, the Citadel resembled a cinema set with its empty buildings, some of which were topped with the three letters CDR (Committees for the Defense of the Revolution); its fake clinic; and its railway. It was the ideal place to simulate urban combat with moving cars and marksmen in ambush on the roofs.

So as to make it more realistic, a life-size model of a car was placed on the railway tracks as a moving target. The *Cuidadela* contained several practice ranges for shooting with rifles, submachine guns, machine guns, grenade launchers, and rocket launchers, to a distance of about 550 yards. The coastal roads that ran through the site also allowed shooting from moving cars. One of the exercises I developed consisted of drawing a weapon, loading it, shooting (and hitting the target), and then putting it away in the holster, all within less than three seconds.

Personally, I rapidly exceeded the obligatory four hours of daily training, imposing on myself a program of running and shooting on my days off so as to hone my skills to the maximum, to set an example, and to maintain my position at the head of the team. I willingly gave up most of my half days of rest and my holidays to work six days out of seven or even more.

As the person responsible for the escort's physical training, it was also my job to select which soldiers of the group would have the honor and privilege of accompanying Fidel Castro on his official trips abroad while the rest, whose performance was less impressive in my eyes, would stay behind in Cuba. Without doubt, this provoked jealousy and led to some guards harboring resentment against me.

In the mid-1980s, I added another string to my bow: I was chosen to do the job of forerunner, the person who went ahead as scout to carry out all the preparations needed to ensure the security of President Castro before he arrived in a given country. For example, the forerunner had to conduct reconnaissance in the capital to be visited, decide on the securest routes, and check that the Cuban delegation had everything they needed and were not exposed to any risk.

It was therefore also up to me to rent houses or make hotel reservations while ensuring that the entrances and exits of these buildings were secure. Suitcase of cash in hand, I sometimes even bought houses, particularly in Africa, when I judged that to be the best way of guaranteeing Fidel's security during the night. I was not alone in this mission. *La avanzada* (the advance party) generally included six officers: a head of the medical team, someone responsible for food, a *Técnica* specialist (from the technical department of the secret police, responsible for placing or detecting microphones), myself, and the head of personal security (at that time Maj.-Gen. Humberto Francis Pardo, who had several thousand men under his command).

Apart from Major-General Francis, the most vital link in the chain was naturally the one that directly represented Fidel's escort—at the time, yours truly. Nothing was more important than the Commander in Chief's security. With my colleague from the *Técnica*, I devoted particular care to uncovering any hidden microphones. In the course of my career, I found two: one hidden in the window frame of Fidel's hotel room in Madrid, the other in the false ceiling of the residence of the Cuban ambassador in Harare, Zimbabwe. In the countries we visited, *la avanzada* obviously received the support of the intelligence officers attached to the Cuban embassy.

Fidel always seemed satisfied with my work. More than once, when I stood on the ground to greet him as he walked down from an airplane, I heard him exclaim, "Ah, Sánchez! Are you here? *Muy bien*, all is in order. Tell me, Sánchez, what do you suggest?"

I would then set out for him all the issues relating to logistics, security, and his movements. I would sometimes advise him, for example, not to go toward the crowd at a certain moment of a particular official visit because our intelligence agents had learned that false partisans hoped to draw him toward them with cries of *¡Viva Fidel!* (acclamations to which Fidel was particularly susceptible), so they could insult him as soon as he was near them. As a general rule, I would also set out the accommodations possibilities I envisaged as he walked down from the plane—but he trusted me to make the final choice.

My career within the "family" of the escort progressed steadily. Lieutenant in 1979, I was promoted to captain in 1983, major in 1987, and lieutenant colonel in 1991. I was sure of one thing: I always did good work. In 1986, Major-General Francis, who as commander of the general personal security department was one of the most important figures in Cuba, had me draw up a report on my vision of the escort of a head of state. He liked my comments so much that after reading them he asked me to give a conference to the whole of the personal security staff, in other words to all the heads of escort of all the Cuban leaders.

On certain occasions, Fidel would also reward my services with a medal. On our return from Brazil in January 1990, where Fidel had attended the inauguration of President Fernando Collor de Mello,* for example, I was decorated for the excellence of my work in Brasília. In November 1992, I won the national contest for the best service pistol marksman from twenty-five meters (about twenty-seven yards), setting an absolute record of 183 points out of 200 and earning the distinction of being the first Cuban soldier to be designated an expert gunman.

As I have said, my role as "first" guard also extended to the sea during the underwater fishing expeditions at Cayo Piedra, where it was my responsibility to protect Fidel from the moray, sharks, and barracudas. However, in a less athletic arena, my most important function was without doubt the keeping of the *libreta*. I would jot down everything Fidel did over the course of each day in this gray pocket-size notebook: what time he got up, what he had for breakfast (and for every other meal), the time he left for the *Palacio de la Revolución*, the time he arrived, the route taken by the presidential cortege through Havana, the names of the people received in audience, the time and duration of each meeting, as well as the subjects addressed.

Whether he was telephoning the leader of the Kremlin

---

*He would be deposed just two years later, in 1992.

Mikhail Gorbachev, meeting the Minister of the Interior José Abrantes, or visiting his friend Gabo (Gabriel García Márquez) in his house in Havana, the subjects discussed had to be jotted down succinctly. This work of scribe was a special vocation. Sometimes it involved the most trivial details; at Cayo Piedra, for example, I had to make an exact list of the number of fish caught by the lord of the manor: ten lobster, four red snapper, three grouper fish, and so on. I had to also write the name, the origin, and the vintage of the wine each time Fidel uncorked a bottle.

When I had a day off, my replacement in *grupo 2*, my partner, noted everything down on loose paper; the following day, I had to put together the information he had collected and copy it down into the *libreta*. From 1977 to 1994, I kept that notorious gray notebook, giving me a detailed, hour-by-hour knowledge of Fidel Castro's life.

When all the pages of the *libreta* were filled, the notebook was wrapped up with string like a birthday present, sealed with wax, and then sent to the documentation service of the *Palacio de la Revolución*, where it was stored away for posterity, next to hundreds of other identical notebooks. The whole of the Commander's life therefore occupies several yards of shelving somewhere within the presidential palace in Havana. There, too, are all the audio recordings made on Fidel's orders (but unknown to his interlocutors); whenever possible, he recorded all his important conversations, either with the hi-fi installed in his office or the minicassettes that we members of the escort always carried in our luggage. Cautious Fidel also ordered that if ever Cuban communism were toppled, these archives must be urgently destroyed.

Fidel's escort might have constituted his only "real" family, but I have to acknowledge that the same was true for me. Entirely devoted to the Revolution, I had little time to spare for my wife and children. It has to be said that I had a fantastic job. Action, travel, spying, counterespionage, all while immersing myself in the nerve center of power: in short, all the ingredients of a good film. Icing on the cake: I acquired a certain fame. As I always appeared in the photo frame or on television behind the *Líder Máximo*, I was a celebrity in my neighborhood. I remember that before we moved into our own flat and were still living with my mother, pretty female neighbors would seize on the slightest pretext to come and visit us—preferably when my wife was not there—to check whether I might not, by chance, be on the premises. Though I would like to reassure my beloved ex-wife that the Revolution and service to Fidel left no time for philandering.

I have often been asked whether Fidel Castro was a father substitute. I always reply that no, he represented much more to me! I drank in his every word, believed everything he said, and followed him everywhere. I would have died for him. At one time, my deepest wish was truly to be killed in the act of saving his life. I had an unshakeable belief in the noble ideals of the Cuban Revolution and could reel off without doubt or hesitation the prevailing anti-imperialist creed. My eyes were opened later, but at that period I was too absorbed in my job and too fascinated by Fidel to exercise my critical faculties in any way.

The atmosphere within the escort was excellent, at least during the reign of Domingo Mainet, in other words before the arrival in 1987 of his idiotic successor, José Delgado Castro, the most incompetent leader—conspiratorial, cowardly, stupid, jealous: the list goes on—that Fidel ever had as head of his escort. Very fortunately, as I have already said, the real head of Fidel's escort was in fact Fidel himself.

At any rate, my colleagues and I always aimed at excellence and, even under the reign of the imbecile José Delgado Castro, I believe we attained it. Our foreign counterparts themselves, including the CIA, said and wrote that the Cuban services as a whole were among the world's elite, ranking alongside the five greats: the United States, USSR, Great Britain, France, and Israel. It is true that we took our inspiration mainly from the American Secret Service and the Israeli Mossad, but we were also influenced by the French service and the British MI5.

The experience of the KGB in terms of the protection of VIPs was, on the other hand, without value or use in our eyes. The Russians could teach us nothing because the public appearances of dignitaries in the Soviet Union were rare, static, orchestrated, and regulated like clockwork, with never the slightest direct contact with the crowd or any improvisation or spontaneity. In short, the very opposite of Fidel, who was instinctive and impulsive, diving into the crowd without warning and exposing himself to all sorts of risks and dangers.

Naturally, we analyzed in the smallest detail all the attacks, successful or attempted, that had taken place against heads of state or celebrities all over the world: John and Robert Kennedy (1963 and 1968), Anastasio Somoza (1980), John Paul II (1981), Indira Gandhi (1984), and the Colombian presidential candidate Luis Carlos Galán (1989). As for the assassination attempt on General de Gaulle (1962) in the suburbs of Paris, we examined it from every conceivable angle, as we did the 1986 ambush on Pinochet in Chile in 1986—which had in fact been devised with the help of Cuba. I remember that my colleagues and I felt sincere admiration for the chauffeurs of the two presidents, who had demonstrated extraordinary sangfroid, reflexes, and courage in saving the lives of their bosses.

Imagining, anticipating, preparing for, and avoiding any attack against Fidel Castro was our permanent preoccupation at that time of cold war, particularly in the 1980s when the American president Ronald Reagan had vowed the death of international communism. The threat was real. We were very aware that one of Fidel's most vulnerable points was his island vacation home of Cayo Piedra, if it were ever discovered. Several types of attack were possible: bombardment of the island via a tourist plane such as a Cessna flying at low altitude and therefore undetectable by radars; an attack from a fast patrol boat bombarding us like a gunboat; or a special operation of enemy underwater divers placing explosives on Fidel's yacht, the *Aquarama II,* by night so as to blow it up when he was on board.

There were no refuges or air raid shelters on the island, and so an evacuation plan was drawn up to offset the danger of a bombardment. The idea was simple: to drive Fidel some two hundred yards from his main house to hide him in a swampy area where, beneath the vegetation that was invisible from the sky, a jetty had been built to provide Fidel shelter until the first

salvo was over. The evacuation of the island would then immediately begin, the idea being to start up all the watercraft and
helicopters present on the island at the same time, so as to confuse the enemy. Of course, Fidel would not be in his yacht but
in a smaller, more discreet boat. A variation on this scenario
had also been devised, in which Fidel would stay on the island
as all the motorized vehicles left so as to create the illusion that
he was fleeing; a Cuban commando would come several hours
(or days) later to pick him up.

Needless to say, there was no scenario that Fidel—who almost
caused a nuclear war to be unleashed during the 1962 missile
crisis*—did not envisage, including regional or world war. A
fallout shelter was therefore built in Havana under the presidential palace, and it was in this bunker that a war council consisting of Fidel, Raúl, the leading ministers, and the commanders
of the three armies—land, air, and sea—would find refuge. This
shelter of at least 1,200 square yards was large enough to contain offices or meeting rooms, a dormitory, a dining room, a
kitchen, bathrooms, and a "war room" from where Fidel would
supervise operations. About six yards underground, a secret tun-
nel over two hundred yards long ran underneath Independence
Avenue and linked the *Palacio de la Revolución* to the Ministry

---

*From October 14 to 28, 1962, the missile crisis pitted the United States
against the Soviet Union when it was discovered that Soviet nuclear missiles
pointing toward the United States had been secretly installed in Cuba. The
crisis was the culmination of the cold war and was resolved directly between
John F. Kennedy and Nikita Khrushchev, without Fidel Castro being consulted.

of Cuban Revolutionary Armed Forces (under the leadership of Raúl Castro), which also housed a fallout shelter.

In the event of war, Fidel's escort would immediately have swapped their Mercedes-Benz for Cruiser Land Rovers armed with RPG rocket launchers, RPK machine guns, and 30 to 40mm caliber grenade launchers. In such an eventuality I would have retained my role as head of car but of a British four-wheel drive carrying eight men: a chauffeur, six guards (including three snipers), and myself. As for Fidel, he would be driven everywhere in an armored military vehicle.

The security of Fidel's family had not been overlooked. In case of international conflict, Dalia and her children would have had the choice of two shelters. The first was an unoccupied house in Punta Brava, the same one where Dalia had been accommodated in 1961 when she arrived in the capital, before going to live with Fidel,* the other hidden within the House of Gallego, a house situated just opposite Unit 160 where Fidel was in the custom of celebrating his birthday with his escort. On the other hand, contrary to the widespread rumors on the subject, the Castros' house in Punto Cero contained no air raid shelters. That made sense: who would be stupid enough to hide in their own home?

We also knew that danger could present itself in the banal form of a meal, which was why all the food consumed by Fidel was, and still is, subject to bacteriological and chemical tests before

---

*Punta Brava is located on the outskirts of Havana, around four miles southwest of the family residence of Punto Cero.

being served to him. These tests are carried out by the famous Medical-Surgical Research Center in west Havana, just half a mile away from the Castros' property. Similar precautions are taken in regard to the cases of wine that Fidel receives as gifts: the escort would choose several bottles at random to check that they did not contain explosives or poison. From time to time, a chauffeur from Unit 160 was chosen to test the drink; just like medieval kings, Fidel had his taster.

Even the food from the Punto Cero complex was subjected to particular monitoring. Vets ensured the good health of the chickens and cows raised on the property while the fruit and vegetables grown in the six hothouses in the garden were systematically washed with ozone in a special method that rid the produce of potential contaminated residue, thereby avoiding cancer risks as far as possible. Similarly, the well water in the garden was regularly tested.

All these precautions give the impression that Fidel Castro was surrounded by enemies and lived under the permanent threat of poison attempts—and it was true! As the American secret services have themselves admitted, for a long time—doubtless until the beginning of the 1990s—the CIA concocted numerous assassination plans, although none of them came to fruition. In the early 2000s, a certain number of secret American archives dealing with this subject were declassified and made public. Nonetheless, that does not mean that Fidel had nothing but enemies. On the contrary, his worldwide followers were an extended family, much larger than that of his guards. I have seen many of them, whether revolutionary leaders, Latin American guerrilla fighters, or Basque terrorists, marching through Havana. These disciples see Fidel as the foremost leader of the developing world and the most experienced anti-imperialist guerrilla fighter; for them, he is more than the head of the family. He is a guerrilla war leader, always ready to dispense wise advice on matters of subversion.

GUERRILLA FIGHTERS OF THE WORLD, UNITE

One of the best-kept secrets entrusted to me in Cuba was that of the existence of the training camp of Punto Cero de Guanabo (not to be confused with Punto Cero, the Castros' private residence). It was here, fifteen miles east of Havana on a military terrain guarded by a nondescript-looking main gate, that the government trained, shaped, and advised guerrilla movements—and even certain guerrilla organizations—from all over the world. Just a few minutes from the idyllic beaches, on 3.8 square miles of rolling terrain covered with vegetation, over fifty buildings in separate "villages" linked by a network of country roads were spread out. There were classrooms, residential buildings, a canteen that could serve six hundred meals an hour, training grounds with obstacle courses, three practice target areas, a quarry for the detonation of explosives, and the frames of two propeller planes (an Ilyushin and an Antonov) in which life-size simulations of airplane hijacking took place. There was also a helicopter, similarly nailed to the ground, which allowed trainees to learn how to get down from such an aircraft after landing, when the blades were still turning, and, also, how to launch a hijacking attack on it.

Here, only the *tropas*—the shock troops—were Cuban. The recruits, for their part, came from Venezuela, Colombia, Chile, Nicaragua—in short, from all over Latin America and even beyond. In a conservative estimate, 90 percent of Latin American guerrilla leaders have passed through Punto Cero de Guanabo. Whether they were members of ELN (Ejército de Liberación Nacional, Colombia's National Liberation Army), FARC (Fuerzas Armadas Revolucionarias de Colombia, the Revolutionary Armed Forces of Colombia), M19 (the April 19 Movement, another Colombian organization), the Peruvian Sendero Luminoso (Shining Path), MRTA (Movimiento Revolucionario Túpac Amaru, the Revolutionary Movement of Túpac Amaru, also from Peru), the FPMR (Frente Patriótico Manuel Rodríguez, the Patriotic Front of Manuel Rodríguez, Chile), the FSLN (Frente Sandinista de Liberación Nacional, the Sandinista Front of National Liberation, Nicaragua), or else FMLN (Frente Farabundo Martí para la Liberación Nacional, the Farabundo Martí National Liberation Front, Salvador), for them Cuba was Mecca and Punto Cero de Guanabo a prerequisite.

The golden age of this "campus of revolution" had occurred in the 1970s and 1980s. At the time, it also played host to soldiers from other regions of the world such as militants or terrorists from the Basque separatist movement ETA (Euskadi Ta Askatasuna, Basque Homeland and Liberty), the IRA (Irish Republican Army), Yasser Arafat's Fatah, George Habash's Popular Front for the Liberation of Palestine, the Polisario Front (a popular movement in Western Sahara), or else the North American Black Panthers. Among its famous guests, we should cite the Venezuelan terrorist Ilich Ramírez Sánchez, aka Carlos the Jackal; brothers Daniel and Humberto Ortega, future Nicaraguan leaders; Abimael Guzmán, the mad terrorist of the Peruvian Shining Path; and, apparently, the "assistant commander," Marcos of Mexico.

Punto Cero de Guanabo was just twenty minutes away from the Palace of the Revolution, which housed Fidel's office on the third floor. However, the place was so secret that I only went there three times, at the beginning of the 1980s. Even though this military zone was placed under Fidel's direct responsibility (rather than that of the Ministry of the Interior or of the Armed Forces), the *Comandante* rarely went there. At that time, the place was run by Gen. Alejandro Ronda Marrero, the head of the *tropas* and a key figure who played a vital role in the secret dealings with the Latin American revolutionary left. It was he, for example, who in the 1970s was the officer dealing with the Venezuelan terrorist Carlos.

The first time I set foot on Punto Cero de Guanabo was in the company of Fidel, during one of his inspection tours. When we arrived that day, General Ronda Marrero was waiting for us outside the headquarters, in the company of three officer trainers. After greeting the *Comandante*, the general took him to carry out his tour of inspection, beginning with the pistol shooting range just behind the building. During our walkabout, we visited in succession Guatemalans, Salvadorans, and Colombians, all guerrilla fighters in their respective countries who were on a training course there. Finally, the tour—which had lasted three hours in total—took us to the long guns (rifles, machine guns, and so on) shooting range, situated on a raised area, with metal targets placed on another raised area about 325 yards away.

Fidel then asked for his black suitcase, kept in the trunk of his Mercedes, which contained his AKM Kalashnikov 7.62. Then he stretched out on the ground to shoot at metal targets. For almost every shot, one could hear in the distance the little metallic sound—*ping!*—that showed he had hit the target despite the considerable distance. Fidel was in fact an excellent rifle shot. He loved to fire shot after shot, "peppering" like a madman as he emptied at one go cartridges that contained rounds of thirty or forty bullets. That day, he fired off so many that the varnish on the lower, wooden part of his weapon began to crack from the heat. So Fidel asked for his second rifle to be brought, the one with a folding butt that he always kept inside his car, at his feet. Then he went back to taking his potshots.

At the end of the day, we went back to the *palacio*. I no longer recall what Fidel said that day to the trainee guerrilla fighters, but he must have inspired them—as he knew so well how to do—with revolutionary fervor by talking to them about the importance of their commitment and their sacrifice for "the cause." One thing was certain: seeing the Commander in Chief in the flesh must have been a major event for all these men—for some, probably the greatest day of their lives.

There is nothing inherently surprising about the existence of a camp like Punto Cero de Guanabo, a veritable guerrilla laboratory. Those who have some knowledge of the history of the Cuban Revolution and of Fidel's personality know that such an infrastructure, dedicated to international subversion, was entirely in keeping with Castrist political thinking and military action.

From the start of the Revolution, the *Líder Máximo* had his sights set on international, even planetary, goals far beyond his domestic context. Fidel's ambitions were not limited to Cuba. Castro intended to export his revolution everywhere, beginning with the Latin American continent, where he wanted to create a "One, two, three, Vietnam" according to the Castrist theory of *foco* (focus), or focalism.

Popularized by Ernesto Che Guevara, this doctrine recommends increasing the number of rural insurrectionist groups, whose actions would spread like fire to the large cities, then throughout an entire country. In 1967, the Frenchman Régis Debray took up the idea in *Revolution in the Revolution*, a book that became phenomenally successful. It has been forgotten now, but in university circles all over five continents this bestseller became the reference work for all guerrilla movements and their future combatants, as much in Latin America as in Africa or the Middle East.

Beginning in July 1959, Fidel moved on to a phase of "practical work," launching very ambitious, all-out initiatives. Just six months after the overthrow of Batista, for example, he mobilized an expeditionary force of more than two hundred Cubans in the hope of unleashing an uprising against the dictator Rafael Leónidas Trujillo on the neighboring volcanic island, the Dominican Republic. With the local army lying in wait for them, the rebels were wiped out. A month later, snap: an identical operation was mounted against the dictator François

Duvalier, aka Papa Doc, on the other side of the island, in Haiti. Another failure, from which there were practically no survivors.

In 1961—the year the Berlin wall was built—Fidel took to the ocean for the first time, delivering cargos of weapons by boat to the fighters of the Algerian FLN (Front de Libération Nationale, National Liberation Front), at war with the French army. During the same period, several guerrilla movements sponsored by Havana rose up in South America: the Ejército Guerrillero del Pueblo (People's Revolutionary Army) was started in Argentina in 1962 and included in its ranks a certain Abelardo Colomé Ibarra, aka Furry, the present Cuban minister of the interior; in Colombia, ELN and FARC saw the light of day in 1964. As for Che, he launched the "African adventure" in 1965 by trying, in vain, to create a gigantic *foco* in the Congo.

This historical note would be incomplete without mentioning the Tricontinental Conference, also known as Trico, that Fidel Castro organized in January 1966, during which he officially designated Havana the epicenter of world subversion. It was an unusual kind of conference: for two weeks, the Trico united "anti-imperialist" forces from all over Africa, Asia, and Latin America. Eighty-two delegations from former colonies, Afro-Asian liberation movements, and Latin American guerrillas were all gathered at the Habana Libre hotel. Among the participants were representatives from the PLO (Palestine Liberation Organization); a Vietnamese delegation; Salvador Allende, future president of Chile; Amílcar Cabral, future hero of Guinea-Bissau independence; and the Guatemalan officer Luis Augusto Turcios Lima.

It was in this context that Fidel opened the training camp

of Punto Cero de Guanabo. True, the death of Che Guevara on October 9, 1967, in the Bolivian maquis marked a turning point: Fidel acknowledged the failure of the *focos* of rural guerrillas because of their lack of preparation, due to an overly romantic approach to revolution. However, this in no way brought into question his fundamental goal of exporting revolution. To achieve that end, he needed to become more efficient, and the trainers of Punto Cero de Guanabo dedicated themselves to that objective.

To give an indication of the seriousness with which international revolution was being prepared in Cuba, the training courses at Punto Cero de Guanabo lasted an average of six to nine months—virtually as long as national service. During that period, students were absolutely forbidden to leave that ultra-secret zone. In addition, in order to guarantee participants' anonymity, the various groups were hermetically sealed off by nationality: they lived in groups of forty or fifty in separate areas, ate in the canteen at different times, and went to the shooting range at different times of day. And so the Salvadorans never ran into the Colombians, who never met the Arabs, and so on. Anyone who disobeyed the rule was immediately sent back to his country. During our tour of inspection of Punto Cero de Guanabo, Fidel met the Guatemalans, the Salvadorans, and the Colombians separately, and none of them knew about the existence of the other groups, just several hundred yards from their own sector. As another precaution, the groups traveled from one point to another in a minibus, and when they encountered another vehicle, they were ordered to plunge their head between their knees.

The *guerrilleros'* curriculum was wide-ranging and of a high quality. Other than Marxism and literacy for some students, there was instruction in how to handle firearms and explosives, map reading, photography, counterfeiting documents, disguise and change of appearance, identity theft, encryption of messages, basic techniques of espionage and counterespionage, urban and rural guerrilla methods, sabotage, terrorist acts, the planning of kidnaps and hostage taking, hijacking of boats and planes, interrogation and torture techniques, logistics, and political strategy.

Military maneuvers were also on the agenda. During their stay, students went off to camp in the forest for periods of ten days in real guerrilla conditions; there, they learned survival in hostile territory and tactical organization of small fighting units—in short, the art of war. These operations took place in one of the two Puntos de Entrenamiento de Tropas Irregulares (Training Centers for Irregular Troops) in the province of Pinar del Río, ninety-three miles away in the far west of the country. That was the only time the apprentices left the base of Punto Cero de Guanabo.

For the left and the extreme left in Latin America, all roads led to Havana. However, it would be simplistic to think that the Revolution was being prepared solely within the "university" of Punto Cero de Guanabo. Since his guerrilla years and the start of the Revolution, Fidel attached considerable importance to the espionage work carried out by his secret services abroad. Though not his only target, Latin America was his main one. In 1975, he created the notorious *Departamento América* under the leadership of Manuel Piñeiro, until then head of the General

Intelligence Directorate. Nicknamed Barbarroja ("Redbeard") because, unsurprisingly, of his ginger beard, this artfully cunning spymaster had the job of detecting, recruiting, and training supporters of the Cuban Revolution, whether students, trade unionists, university lecturers, politicians, or even CEOs. The goal was to create, all over the continent and for generations to come, agents who would influence and engage in propaganda and even moles who would infiltrate governments. One example among thousands: in the 1980s, the Venezuelan economist Adina Bastidas was recruited by the *Departamento América* when she was an adviser to the Sandinista government of Daniel Ortega in Nicaragua; twenty years later, between 2000 and 2002, here she was, vice president of Venezuela in the government of Hugo Chávez. Another example of a recruit of the *Deparamento América* was Alí Rodríguez Araque, an ex-*guerillero* who had become minister of energy and oil, then foreign minister and minister of economy, in the same Chávez government.

One day in 1989, I saw Redbeard striding into Fidel's anteroom at the *palacio*. He was accompanied by the Brazilian trade unionist Luiz Inácio Lula da Silva, who was running for the presidency of his country for the first time. While the electoral campaign was in full swing in Brazil, Lula apparently thought it useful to make a stopover in Havana to meet Fidel. Redbeard's first words still resonate in my mind: "May I introduce you to the future president of Brazil?" he announced. His prophecy came to pass, but not until twelve years later. The spymaster never knew: he died in a car accident in 1998, at a time when he was about to embark on writing his memoirs. As for Lula, who was president of Brazil from 2003 to 2010, he was never heard to express the slightest criticism or reservation about the Castrist regime, even though during his term of office it held dozens of political prisoners. . . . Worse, in 2010 after the death in prison of the Cuban dissident Orlando Zapata after a hunger strike, Lula—in Cuba at the time—declared that he did not agree with such methods. He was talking about hunger strikes.

To judge the efficacy of the Cuban espionage system, one need only look at the case of Chile. Before the Nicaragua of Daniel Ortega in the 1980s and Venezuela of Hugo Chávez in the 2000s, the Chile of Salvador Allende at the start of the 1970s was without doubt the country in which Cuban influence had penetrated most deeply. Fidel devoted enormous energies and resources to it. I was obviously not in Fidel's direct employment during the crucial years of the People's Unity government of Salvador Allende (1970–1973), but from listening to Redbeard, who was always hanging around the presidential palace, and Chomy (José Miguel Miyar Barruecos, Fidel's secretary) talking to the latter about Chile, I eventually absorbed the history as though I had lived it alongside them.

First of all, let us get one fact straight: despite what so many people said, Allende was not "Castro's man," nor his puppet. On the contrary, at the time, Allende's accession did not really serve Fidel's purpose. The Chilean had come to power through democratic means, demonstrating that for the Latin American left there was a real alternative to armed struggle: elections. Fidel's real protégés were Miguel Enríquez, the leader of the Movement of the Revolutionary Left, and Andrés Pascal Allende, cofounder of that radical movement and also nephew of President Allende. For Fidel, these two young Marxists who had partly trained in Cuba embodied the real future of Chile.

On that basis, the tactics of the ever-Machiavellian Fidel were simple. They consisted of cultivating and developing the image of these two hopefuls among Chilean youths. In the medium or long term, the objective of Fidel Castro, who always projected himself ahead into the future like a chess player thinking three or four moves ahead, was to impose one or the other of them as the natural leader of Chile the day circumstances allowed Allende to be succeeded. With a little patience, Cuba would thus have an unconditional ally in Santiago de Chile.

While waiting to fulfill that goal, Manuel Piñeiro and the Cuban services penetrated and infiltrated the entourage of Salvador Allende. First of all, they recruited the journalist Augusto Olivares, then media adviser to President Allende and head of public television. According to Redbeard, Olivares, nicknamed El Perro (the Dog), was "our best informer" in Santiago, and Piñeiro often liked to boast that "thanks to him, Fidel was always the first to know what was happening inside the Moneda [the Chilean presidential palace]. Sometimes even before Allende!"

What is more, the Cubans had Beatriz Allende, the president's daughter, twisted around their little finger. She had even married a Castrist diplomat posted in Santiago de Chile. Coincidentally or not, it was she who persuaded her father to get rid of the policemen of the presidential guard, inherited from the previous government, to replace them with a new, more informal escort. Composed of militants of the left and christened the Group of Personal Friends, it included among its ranks two famous Cuban agents, twin brothers Patricio and Tony de la Guardia.

Whatever the case, the coup by Gen. Augusto Pinochet on

September 11, 1973, ruined all the reconnaissance work carried out by the Cuban espionage services. Augusto Olivares, Allende's media adviser, committed suicide at the same time as the Chilean president in the Moneda on the day of Pinochet's putsch. The revolutionary leader Miguel Enríquez was killed by the police in 1974. His associate Andrés Pascal Allende managed to escape to Cuba, where he still lives today. Finally, Beatriz Allende, who had also taken refuge in Havana, killed herself in 1977.

However, the Commander in Chief's interest in Chilean affairs was not extinguished with the death of Allende and the establishment of an extreme right-wing dictatorship in Santiago, for at the precise moment Pinochet took power in 1973, hundreds of Chileans were in Cuba, where they were studying agronomy, medicine, or engineering. Since they were blocked in Havana, Fidel offered them politico-military instruction by sending them to the training camp of Punto Cero de Guanabo, where they were quickly joined by other compatriots from the Chilean revolutionary left who were also in exile in Cuba. Among these new pro-Castrist recruits was Juan Gutiérrez Fischmann, aka El Chele (the Blond). Son of a Bolivian architect and a Chilean woman and already living in Cuba, he was noteworthy on several counts. First, in 1983, El Chele grew close to the immediate circle of power by marrying Mariela Castro, Raúl's daughter, whom he would divorce a few years later after having a child with her. The same year, the Blond cofounded the FPMR, a guerrilla movement that would carry out the spectacular failed attempt against Pinochet in 1986 with *tropas* officers and under the supervision of Gen. Alejandro Ronda Marrero. Long sought by Interpol (who have been unable to bring him to court since 2009) for his participation in various assassination attempts and kidnappings of right-wing Chilean politicians, including the assassination of senator and ex-adviser of Pinochet, Jaime Guzmán, in 1991, the *guerillero* Juan Gutiérrez Fischmann is currently living in Havana—even if the Castrist regime, now under the leadership of his ex-father-in-law Raúl Castro, denies it.

Like the Chileans, generations of Latin Americans have come to take advice, or orders, from Havana. Nothing surprising in that: in the eyes of South American guerrillas and even the left in general, Fidel Castro is an inspiring example—a compass, guide, and mentor. Indeed, no one else possesses as much experience garnered over as long a career. In Latin America, his CV is unequalled. Overthrowing a dictatorship in 1959, he inflicted an unprecedented humiliation on the United States (in the Bay of Pigs in 1961) and then hurtled the planet to the edge of nuclear war during the missile crisis in 1962. Castro battled eleven American presidents and determined the outcome of at least two historic events of the cold war, as we will see later: the Sandinista revolution in 1979 and the Angola war in southern Africa in the 1970s and 1980s.

Whether we like it or not, Fidel Castro is one of the most influential political figures in the history of Latin America, just behind the *libertadores* Simón Bolívar (1783–1830) and José de San Martín (1778–1850), emblematic heroes of South American independence. To give an idea of Castro's charisma and ascendancy over the Latin American left, I shall reveal an event—never before publicized—that I witnessed at the *Palacio de la Revolución* and which shows the degree of similarity between Fidel and the Colombian guerrilla fighter. As background, I need to go back to the creation of one of the most original guerrilla movements of the continent: M19, which arose in Colombia in 1974 and which was launched to the fanfare of a publicity campaign in the principal cities of the country.

Between January 15 and 17 of that year, advertisements were published in the main newspapers announcing, in an enigmatic, anonymous manner, a great event. In *El Tiempo*, Bogotá's leading daily, a marketing campaign proclaimed: *¿Parásitos? ¿Gusanos? ¿Falta de memoria? ¿Inactividad? ¡Ya viene M19!* (Parasites? Worms? Memory loss? Lack of activity? The M19 is coming!) Speculation among the public was rife. Some people presumed that a new miracle drug, the M19, was going on sale in pharmacies.

On the evening of January 17, 1974, just as national monuments were closing, an armed commando stole the sword of the *Libertador* exhibited in the Quinta de Bolívar, the house museum in which the hero had lived for a certain time. Before they left, the *guerilleros* painted their signature onto the white walls: M19. And thus the guerrilla group was launched, with this scandalous, nose-thumbing gesture. Its distinguishing feature: it was an urban, intellectual guerrilla movement, unlike the FARC and the ELN, the two other rebel organizations in the country, both rural in origin.

The theft of Simón Bolívar's sword was, to say the least, the talk of the town, and for seventeen years Colombian journalists tried in vain to track down the sacred relic. And then, around five p.m. one fine day in 1980, when I was on duty in the ante-room of Fidel's office, Jaime Bateman, one of the founders of M19 and the main protagonist in the organization of the sword theft, was announced at the Palace of the Revolution. That day, Fidel did not stand waiting for his visitor in his office, as was his custom, but walked across the anteroom to place himself in the corridor, visibly impatient to welcome Bateman. Was the occasion truly so special? Yes, it was. A minute later, Jaime Bateman emerged from the elevator, at the other end of the corridor, accompanied by Redbeard, and made his way toward us. He was holding a long object wrapped in a piece of simple black cloth. It was a solemn moment. Jaime Bateman was holding the Excalibur that had been stolen six years earlier. Once in front of the *Líder Máximo*, he took it out before our astonished eyes and presented him with the "holy grail" hori-zontally, holding it with both hands.

"*Comandante*, here is the sword of the *Libertador* that we took from the museum to put into better hands," said the Co-lombian *guerillero*, clearly moved. "So that you can take care of it until the day it is possible to return it."

"*Compañero*, now I am the guardian of the sword!" replied Fidel, staring into his eyes.

Then the *Comandante* brought us into his office—Bateman, Redbeard, Eugenio Selman (his personal doctor), and me. At that moment, there were five of us who knew that the sacred sword of Simón Bolívar was in Havana, in Fidel's hands. He would keep it for twelve years, hidden somewhere in his office or in his adjoining bedroom, without anyone else knowing about it. Almost a decade passed, and then in 1989 the M19 laid down its weapons with the intention of entering political life. However, the Colombian government demanded a precondition in exchange: M19 had to give back the sword. And so, just as Jaime Bateman (who died in 1983) had come to entrust it to Fidel, another leader of M19, Arjaid Artunduaga, came to recuperate it from the hands of the *Comandante* in January 1991, so that it could be secretly repatriated to Bogotá. After an absence of seventeen years—including a stay of twelve years in Fidel's office—the sword was securely placed in a safe in the Banco de la República in Colombia while a replica was exhibited at the Quinta de Bolívar.

Since then, the theft of Simón Bolívar's sword has continued to produce heated discussion: Colombian newspapers have repeatedly made "revelations" about what really happened to the relic during the seventeen years it was missing, with much publicized "exclusive" testimonies. Former members of the Colombian guerrilla movement even spoke out on the subject. In 2013, thirty-nine years after the news story that had so perturbed Colombia, I saw Antonio Navarro Wolff, a historic leader of M19 who subsequently became a senator of his country, explaining without giving any further detail that "the Cubans" had previously looked after the sword. This guerrilla fighter, who must have known the truth, never once mentioned Fidel's name, so as to protect the image of the *Líder Máximo*—who would never get involved in some vulgar foreign burglary. This incident demonstrates the powerful sense of gratitude and loyalty that the Colombian guerrilla movement, like most of the Latin American left, felt toward Fidel Castro, even long after they had laid down their weapons.

A natural leader in Latin America, *El Comandante* also played a role in the politics of North Africa and the Middle East. From the beginning of the Revolution, he cultivated and developed his networks in these two regions of the world and made the Palestinian cause his own. In addition, numerous Palestinian students came to study medicine in Havanan universities while the fighters of the PLO came to do military training courses at Cuban training camps.

Cuba was also a haven for fugitives on the run from Fidel's enemies. During my career with the *Comandante*, I learned, for example, that the Puerto Rican Victor Manuel Gerena was on our territory. Linked to the Macheteros—a clandestine pro-independence organization that demanded the emancipation of Puerto Rico from the United States—he was the object of an FBI search since 1984 in connection to the armed holdup of a Wells Fargo bank security truck. At the same period—during the Reagan years—Assata Shakur (the aunt of the deceased rap singer Tupac Shakur), accused of the murder of a white policeman in 1971, also took refuge in Cuba. After escaping from a high-security American prison in 1979 and spending years on the run, the famous Black Panthers militant landed in Havana in 1984, where Fidel granted her political asylum, much to the irritation of the American Congress. She still lives there.

Fidel also established links with the Basque separatists from the ETA, whom I often encountered. In Havana, the Etarras (as they were known) were in their element, welcomed with open arms by Fidel. At the time, they were always received in the building of the Department of Urban Struggle for the *tropas*—the

Cuban shock troops—situated in 222nd Street in the Havanan quarter of Coronela. I remember their names in full: José Ángel Urtiaga Martínez, José Ignacio Echarte Urbieta, José Miguel Arrugaeta, and Miguel Ángel Apaletegui, known as Apala.

The Basque separatists of ETA brought us a lot. They mastered to perfection the art of exploding homemade bombs via remote control. Fidel therefore asked them to teach these procedures to the specialists of the *tropas* who, in their turn, taught them to the guerrilla fighters from Colombia, El Salvador, and Guatemala during the training courses at Punto Cero de Guanabo, where there was a quarry expressly designed for testing explosives. It was here that the Etarras developed their famous rocket launcher, known as the Jotake, a weapon that was subsequently used during attacks in Spain and . . . which was ultimately found in the hands of the FARC in Colombia.

At that time, Fidel directly controlled everything relating to ETA; nothing was decided without his approval. During negotiations in 1984 on the resolution of the Basque question, Cuba signed an agreement with the Spanish government (then headed by the socialist Felipe González) and Panama (under the leadership of Manuel Noriega) that granted political asylum in Cuba to the Etarras. In summary, ETA terrorists were allowed to settle in Cuba, on the condition that they gave up their weapons and no longer conspired against Spain. On his side, Fidel promised that he would control their maneuvers and that he would inform Spain if they took the slightest false step.

The snag was that shameless lying was one of Fidel's many talents. Later, confronted with Madrid's growing suspicions, the *Comandante* insisted on the fact that the Basques had "never used the Cuban territory for activities against Spain or any other country." He even specified that "Cuba scrupulously respects the spirit of the agreement." Now, not only was Havana welcoming more Basques than Madrid suspected but, in addition, far from being watched, these exiled Etarras were actively collaborating with the Castrist regime by offering their know-how in terms of terrorism. Other than the art of handling explosives, these experts in clandestine urban struggle also taught Fidel's officers the arts of kidnapping, shadowing, and evasion techniques.

That was not all. The Etarras also served as clandestine envoys in Latin America. When the *Comandante* needed to send a secret message to one of his contacts on the continent, he would send a Basque messenger to meet the trade unionist, politician, or guerrilla leader. Equipped with a Cuban passport but passing for a Spaniard, the Basque was obviously much less identifiable than a Cuban with his highly distinctive accent.

One day in 1993, Fidel decided to go to the main "protocol house" of the *tropas*, so off we went in convoy, in the Mercedes. In Cuba, protocol houses are villas of which the government has discretionary use to accommodate passing guests, celebrities, or spies visiting the island. They guarantee greater confidentiality than the presidential palace, which was why Fidel liked them.

When we arrived, I was introduced to the high-level Basque leader Jokin Gorostidi Artola, the official head of the Basque deportee board that was officially responsible for establishing contacts with the diaspora of Basque terrorists in exile, under cover of the international agreement.

Fidel and Jokin sat down in the sitting room of the protocol house, situated right next door to that of the Castro couple. It was obvious that Jokin was a Castrist sympathizer. Together, the two men first discussed the comings and goings of Etarras between Cuba and South America, theoretically forbidden under the international agreement. Then they talked business, for, above all, Fidel wanted the Basques to carry on circumventing the American embargo at that difficult time—the beginning of the 1990s—when the economic situation of the island was so catastrophic that it threatened the Revolution.

"Jokin, it is very, very important that you help us create companies outside Cuba," insisted Fidel, always convincing and impressive, not least through his physical presence. "It's crucial. That way, we can buy products that the harsh American blockade prevents us from acquiring."

Jokin was very understanding and keen to help Fidel, going beyond his official mandate to do so. In any case, ETA had already been cooperating discreetly with Cuba in the economic domain. Since the early 1980s, the Basque organization had owned a fish import-export business in Cuba, Gadusmar, as well as a boiler and polyester tube manufacturing company. The latter also had a branch in Venezuela, another in Bolivia, and a third in Panama called—if my memory serves, and I believe it does—Kaidetarra. The purpose of these enterprises was to finance both Basque separatism and the Cuban Revolution.

And so, from the Spanish Basque country to Palestine and from Chile to Colombia, Fidel interfered in secret, dispensing advice and radio-controlled guerrilla fighters. His fervid desire was to change the course of history once again, just as he had done in 1959 in his own country. As patient as a chess player, he pushed his pawns forward without decisive victory. And then, after twenty years of effort, the *Líder Máximo* finally experienced success. And what a success! Over 1,800 miles from Havana, a remake of the Cuban Revolution was being staged: Managua, the capital of Nicaragua, fell into the hands of the "Sandinista revolution," and, like Batista two decades before, the infamous dictator Anastasio "Tacho" Somoza peremptorily abandoned his bunker, the capital, and that volcanic country. The international press celebrated the triumph of the rebels of Central America led by two brothers, Daniel and Humberto Ortega. Yet nobody seemed to know about the role that Fidel had played in the wings—nobody except ourselves, a handful of ministers, generals, and his escort. From his Havanan war room, Fidel had been following the situation for several months, overseeing the advance of the rebels and, eventually, the fall of the last dictator of that banana republic.

NICARAGUA, FIDEL'S OTHER REVOLUTION

"Sánchez, tráeme un whiskycito, ¡en las rocas!" ("Sánchez, bring me a little whisky, on the rocks!") That was also occasionally part of my job, preparing the Commander in Chief's scotch when he was working alone in his office. Without being a great tippler like his brother Raúl, Fidel still drank every day. He liked scotch served with ice or water in a large glass, or else this "little whisky"—that is, a single shot with nothing else in a small glass.

When I brought him his drink that day, I found him plunged in *Newsweek*: he read English fluently and was reading an article that traced the history of the tyranny of the Somozas in Nicaragua.

It was the beginning of 1979 and the dictatorship of that little Central American republic was in its last throes. For more than four decades, the Somoza clan had been shamelessly exploiting the Nicaraguan people; since the assassination in 1934 of Augusto Sandino, the first legendary Nicaraguan guerrilla fighter, that family had been running Nicaragua as though it were its *finca* (farm). The family owned everything: mines, the best terrain, cement works, pasteurization factories, coffee plantations, livestock farming, fisheries, and even parking meters in the capital! Trained by the American marines, the national guard imposed order through brute force, with the blessing of Washington. "Somoza might be a son of a bitch, but he is *our* son of a bitch," Franklin D. Roosevelt once declared, referring to the elder Tacho Somoza, dictator since the 1930s.

When the latter's son, bearing the same name, succeeded him in the 1960s, Washington continued to support without too many qualms this new "son of a bitch" who, in 1972, did not hesitate to misappropriate the international aid granted to victims of the earthquake that had just destroyed sixty thousand houses in the capital, killing twelve thousand people. At that moment, the Sandinista guerrilla movement—founded in Havana in 1961 as the FSLN—sprang into life; until then, its activities had been limited to the mountainous, sparsely populated regions.

When he had finished his reading of *Newsweek* and his small whisky, Fidel indicated to his aide-de-camp, Pepín, that he was ready to leave. Ten minutes later, there we were in the elevator that led directly from the third floor to the basement parking lot where the vehicles of the escort were lined up, ready to leave. Soon our cortege was driving away in procession into the Havanan dusk: that moment at twilight I love when the tropical air suddenly grows cooler and the streets burst into life. We were driving at a leisurely pace toward the quarter of El Laguito, where most of the protocol houses were situated. It was very close to Unit 160 and also to the house of Gabriel García Márquez. We parked outside protocol house no. 14 and went in, and that's where the main leaders of the Nicaraguan revolution were waiting for us—or, rather, waiting for Fidel.

Like most of the protocol houses, it was a villa with a swimming pool. In the living room, the Nicaraguans were sitting in leather armchairs placed around the coffee table. When they caught sight of Fidel, they stood up as a single man; with his six feet and two and a half inches, he towered over the *Nicas*, generally of modest height. It was not their first visit to Havana, far from it, and so I knew them all. Gathered here were all the future heroes of the Sandinista revolution: Tomás Borge, the stocky fortysomething who was the oldest of this band of men in their thirties; Henry Ruiz Hernández, aka Modesto, a mathematician whose feats as a guerrilla fighter were already legendary; Bayardo Arce, a journalist who led the rebels in the region of Matagalpa; Jaime Wheelock, the grandson of an American businessman who had studied political science in Chile under Allende; Carlos Núñez Téllez, the most radical despite his youth; and finally the Ortega brothers, Daniel and Humberto, who would soon become the Nicaraguan president and minister of defense, respectively. Before going into the room, Fidel reminded me to record the conversation, as was his custom, sometimes secretly and sometimes in full view of everybody present. I therefore placed the little cassette recorder on the coffee table and monitored the running of the tapes, which I replaced as often as necessary. Then I tried to make myself scarce in a corner, while continuing to listen attentively to the conversation.

As on previous occasions, the meeting went on and on; they talked until four in the morning. Fidel was a night owl, and he was in the habit of beginning a discussion around seven p.m. and finishing it at dawn. During the conversation, I noticed that the *Líder Máximo* seemed to appreciate Jaime Wheelock, who stood out from the crowd because of his eloquence. For my part, it was Commander Humberto Ortega who held my attention, probably because I sensed that, like me, this man was a soldier through and through. Fidel listened to the news from the "ground," after the failure of the first general offensive against Somoza during the previous September. This badly co-ordinated popular uprising had not had the desired result: it had been ruthlessly crushed by the ten thousand soldiers of the national guard, who had not hesitated to bayonet civilians to death. The final toll was around five thousand dead.

Reorganization was called for and the *Comandante* gave himself to the task by devoting all his energy to persuading the rebels to get on with each other. "*Compañeros*, sacred union is the only way to attain our objectives," he insisted. Now, at that time, the leadership of the FSLN was divided into three branches. The Prolonged Popular War Faction was the oldest, represented by Borge, Ruiz, and Arce, proponents of rural guerrilla warfare. The Marxists Wheelock and Núñez Téllez belonged, for their part, to the Proletarian Faction: since the split with the previous group in 1973, their priority had been to involve students and workers in the towns, alongside the insurgent rural groups. Finally, the *terceristas*—Third Force—constituted the largest grouping as well as the best organized and the least dogmatic, comprising five thousand armed men under the command of the Ortega brothers.

Based on his own experience, Fidel knew better than anyone that this division made the prospect of rapid victory less likely. So, having listened to all the points of view, he set out his own thinking, presenting it from every angle, using the example of Sierra Maestra, detailing the political aspects and the military advantages of his vision. Gradually, the "snake charmer" gained psychological ascendancy over his audience, eventually persuading them to his point of view.

Historians have not realized to what extent Fidel's involvement was crucial in the Nicaraguan revolution. They have written about the financial aid given by Venezuela and Costa Rica, but they have not sufficiently highlighted the role of the Cuban leader. Without his force of conviction, the three factions would not have fallen into agreement so quickly. The proof of that? Because Communist leader Schafik Handal and his *guerillero* compatriot Joaquín Villalobos did not achieve the same cooperation in El Salvador—despite the intense efforts of Fidel, who regularly met the two men in Havana at the same period—the Salvadoran guerrilla movement never managed to overthrow the authorities during its long and bloody civil war from 1979 to 1992.

After making the signing of their sacred union agreement public in March 1979, the Sandinistas launched the "final offensive" in June. Nine months after the failure of the first uprising, a new, nationwide assault was launched. In the north, towns and villages changed hands every forty-eight hours. Popular areas formed pockets of resistance and in the south, where the guerrilla fighters had for several months sought sanctuary, the rebels widened their hold and marched on Managua, which was paralyzed by a general strike declared on June 4. The insurgents staged spectacular coups and acts of sabotage everywhere. Bridges were blown up. The Pan-American route that crossed Nicaragua from north to south was blocked. The rebel army included within its ranks a thousand "internationalist" volunteers come to lend it their strength, as well as a respectable quantity of Cuban "advisers." It would, however, take fifteen thousand dead and thirty thousand wounded (in a country on the brink of ruin and with a population of barely two million) before the capital was taken by rebels. On July 19, 1979, Somoza abandoned his "bunker" and took off for the golden exile of Miami, accompanied by his exotic parrots and seventy members of his entourage. Fourteen months later, after having recently gone to a new political exile in Asunción (Paraguay), to which another tyrant, Alfredo Stroessner, had welcomed him, Somoza died at the age of fifty-five in a spectacular assassination: Argentinian guerrilla fighters, trained in Cuba by the instructors of the military campus of Punto Cero de Guanabo, fired a rocket launcher that pulverized his car in the middle of the street just after it left his house.

For the time being, Fidel savored his victory; after two decades of effort, he had finally managed to export his revolution. At first, a Sandinista junta took the reins of power, with Daniel Ortega as its "coordinator," until he was elected to the presidency in 1984. His brother Humberto was appointed minister of the armed forces while Tomás Borge became minister of the interior, Jaime Wheelock minister of agriculture, and Henry Ruiz minister of external relations. Bayardo Arce was appointed coordinator of the political committee of the FSLN National

Directorate, and Carlos Núñez Téllez first president of the National Assembly.*

The images of jubilation in Managua inevitably reminded Fidel of his triumph, twenty years earlier, in Havana. From Cuba, he continued to dispense advice under the counter, as it were, to the Sandinista junta, although he kept a low profile, like any self-respecting espionage agent, so as not to arouse the suspicions—and irritation—of Washington. He even waited an entire year before going to Nicaragua, scene of one of his most striking successes.

Twelve months after the Sandinista revolution, we flew toward Managua in the presidential plane with, in addition to Fidel and his entire escort, the spymaster of the *Departamento América* Redbeard, and the Colombian novelist Gabriel García Márquez. The view of Managua through the airplane windows as we approached it, with its series of geometric volcanoes, was as unexpected as it was breathtaking.

The visit lasted a week. Fidel decided to explore the whole country as he had done previously in Chile under Salvador Allende. Everywhere he wanted to see evidence of "his" victory. Our cortege stopped in the tiniest villages as well as the main

*Daniel Ortega returned to power in 2007 and is the current president of Nicaragua. He is still an ally of Cuba. His brother Humberto left politics in 1995 to devote himself to business. Appointed ambassador of Peru in 2007, Tomás Borge died in 2012. Jaime Wheelock heads a nongovernmental organization, the Institute for Development and Democracy. Henry Ruiz is fighting against the current Ortegan corruption of power. Bayardo Arce is an economic adviser to President Ortega. Carlos Núñez Téllez died in Cuba in 1990.

towns: Estelí, León, Matagalpa, Granada, Rivas, Masaya. One day, we even went as far as Bluefields on the Atlantic coast, a journey of sixteen hours. Fidel went on more and more walkabouts—with me always just a yard away! To blend in better with the crowds, I swapped my khaki uniform for civilian clothes, thereby passing for a native of the country.

It was a fast-paced journey, rich in emotions. One day, we climbed up as far as the Masaya volcano, one of the most active in the country. The spectacle of the lake of lava at the bottom of the crater was phenomenal. The following day we want to Granada, on the edge of Lake Nicaragua, where our hosts attracted bull sharks (a rare species of freshwater shark) by throwing large buckets of scarlet blood into that immense lagoon.

However, the most extraordinary memory was the military procession itself on the first anniversary of the Sandinista victory, on July 19, 1980. Carlos Andrés Pérez, social democrat president of Venezuela and friend of Fidel, was also present, as was Michael Manley and Maurice Bishop, the prime ministers of Jamaica and of Grenada. The president of the Spanish government, Felipe González, had also traveled there. I was, as usual, in immediate proximity to Fidel on the official rostrum. The procession began with the armored cars and the jeeps, followed by the infantry soldiers of the *Nica* army, when, to general astonishment, a squad of young—and even very young—volunteer fighters appeared. During the whole course of my career, I had never seen such a thing: some of these *muchachos* were barely ten years old and the oldest were fifteen. Their rifles seemed disproportionately big and heavy. The image remains imprinted on my mind. Today, thirty-five years later, thinking of these child soldiers, who were my son's age at the time, gives me goose bumps. On the rostrum, I remember having discreetly observed Fidel's reaction from a corner of my eye: his expression was stone-like and inscrutable.

The surprises did not end there. That same evening, the Sandinistas arranged the best possible accommodations for Fidel, in a residential complex that had until recently belonged to the Somoza clan: eight or ten villas arranged in a circle around a swimming pool. Fidel occupied the largest. A fence protected the area, already surrounded by dense vegetation and a section of tropical forest that resonated with the rhythmic croaking of frogs at night. A military guard post dominated the entrance to the site, where *Nicas* were posted, though they were rather inexperienced in comparison to us Cubans, who already had two decades of practice behind us.

That evening, Fidel retired home on the stroke of eight p.m. I then undertook a reorganization of the security of the accommodations, beginning with placing one of our escort behind the house of the *Comandante* while I, for my part, took up the most important position, in front of the main entrance. From there I organized, as was the rule, the convoy of cars so that it was ready to leave at any moment, and, finally, carried out a general inspection to ascertain that the *Nica* guards were correctly deployed in a ring all around the site. Then I went back to the front steps of the house, where I began chatting with a Sandinista soldier.

All of a sudden—*bang!* A rifle shot rang out at the edge of the wood. A brief silence and then a second shot: *bang!* A fraction of a second later, a fusillade burst out—*bang, bang, bang, bang! Ratatatatatat!* Shots were unleashed in every direction for fifteen interminable seconds. Someone shouted, "Stop your fire!" The shooting ceased. I immediately ran to find out what was going on, expecting to find a corpse or a wounded man, covered in blood. But instead I discovered it was a rather nervous guard who had taken fright at the sound of a branch cracking beneath the weight of a passing cow. He had begun shooting, provoking a contagious free-for-all of rifle fire. Flabbergasted—and amused—by the amateurism of the *Nicas*, I turned toward Fidel, who was already waiting for me on the doorstep.

"*Sánchez, ¿qué pasa?*"

"It's nothing, *Comandante*. It was just a *Nica* who got scared when he asked the cow, 'Who goes there?' As the animal didn't reply to the summons by saying, 'Um, it's me, the cow,' he drew his gun and everyone panicked."

Fidel burst into a volley of laughter such as I had rarely heard.

After a week in Nicaragua, we went back to Cuba, where other festivities awaited us: the national holiday which, that year, commemorated the twenty-seventh anniversary of the attack on the Moncada barracks on July 26, 1953. I barely had time to go home to see my wife and two children before I was already on my way to the town of Ciego de Ávila, about 250 miles east of Havana. Before the crowds of people waving their Cuban flags, Fidel began his speech with these words:

"*¡Compatriotas!* New things are happening. Last year we celebrated our national holiday a week after the great Sandinista victory in the presence of numerous Nicaraguan guerrilla fighters who had come to Cuba. [applause] This year, the relationship between our two people has deepened. [applause] We have just arrived back from Nicaragua. It is therefore inevitable that this country is uppermost in our mind. What is happening there concerns all Latin Americans. Understand the significance and take stock of the joy, enthusiasm, optimism, and emotion at witnessing a second Latin American country freeing itself from imperialism, [applause] to which must be added a third, Grenada. [applause] Now there are three of us that have shaken off the yoke of imperialism radically and permanently. [applause]"

Radically? No doubt about it. Permanently? Not exactly. On March 13, 1979, the Marxist revolutionary leader Maurice Bishop overthrew, almost without violence, the authoritarian regime of Prime Minister Eric Gairy, who had been the president of Grenada since the independence that had been won five years earlier from Great Britain. Grenada immediately fell into the Cuban orbit, thanks to the excellent personal relationship between Maurice Bishop and Fidel Castro, who supplied arms, advice, and military personnel to his alter ego. In 1983, however, the landing of American marines would put an end to the brief revolutionary experience of the Caribbean islands of Grenada.

As for the Sandinista revolution, it would be rapidly jeopardized by dissension. From 1980 on, the daily newspaper *La Prensa*, mouthpiece of the moderate opposition, denounced the authoritarian downward slide of the revolutionary government and the attacks on the freedom of the press. The Church, initially favoring the Sandinistas, also withdrew. The arrival of Ronald Reagan in the White House at the start of 1981 complicated the scenario yet further. Anti-communist and anti-Castrist, he suspended the economic aid given to the Sandinistas by the Carter government while secretly financing the Contras. This counter-revolution was driven by former members of the national guard as well as a section of the peasantry disappointed by the revolution, and it was financed and armed by Washington, which made numerous incursions from neighboring Honduras. Between 1982 and 1987, the country was embroiled in a civil war (twenty-nine thousand dead and thirty thousand wounded) similar to the war that raged in neighboring El Salvador (more than a hundred thousand deaths from 1979 to 1992).

For a decade, Central America was a bloody battlefield, the new theater of the cold war in which the United States opposed Russia and Cuba. A stakeholder in the conflicts in Nicaragua and El Salvador, Fidel personally supervised the arms trafficking that passed through Cuba to supply his allies in these two countries. Without entering into the details of the secret routes or of the estimated number of arms that passed through Havana en route for Nicaragua during those years, I will limit myself to relating the scene I witnessed twice at the military airfield of Baracoa, situated beyond the western exit to Havana, off the Pan-American route. It was here that the planes and helicopters used by the Cuban leaders customarily took off and landed. One evening—it was around 1984 or 1985, at the time when General Ochoa was the head of the Cuban military delegation in Nicaragua and was advising the army of the Sandinista government—Fidel left his office to go to this airfield where, at the end of the runway, was a meeting room for dignitaries and hangars for the aircraft.

When we got there, Fidel's brother Raúl, the defense minister, was already present, accompanied by General Carrera, commander of the base. After the customary greetings, the two brothers sat down in the meeting room, without General Carrera but in the presence of the head of the escort Domingo Mainet and myself. There, in private and away from prying ears, Raúl outlined to his brother the methods by which war weapons would be loaded, transported, and secretly delivered to Ochoa. The latter, Raúl explained, was already stationed in the north of Nicaragua, near the border with Honduras, on the banks of the Río Coco, where under cover of darkness a few hours later he would receive the "merchandise" on a secret runway. Always anxious to check the smallest details and take stock of situations himself, Fidel listened attentively, preoccupied with one goal: making sure that his brother's plan was flawless and that, should the trafficked goods be intercepted by the enemy, it would be impossible to establish the slightest link with Cuba.

After he had been reassured by Raúl on this point, the four of us went out onto the tarmac, where several military trucks had just arrived to deliver wooden crates containing war equipment, notably Kalashnikov rifles. It was dark and the place was badly lit, for most of the lights on the runway were extinguished, apart from the blue approach lights; nonetheless, I could still see that the tail of the machine—an old but imposing Britannia with propellers—had been masked with the colors of Honduras! Fidel greeted the pilots and continued asking Raúl questions; when he was happy that the operation was failsafe, he gave the signal to return to Havana. Several weeks later, I was witness to the same scene with the same protagonists and the same "Honduran" plane. The excursion lasted only an hour, but it allowed me to see that all arms trafficking in Cuba was subject to the green light of the Commander in Chief.

In any event, the peace efforts of the skillful president of Costa Rica, Óscar Arias, ended in the signing of the Esquipulas II agreement. Drawn up over several years under his auspices, it was signed in 1987, the year in which Arias received the Nobel Peace Prize. Esquipulas II gradually brought an end to all the conflicts in the region, from Nicaragua to El Salvador and including Guatemala. The agreement provided principally for the organization of elections in Nicaragua, which were due to take place in February 1990, three months after the fall of the Berlin wall and in a very different, post–cold war climate.

I had heard Fidel expressing his concern on this subject many times in Havana. He became aware of the growing unpopularity of the Sandinistas before anyone else, thanks to the "Cuban advisers" (in reality intelligence agents) that he had put in place around President Ortega. In power for a decade, Ortega's government was not just suffering from the wear and tear of age and the civil war—above all, the people blamed their leaders for having appropriated all the Somozas' assets and for living comfortably off them without really worrying about boosting their compatriots' economic status.

One year before the organization of the elections, to which the Sandinistas had not yet given their support, Fidel brought up the subject with the head of the America Department, the notorious Manuel Piñeiro, the Redbeard.

"Piñeiro, you must convey the message to our Sandinista friends that I think it prudent that they do not hold these elections, because from what I see, there is much to lose and very little to gain," Fidel told him in the office of the *palacio*, where I was also present.

This laconic way of expressing things was typical of Fidel's style: he did not necessarily give precise orders but would often rather deliver opinions or formulate simple, seemingly tenuous outlines—that were in fact injunctions that he expected to see put effectively in place.

This time, however, Fidel no longer had any involvement in the peace process that had been set in motion in Central America. On February 26, 1990, Ortega and the Sandinistas were ousted by Violeta Chamorro, the widow of the editor of the daily *La Pensa*, assassinated by Somoza's henchmen twelve years earlier. She became the first female president of Nicaragua, with an unchallenged result of 55 percent of the vote.

After the Nicaraguan election, I frequently heard Fidel ruminating over that defeat. He would repeat to Redbeard, who had been unable to convince the Sandinistas to block the holding of free elections, "I told them, the Sandinistas . . . I tried to warn them . . . I knew there was popular discontent. . . ." Then, no sooner had Redbeard left the room than Fidel would rage about him: "What an incompetent fool!"

FIDEL IN MOSCOW,
SÁNCHEZ IN STOCKHOLM

Fidel was not particularly crude. His language in public had always been temperate, with the exception of a few speeches in the early years of the revolution in which he described the presidents of America as *hijos de perra* (sons of bitches) or as *hijos de puta* (essentially the same, of the noncanine variety). In more private circles, he sometimes expressed his annoyance with a *coño* (literally "cunt," but used similarly to the American "fuck") to remind people that, in the face of imperialism, Cubans had *cojones* (balls) or to say of an enemy, *¡Qué se vaya al carajo!* (Let him go screw himself!) Ronald Reagan and his successor George H. W. Bush were without doubt the American presidents he most maligned. There were reasons for that: in the 1980s, the Reagan administration had, from its election to power, represented the greatest danger to Fidel. Fiercely anti-communist, the president had financed the Contras in Nicaragua; sent the U.S. Marines to Grenada; and, in Africa, given military support to the soldiers of the National Union for the Total Independence of Angola (known as UNITA, the abbreviation of the

Portuguese version of the name) who were fighting the Cuban army on the ground.*

One of the characteristics of the 1980s was the proliferation of international events, from the boycott of the Olympic games in Moscow (1980) to the fall of the Berlin wall (1989), along with the Falklands war (1982); the end of dictatorships in Argentina (1983), Brazil (1984), and Uruguay (1986); and the Battle of Cuito Cuanavale (1987–1988) during the Angola war, which resulted in Cuba blocking the advance of the South African army.

The event that had the most effect on me personally was the sudden death of Leonid Brezhnev, who had presided over the USSR since 1964 and who succumbed to a heart attack on November 10, 1982.

Several days after having received news of the death, we took off for Moscow to attend the funeral of this leader of a "brother country," leaving our tropical heat for the freezing cold of the banks of the Moskva. However, before reaching the Soviet Union on board the presidential Ilyushin-62 with its colors of the airline company Cubana de Aviación, our plane made a technical stopover at Shannon Airport in Ireland. As soon as it came to a halt, our plane was immediately surrounded by twenty or so soldiers who mounted guard, rifles slung over their shoulders. We were watching this spectacle from the win-

---

*Led by Jonas Savimbi and financed by the United States and South Africa, UNITA fought the Marxist-Leninist government of the People's Republic of Angola, supported by the USSR and Cuba. Like the conflicts of Central America during the same period, the Angolan civil war from 1975 to 1992 was one of the main theaters of the armed conflict of the cold war.

dows of the plane when Fidel suddenly decided to disembark to enjoy an Irish coffee in the transit zone. It was sheer bravado: for the *Comandante*, it was a way of saying that nothing could stop him from making an incursion into enemy territory—on this occasion, that of Ireland, next door to British prime minister Margaret Thatcher, an indefatigable ally of Ronald Reagan.

And so, our small delegation went off in search of Irish coffee! There were eight of us: Fidel Castro, the interpreter Juanita Vera, the aide-de-camp Pepín Naranjo, the head of the escort Domingo Mainet, the Minister of the Interior Ramiro Valdés, the doctor Eugenio Selman, and two bodyguards. For me, this expedition constituted a dangerous moment because, while I always had to be armed when I accompanied Fidel, here that was strictly forbidden. If the police had found out that one of us was carrying a weapon, the discovery would have provoked a serious diplomatic incident.

In the Jetway leading from the plane, Valdés turned to me to ask me if I was indeed armed. I replied by opening my long winter coat, in which I had just pierced a hole through the pocket and the lining. In my left hand I held a mini Uzi, the smallest pistol machine gun produced by the Israeli manufacturers, with its diabolical firing rate: twelve hundred shots a minute! At the end of the Jetway we turned left, crossing the shopping zone, and sat down next to Irish passengers who were astonished to see Fidel, instantly recognizable with his height, his beard, and his military uniform. We just had time to order and swallow our hot drinks before we returned to the cabin of the Ilyushin. Fidel Castro's only visit in proximity of Great Britain had lasted less than ten minutes!

———

After filling up with fuel, we took off again, flying over a Europe that was split into two by the cold war, east and west. Five hours later, the plane landed in the drab gloom of the grieving capital of the USSR. It was so cold that the personnel of the Cuban embassy went off to buy me fur boots to replace the ones I had on, unsuitable for the climate. A Spanish-speaking chauffeur from the Russian security service operated as guide and interpreter. Back at the embassy, this colleague from the KGB watched me as I put on my new boots and then suddenly blurted out: "They're so expensive that even a doctor can't afford to buy them. . . ." He went on: "In our country, a doctor earns much less than a mechanic. So there are lots of doctors and engineers who prefer to work in a factory." At the time, I couldn't understand what he was saying. Seeing my perplexity, he continued: "Here, it's better to have a university degree if you want to get a job as a skilled manual worker." With a friendly smile I replied, "So if all the engineers want to become workers, who are the engineers?" I began asking myself questions. . . .

Later, we went to drop off our luggage at the hotel, then rejoined the *Comandante* in Lenin Hills (today called Sparrow Hills), where the Soviets always put a dacha (a country house) at Fidel's disposition. In the USSR, the KGB took on most of the responsibility for Fidel's security, making my workload a little less intense.

The following day we went to the House of the Trade Unions, where the embalmed body of Leonid Brezhnev was displayed for three days on a red bier decorated with flowers, numerous wreaths, and the countless medals of the deceased leader. Musicians wearing black played Rachmaninoff without a break. After the last homage of ordinary Muscovites came those of Soviet dignitaries and statesmen from all over the world. I recognized Indira Gandhi, Saddam Hussein, and Yasser Arafat, as well as the Polish general Wojciech Jaruzelski and all the leaders of the other Soviet bloc countries. I do not believe Fidel was particularly affected by the death of the austere Brezhnev, even if he gave the opposite impression. I think he had much more natural affinity with the jovial Nikita Khrushchev—but that was not the essential point. The mutual alliance of our two countries was unconditional; for Moscow, Cuba was a vital element in the East-West balancing act, both because it was the sole communist ally in the Western world and because it was situated less than 125 miles from the American coast. And for Havana, Soviet military and economic assistance was, quite simply, vital: without it, Cuba would probably not have withstood American pressure for so long.

The moment arrived when the funeral cortege crossed the capital for the burial in Red Square. Yuri Andropov, former boss of the KGB and new master of the Kremlin, gave the eulogy. After the ceremony, I returned to the hotel with the chauffeurs of the Russian security services; no sooner had we got to our destination than the latter rushed to make purchases in the shop next to the lobby, theoretically reserved for foreign visitors, stocking up on deodorant, toothpaste, and soap manufactured in the countries of Comecon, the Council for Mutual Economic Assistance that united the countries of the Soviet bloc: the USSR, Bulgaria, Romania, Albania, Hungary, Poland, Czechoslovakia,

East Germany, Cuba, Vietnam, and Mongolia. "You have to take advantage when there are goods for sale," they explained to me, "because the only time shops have merchandise is when foreign delegations are visiting Moscow."

The poverty in the USSR jumped out at you, particularly when you left Moscow for the countryside, where the peasants were dressed in clothes that resembled those worn at the time of the Second World War. In the capital, shortages were worse than in Havana, and yet the Soviet model for constructing a socialist state was supposed to be the most advanced. Somewhere deep down, the shadow of a political doubt took hold in my mind. Was the communist system really more efficient than that of capitalism? If that was where the Soviets had got to after sixty-five years of revolution, was following their example truly a good idea? It was a tiny, elusive doubt and I immediately chased it from my mind to plunge back into action, in service of Fidel and the revolution.

After Brezhnev's funeral, a period in which we took many trips to Moscow began—because Soviet dignitaries started dying, one after the other. The brilliant Yuri Andropov who headed the KGB for eighteen years died in 1984 at the age of seventy, after just fifteen months at the Kremlin. The reign of his successor, Konstantin Chernenko, already ill during his term of office, was even briefer—just thirteen months! The old apparatchik died in 1985, at the age of seventy-six. The sprightly fifty-four-year-old reformer Mikhail Gorbachev succeeded him: this protégé of Andropov then launched his famous policy of glasnost (transparency) and of perestroika (economic reconstruction)—of which

Fidel soon expressed all his contempt by describing it as "another man's woman."

During the winter of 1986 we were back in Moscow, and Fidel was trying despite everything to forge links with Gorbachev, when terrible news flashed onto the news ticker of the press agencies: the previous evening, on February 28, 1986, the Swedish prime minister Olof Palme had been assassinated in a street in Stockholm. At exactly 11:21 p.m., Palme came out of a cinema in the capital with a woman. Two shots were fired into his back as the couple were walking back to his home; one hour later, Swedish doctors pronounced him officially dead. The man who fired the shots would never be found and Palme's murder remains a mystery today. At any rate, the entire world found out that in the peaceful Scandinavian democracy, the head of the government was in the habit of walking about without any security presence whatever. . . .

Fidel Castro was thunderstruck by the news of the death of his ally. The Swedish leader—simultaneously socialist, third world–ist, and anti-imperialist—had openly demonstrated his support for the Cuban Revolution and as far back as 1972 Palme had provoked the anger of Washington and a breaking off of diplomatic relations with the United States for a year because of his participation, in his capacity as prime minister, in a demonstration against the Vietnam War. Even worse, on the radio he had compared the American bombing of Hanoi with that of Guernica during the Spanish Civil War and to the massacre of the Jews at Treblinka by the Nazis. Then, in 1975, the daring Swede was the first head of state of a Western country to go on an official visit to Cuba, where Fidel Castro had given him a triumphal welcome in Santiago de Cuba, the second largest city in the country. There, the two men had celebrated the national day of July 26 together.

Just a few hours after the announcement of Palme's death, Fidel expressed the desire to attend the funeral of the Swedish prime minister. Over the following days, we had to exploit every means we could think of to remove the idea from his head, the subject of countless discussions between Fidel's private secretary Chomy, who had been alongside the guerrilla fighter in the Sierra Maestra; the aide-de-camp Pepín Naranjo; Carlos Rafael Rodríguez, friend of Fidel and a diplomat who played a decisive role in Cuba's relations with the Soviet bloc; and myself. We were all agreed: from the point of view of security, Fidel's presence in Stockholm was inadvisable. Indeed, we did not know at the time—and still do not know today—the killer's identity and motivation. Who knew if those who had ordered Palme's assassination did not also want to make an attempt on Fidel's life? In the end, the *Comandante* came over to our point of view and chose Rodríguez to represent him in Sweden.

"Sánchez will go with you to take care of your security," he added. Fidel trusted me, and he was right to do so: taking advantage of a trip abroad to defect would not have entered my mind. At the time, I was perfectly happy in my work in service of Fidel and also impatient to rejoin my family in Havana after each mission away.

And so, the diplomat Carlos Rafael Rodríguez and I took off for Stockholm, via Copenhagen. Once at the Cuban embassy,

I realized again to what extent being Fidel's bodyguard conferred a special status. The ambassador asked my opinion on numerous subjects, as though he was talking to Fidel himself . . . and I have to admit, it was rather nice. On the other hand, the embassy employee who served us an aperitif was not quite as considerate! When she asked me what alcoholic drink I would like, I replied that I never drank. The ambassador insisted, however, and so I finally ordered a Napoleon brandy, inspired by the example of Fidel, who liked that spirit as well as whisky. The domestic servant lectured me in public: "Brandy is not an aperitif, it's an after-dinner liqueur." Stung to the quick, I swallowed my annoyance and replied like a shot, in a tone of humor: "You know what? When etiquette was invented, they forgot to ask my opinion. That's a shame, because with brandy, I drink it before, during, and after meals, you understand?" Two days later, as we were leaving Sweden, I discovered that the wife of the Cuban ambassador, who had taken my comment at face value, had slipped a bottle of brandy into my suitcase as a surprise.

I also remember that before we left, I wandered around the streets of Stockholm, retracing the steps of Olof Palme from the cinema exit to the place where the prime minister had been shot down a few days earlier. The pavement was spilling over with flowers.

The Swedish capital made a strong impression on me, not so much because of its prosperity but rather because of the simplicity of the human relations between the people and their leaders. While I was there I learned that most ministers took the bus, the metro, or the commuter train to go to work. And that Olof Palme himself had regularly cycled around the capital on his bike; he had not wanted to benefit from any privilege—not even that of a bodyguard—in the name of his freedom and of the equality of citizens before the law. I was bowled over. It was exactly the opposite of the Cuban system in which Fidel, protected twenty-four hours a day, never went anywhere without a strict minimum of ten *guardaespaldas* (bodyguards).

RAÚL'S CLAN

In the mid-1980s, alongside my guard duties, I was completing higher education studies at MININT in company with officers from the various military regions of our country. On the curriculum of that continuing education course were classes in political history, criminal law, psychology, and counterespionage. One day, at the end of a class devoted to the recruitment of foreign agents, a student officer—I can still remember his name, Roberto Dobao—came over to me to announce that Ramón Castro wanted a private talk with me. Intrigued, I asked him, "Ramón, the brother of the Commander in Chief?"

"That's the one!"

The student explained that he was working at the Valle de Picadura dairy farm, an agroindustrial farm run by Fidel's eldest brother. Ramón, having found out that Officer Dobao was taking courses with "Fidel's bodyguard," had asked him to approach me discreetly. I was both surprised and intrigued by this request and I willingly accepted. Several days later, on a day off, Dobao and I were en route for Valle de Picadura, about thirty miles east of Havana.

Ramón was Fidel's "other brother." They were almost the same age (Ramón was two years older), the same stature (over six feet two), and wore the same beard. In short, they were physically similar, but the resemblance ended there. Totally uninterested in politics, the eldest Castro had never occupied a government post. *Guajiro* (farmer) through and through, he had quietly devoted his life to agriculture, first by taking over the huge estate of their father, Ángel Castro, situated in the east of the country near Santiago de Cuba, then as a high-level official in the Ministry of Agriculture, and finally as director of the special dairy farm in Valle de Picadura, one of the foremost state industrial farms of Cuba, then producing mainly fruit juice and milk. I had been there several times with the *Comandante*, for Fidel liked to observe for himself the progress of the revolution in the agricultural sector, of which he thought himself an expert.

It took about an hour to reach the place from Havana. No sooner were we there than Ramón came down from his office and took me aside to talk, in the shade of a mango tree. It was odd to be meeting Fidel's brother without my boss. Ramón was visibly preoccupied: "Thanks for coming, Sánchez," said the farmer whose handshake was even firmer than Fidel's. He immediately set out the reason for his distress, using the familiar "you" form.

"Listen, I've been trying to get hold of my brother for months, but it's impossible. . . . I don't know what's going on. I've left messages everywhere, including at the *palacio* . . . no reply! I really need to speak to him. So could you have a word with him for me?"

"Of course, *señor*, I promise to do what I can," I said, using the formal "you" form since I wasn't in the habit of addressing just anyone with the familiar form, especially not official figures such as Ramón.

When we got to the *palacio* the following morning, I took the opportunity of being alone in the elevator with the *Comandante* to talk about Ramón.

"*Comandante*, yesterday I was at Valle de Picadura and I found your brother very upset and sad. . . . I think he would like to talk to you. . . ."

"I know, I know . . . I know about it, Sánchez. . . . Don't worry, I'll talk to him," replied Fidel, bringing the conversation to a close.

I didn't know what vital news Ramón had to tell his brother but, in any case, I knew the latter had taken account of my message; a few days later, my classmate came to thank me profusely on behalf of the eldest Castro. The anecdote ends there, but the episode continues to intrigue me, even now: has anyone else ever had to go through a third party to speak to their own brother?

Throughout his life, the *Comandante* did not set much store by his siblings, as numerous as they were unknown. Ángel Castro (1875–1956) and Lina (1903–1963), a landowner and his young domestic servant whom he wed in a second marriage, had seven children: Angelita (born 1923), Ramón (1924), Fidel (1926), Raúl (1931), Juanita (1933), Enma (1935), and Agustina (1938). Fidel was always fairly close to Angelita, who died in 2012, and they had a friendly relationship without it being deeper than that. As for Juanita, *¡Qué se vaya al carajo!* (Let her go screw herself!) might have been the sentiment of the *Comandante* for this unmarried sister, whom he never once mentioned in my presence. She had fled Cuba in 1964 at the age of thirty-one to live in Miami, from where she frequently denounced communism, Castrism, and totalitarianism. Fidel had deleted her, as though she no longer existed. He also had little to do with Enma, for good reason: she spent most of her life in Mexico, where she married a Mexican businessman in the 1950s. Finally, the discreet and pious Agustina, long married to a pianist who is now deceased, has also always been distant from her famous brother. When all is said and done, only Raúl, five years younger, is truly close to Fidel, despite various serious differences in personality. "As children, Ramón was easygoing, Fidel rigid, and Raúl a clown," their sister Juanita noted. "Raúl had many friends and playmates. Fidel, on the other hand, was solitary, introspective, and selfish."*

Another difference: if a rumor widely propagated in Cuba and the United States and repeated by certain biographers of Fidel is to be believed, he and Raúl did not have the same biological father. The defense minister was supposedly the illegitimate son that their mother Lina had with the commander of a security post in Birán, the Castros' native village. Is it true? I have no idea. All I can say is that Raúl in no way resembles his two older brothers. Smaller, unshaven, he also has slanted eyes,

---

*Juanita Castro and Maria Antonieta Collins, *Fidel and Raúl, mes frères: L'histoire secrète* [Fidel and Raúl, My Brothers: A Secret History] (Paris: Plon, 2011).

hence his nickname of El Chino, the Chinaman. On the other hand, he has a marked resemblance to his younger sister Juanita, who was born two years after him.

Since childhood, Fidel and Raúl had been hand in glove. The latter had followed the former in all his adventures, from the attack on the Moncada barracks in 1953 until his accession to power. For Raúl, Fidel was a sort of substitute father, perhaps because the real father, Ángel, a strict patriarch originally from Galicia in Spain, was that distant, brutal man described in certain biographies. Fidel was also a strict "father"—but a father that Raúl respected and admired, even idolized. The truth is that the *Comandante* possessed all the talents that Raúl did not have: charisma, intellectual agility, political vision, persuasiveness, ease with speaking, and a gift for communication.

All his life, Raúl has been under Fidel's influence. In the Sierra Maestra, he did everything to prove his valor and courage and to win his brother's esteem. According to historians, he executed traitors and enemies with his own weapon and presided over execution squads without displaying the slightest emotion. Raúl has more blood on his hands, professionally speaking as it were, than Fidel. At any rate, his nature is just as repressive as that of the *Líder Máximo*, if not even more so; his zeal paid off, and in 1958 Fidel judged Raúl capable of commanding at the front, like Che Guevara. He therefore entrusted his brother with the opening of a new guerrilla front, the "second eastern Frank País front" situated in the east toward the town of Santiago de Cuba. Raúl acquitted himself with flying colors.

A mediocre student at school who became a rather taciturn adult, this lover of cock fighting—an activity then in vogue but now outlawed—found himself on the battlefield. Tough and dogmatic, methodical and organized, it was there that he earned his stripes as future defense minister—a post that he occupied for forty-nine years, until 2008.

Raúl had an absolute loyalty toward Fidel. He was also the only person in the world that the *Comandante* trusted 100 percent. The two functioned in tandem. For example, when there was good news to announce such as the promotion of new leaders, it was always the number one who took care of it—but when an official was to be stripped of his post and rebuffed in public, the number two always took over. To the gallery it looked like "good cop, bad cop," and in fact the pair were in agreement about everything. They spoke every day on the phone, met several times a week, and—not a minor affair—they would not miss the other's birthday for all the world. Raúl's innumerable visits to the presidential *palacio* gave me ample occasion to observe the relationship between the two brothers.

It would be a mistake to downplay Raúl's historical role. First of all, he was the first to encounter the Cuban communist movement under Batista. Then, it was he who had introduced the Argentinian Ernesto Che Guevara to his big brother. Indeed, some people consider Raúl the real architect of the Castrist system. Unlike his brother—visionary, energetic, impulsive, but totally disorganized—Raúl was a natural, and uncompromising, organizer. His great achievement was to have methodically transformed a guerrilla movement into an army of professionals capable of operating across oceans and defeating a foreign army, as it did in Angola. It was also he who imposed an iron discipline on the military and who organized the dominance of the military over 60 to 70 percent of the national economy, including the lucrative sector of tourism. Headed by "Raúlist" generals, the GAESA (Grupo de Administración Empresarial S.A.) holding company controlled dozens of large companies in every sector: Cimex (real estate, banks, restauration, gas stations, supermarkets, and more than two hundred shops), Cubanacan (tourism), Gaviota S.A. (hotels), Servicio Automotriz S.A. (tourist car service), Tecnotex (import-export of technologies and services), Agrotex (agriculture), Sermar (dockyards), Geocuba (cartography), and so on. From behind the scenes, Raúl was therefore an essential cog in the system.

For all that, the second in command of the revolution did not take any decision, even the most insignificant, without first referring it to the leader. I once saw him in Fidel's office having his brother validate the choice of new battledress for the army. At the time, Raúl was even submissive in terms of his relations with us, his brother's guards—he was well placed to know that we represented the most important structure in the hierarchy of power. The defense minister held us in such high esteem that when he went to join Fidel in a public place, he dismissed his own escort to place himself directly under our protection.

What is more, he did not allow anyone—not even a minister or a general—to go against the slightest order given by Fidel's escort. When one of us asked an official, of whatever rank, to please stand aside to let us through, woe betide him if he protested because Raúl, who watched everything out of a corner of his eye, would immediately notice and mark down a mental black mark against him. I also noticed that during official receptions at the presidential palace, he would sometimes "play the police" himself: if he thought there were too many courtiers around Fidel, he would speak individually to certain of them—including ministers—to tell them they should now leave his brother a little oxygen and space. Then, after having discreetly got rid of the unwelcome guests, he would turn toward us security officers, almost as though he were seeking our approval.

In public, Raúl presented the image of a friendly, affable, approachable man. Particularly fond of iced vodka, this inveterate drinker was also a party lover, an aficionado of jokes who was, according to some, blessed with a real sense of humor. Of course, all of that was nothing more than a façade. For my part, I always found him rough, curt, almost unpleasant. Politically, he was a hard-liner focused on repression; since he has succeeded his brother as head of state, police brutalities have not decreased—far from it, contrary to the notion the government has cleverly managed to instill in world public opinion.

Raúl's humor was often dubious. I can still see him, in the early 1990s, turning up at the airport to wave good-bye to the *Comandante* at the foot of the airplane, as he did each time the latter went abroad. I should point out that, in this case, part of Fidel's escort remained in Cuba. We were about to embark when the number two shouted out to the number one: "Don't worry about your escort, I'll put those who stay behind to work.

No vacations with me!" As the doors of the Ilyushin closed behind us, I thought, "What an idiotic joke. . . ." Apparently he did not know that Fidel's escort rarely sat twiddling their thumbs. When the *Líder Máximo* was abroad, not only did the guards carry on with their normal training but, in addition, they took the opportunity of carrying out overdue tasks such as cleaning weaponry, maintaining vehicles, checking the condition of equipment to be used in case of war, the examination of air raid shelters, and many other duties.

However, there is one thing one cannot take away from Raúl: his sense of family. It was he, and nobody else, who for a long time put up Fidelito and Jorge Ángel, his brother's first sons—legitimate and illegitimate—under his own roof because he knew they were not welcome at Punto Cero with Dalia and Fidel. And it was he who from the beginning arranged that the first wife of the *Comandante*, Mirta Díaz-Balart, who has lived in Spain for more than fifty years, was able to return to the island to maintain contact with her son, Fidelito.

Raúl was the pater familias of the Castros. On Sundays, he and his wife, Vilma, would often put on great barbecues that brought together children, grandchildren, cousins, brothers, and sisters. Sometimes Fidel would join the family, and even if he did not stay long, these reunions gave his sisters the rare opportunity to see him. The surroundings were pleasant: after having lived in a four-story building in the quarter of Nuevo Vedado, Raúl, Vilma, and all their clan had moved close to Fidel and Dalia's, to La Rinconada. Before the revolution it had been a rich coffee trader's property. Situated on 222nd Street, it was surrounded by a huge, tree-filled territory, adorned with luxuriant vegetation, and also boasted two high-quality sports terrains: a pitch for baseball and one for frontenis (a variant of the Basque pelota game played with tennis racquets and mainly popular in Mexico, Spain, and Argentina).

Raúl had met Vilma Espín in the guerrilla movement, when she was twenty-seven. One of the first militant anti-Batistas, this courageous, pretty young woman set her sights on this man, a year younger than her. After the Triumph of the Revolution, they married. Fidel's sister-in-law then became one of the most emblematic female figures of the revolution, alongside Celia Sánchez, the aide-de-camp and mistress of the *Comandante*. Propelled to the head of the *Federación de mujeres cubanas** in 1960, she took on the role of "first lady" when Fidel judged it necessary to be seen in public with a woman beside him.

Smiling, likable, radiant, Vilma carried out her mission perfectly. But appearances are deceptive: she, too, had a double personality. During the trial of General Ochoa in 1989—with whom Raúl and she had been close friends—it was she who, before the Council of State over which she presided, had pronounced in a firm voice the terrible words: "Let the sentence be carried out!" The sentence was the death penalty.

In the interests of truth, I must also say that in private Vilma was an excellent mother, devoted to her husband, attentive and available to her four children: Deborah, Mariela, Alejandro, and Nilsita. Unlike the offspring of Fidel and Dalia, isolated from public life, Raúl's children (with the exception of the youngest)

---

*Federation of Cuban Women, a mass organization that comprises some four million members.

all became involved in politics. Maybe they will play a leading role after the deaths of their father and uncle.

Adviser to the Ministry of Education, Deborah, born in 1960, was married for a long time to a pivotal establishment figure, Luis Alberto Rodríguez López-Callejas. Father of her two children and member of the Central Committee of the Communist Party, this brigadier was the executive president of the GAESA holding company, which controlled most of the Cuban economy. In that connection, he knew better than anyone the secrets of the government's financial packages. According to Café Fuerte, he is now divorced, at Deborah's request, because of his repeated infidelity. I do not know if it's true. Their son Raúl Guillermo, nicknamed Raulito ("little Raúl"), is the current personal bodyguard of his grandfather. Born in 1984 and nicknamed El Cangrejo (the Crab) because of a malformed finger, he occupies the same position with Raúl as I did with Fidel—he, at least, does not in theory run the risk of being thrown into prison as I was.

Mariela, the second daughter, is more flamboyant than her elder sister. Born in 1961, she has for many years been the head of the National Center for Sexual Education. A militant in favor of gay marriage, this sexologist with progressive ideas has long taken part in international conferences on homosexual rights, which gives her a worldwide platform. "She introduced perestroika in my family," Raúl joked one day about his daughter and her bourgeois-bohemian lifestyle. In February 2013, Mariela Castro became a member of parliament, doubtless desirous of playing a role in "post-Raúl" Cuba.

Mariela has always been immersed in politics. Before marrying the photographer and Italian businessman Paolo Titolo, she was married to Juan Gutiérrez Fischmann, with whom she had a daughter. I have already mentioned him: founding member of the armed Chilean group FPMR, he settled in Cuba after Pinochet's coup d'etat in 1973. Militarily trained at Punto Cero de Guanabo, he was one of the architects of the famous assassination attempt on General Pinochet in 1986. He was also one of the main people accused in the 1991 fatal attack against the Chilean senator Jaime Guzmán, who supported Pinochet. Despite the denials of the government, Gutiérrez Fischmann, who remains officially untraceable, is living peacefully in Cuba.

After Deborah and Mariela came Alejandro—who shares the name of one of Fidel and Dalia's five sons. Born in 1964, Alejandro is a colonel in MININT (as previously mentioned, MININT is an abbreviation for the Department of Interior). In his capacity as head of coordination of intelligence between the two most important ministries in the country, MINFAR (Ministry of Cuban Revolutionary Armed Forces) and MININT, Alejandro is one of the closest advisers of his father, Raúl. In other words he has full access to all the secrets held by the various Cuban espionage services.

I remember him as a hyperactive kid. He was ten years old when I went to work for Fidel, and we members of the escort nicknamed him El Loquito (the Little Madman) because he played noisily on the patio of the house where Raúl's family then lived, hurtling ahead without warning on roller skates, bike, or electric motorbike, narrowly missing knocking over whoever passed by. Afterward, I lost sight of him. He resurfaced in the mid-1980s when we learned that he had joined the Cuban military expedition that had gone to fight in Angola. He later returned from Africa with an eye missing, after an accident that had occurred outside the combat zone, earning him the nickname El Tuerto, the One-Eyed Man.

And then, turning on my television at home in Miami one day in November 2012, who should appear on the screen? The One-Eyed Man! For his first steps onto the world stage, this international relations graduate had gone to Moscow to introduce the Russian edition of his book (*The Reign of Terror*), an indictment of the United States. Interviewed in Spanish by a Russian TV channel, it cannot exactly be said that he lit up the screen with his monotonous delivery and pronounced lisp. His lack of charisma and eloquence are as obvious as his father's—but that does not mean he might not go far. Col. Alejandro Castro Espín has the reputation of focusing on compromising cases that can get rid of anyone who gets in his way; inflexible, he apparently had the partner of his own sister, Nilsita, arrested on corruption charges.

I am curious to know whether Alejandro uses the same techniques as his uncle Fidel to manipulate and blackmail his enemies or put them into compromising positions: telephone bugs and secret video recordings that capture the sexual frolics of foreign diplomats in Havanan hotels. Based upon my knowledge of how the Castro regime functions, I imagine he does.

A MANIA FOR RECORDING

Fidel recorded everything. On the third floor of the *Palacio de la Revolución*, in a small area next to his office, was a set of professional recording equipment comparable to that seen in the 2006 film *The Lives of Others*, with two tape decks and two sets of headphones. Unless directed otherwise, the order was to start the tapes rolling each time Fidel had a private meeting with someone, whether Cuban or foreigner, and whether politician, minister, or general. Stenographers, their eyes riveted on the needle of the volume unit meter, controlled the volume and juggled tape decks when a ribbon got to the end of the reel. From the escorts' premises—also adjoining Fidel's office—I was the one responsible for switching the three hidden microphones on and off, by means of three keys that fitted into three locks hidden in a little cupboard that was also locked. It was also to me that Fidel would murmur, *"Sánchez, no grabes"* ("Don't record, Sánchez"), if he judged it pointless to do so. In that case, I would not turn any keys and refrained from mobilizing the stenography service. It must be added that the room of the Council of Ministers, situated on the other side of the corridor less than ten yards from Fidel's office, was itself stuffed with microphones, allowing the meetings of the Communist Party politburo to be immortalized.

Starting from the basis that everything that was said could be used and turned against his interlocutor, these recordings were methodically converted into cassettes or, from the 1980s on, CDs, and then carefully archived. Even years later, they could be used to confront someone with his contradictions. The same principle applied to all Fidel's important telephone conversations; he could eventually use them to put pressure on or compromise his interlocutor.

True, most of these sound documents sat permanently in the archives and would never be made public, perhaps leading to the conclusion that it is all the fruit of my imagination. But fortunately—if I dare put it like that—several years after I left, Fidel Castro himself proved that I am inventing nothing. In 2002, he could not resist the temptation to make public the phone conversation he had just had with the then Mexican president, the conservative Vicente Fox. It was the day before a United Nations summit organized in Monterrey in Mexico and the head of state, with astounding naïveté and almost obscene clumsiness, telephoned Fidel to suggest to him, with heavy insistence, that he make his visit to Mexico, planned for the day after next, as short as possible—so as not to disturb the other participants. Icing on the cake: Fox asked him to abstain from any statements likely to displease George W. Bush, who was on the point of invading Iraq.

As I have explained, opposing Fidel head on is the last thing one should do if one wants to obtain any kind of result with him—and the first, if one wants to antagonize him. Which is exactly what poor Fox, whose understanding of psychology seemed minimal, to say the least, did. Stung to the quick, Fidel then decided to broadcast the whole of their sixteen-minute telephone conversation: from the next day, it was played in a loop on Latin American television and on YouTube, where it is still available. The left-wing press castigated Fox with relish, describing him as a "lackey of Washington." In truth, that was all he was: his words were those of a servile creature submissive to the United States, giving him a disastrous image in that region of the world, where anti-Americanism was never far from the surface. In two shakes of a lamb's tail, Fidel had "assassinated" Fox with ridicule. As far as I know, it is the only time such a recording, carried out in the room adjoining his office, had been brought to public knowledge. And yet there are thousands of them.

As much as possible, Fidel Castro also recorded his private conversations when he went abroad. I well remember our trip to Ecuador in August 1988, on the occasion of the inauguration of Rodrigo Borja, the new social democrat president of this Andean country known for its political instability. In Quito, capital of the Altiplano situated at an altitude of 2,800 meters, Fidel first went to visit his friend Oswaldo Guayasamín, a famous contemporary Ecuadorean artist whose work, inspired by American Indian art, deals with poverty, oppression, and racism. And Fidel, of whom he has painted numerous portraits. That day, the *Comandante* had taken an hour of his time to pose beside the easel of the man he called *mi hermano* (my brother), a phrase reserved for his few real, intimate friends such as Gabriel García

Márquez. Later, Guayasamín came to Havana to finish the portrait that had been started in the painter's fabulous modern house. I remember something he said on that occasion: "Fidel must show his hands because Fidel's hands talk."

The other memorable moment of that trip was an extraordinary episode during the presidential inauguration ceremony at the National Congress. Just as the exiting right-wing president, the very controversial León Febres Cordero, who was an ally of Washington, began his speech, the members of parliament started shouting, "Corrupt! Thief! Son of a bitch!," in an indescribable hullaballoo. Fidel's eyes widened and his face wore an expression of astonishment that I had never seen before. . . . The performance extended as far as the street, under the spotlessly blue sky of the Altiplano, where demonstrators were also shouting down the ex-president. Given the surrounding tension, we decided to evacuate the *Comandante* through a hidden side door.

Finally, to return to the subject of recordings, Fidel took advantage of this trip to Quito to meet with the president of Costa Rica Óscar Arias, who was also there at that time, having recently been awarded the Nobel Peace Prize for 1987 for his mediation in the conflicts in Central America. We went to the house that had been put at his disposition by the Ecuadorian authorities, the whole of Fidel's escort, except me, staying outside. The two heads of state then went into a living room to embark on a discussion about Central America, for Arias was counting on Castro's support to finalize the ongoing peace process, particularly in Nicaragua.

The first thing Arias told him was that he wanted the conversation to remain private—but I took my instructions from

Fidel, not from the Costa Rican president. I therefore followed the wishes of *El Jefe* and started the Sanyo mini-recorder, which I took everywhere with me, as usual. I do not know why or how but, before the interview had even begun, the recorder hidden in my shirt pocket suddenly made a clicking noise! Arias heard it and politely requested Fidel to show me the exit; they then remained alone in private discussion. However, I had noticed that there was another door, situated at the back of the living room. So I tiptoed around via the corridor and discreetly placed the recorder, hidden in a briefcase, on a table near that back door, managing to record the whole conversation—even if the quality was very bad. Rather than reproaching me for my zealousness, Fidel was enthusiastic about getting a sound recording of his meeting; on our return to Havana, he asked the technical department of the secret police, the *Técnica*, to "clean" the tape to get rid of the ambient noise and improve the general sound quality.

As for the placement of mikes and cameras in the houses, apartments, cars, offices, factories, and streets of Cuba, it was the *Técnica*—or State Security, or G2—who took care of it. Not to be confused with the *Departamento Chequeo* (which, for its part, looked after surveillance and tailing), the *Técnica* was also called Department K (like Kafka!) according to its different functions—the KC unit checked postal mail, the KT unit was responsible for *chequeo telefónico* (tapping of telephone lines and microphones placed in hotel rooms, offices, cars, and private homes), the KJ unit looked after *chequeo visual* (video tailing and surveillance), and finally the KR unit managed the *chequeo ra-*

diofónico, that is, the tapping of the numerous two-way radio receivers in Cuba, in both ministries and the homes of certain private individuals who were passionate about radio.

I can also reveal that surveillance cameras were placed in immediate proximity to the fortress of La Cabaña, the colonial building that overlooked the old port, where KJ agents continuously scrutinized—with the help of a powerful telelens—the movements of people at the entrance to the United States "Interest Section" situated 1.8 miles away on the seafront. After diplomatic relations were broken off in January 1961, Washington has no longer had an embassy in Havana, although informal relations have been maintained via the Interest Section since 1977.

A KJ team also operated from a building of Unit 160—the escort's logistics center that housed the garage for the Mercedes fleet, Fidel's private cinema, the house where he met his mistresses, the food stores of the elite, and so on, and which looked directly onto the private apartment of the Swiss ambassador situated on the other side of the street. Even better: the ordinary-looking "policeman" posted at the entrance to this residence was in fact a counterespionage officer who monitored the comings and goings from that address, frequented by numerous Westerners.

Foreigners should be aware that in Cuba nobody escapes the surveillance of State Security. Several hotels in Havana are equipped with rooms specially rigged up by the *Técnica* in order to listen to conversations and film the privacy of "targets" worthy of interest, such as businessmen, diplomats, politicians, university lecturers, and arts and literary figures. To cite a few examples:

the twentieth floor of the Havana Libre hotel, the fourteenth floor of the Hotel Riviera, the Nacional, and the Cohiba. There are others. When the Cuban state invites foreign dignitaries, as it often does, it is easy to put them up in one of these special rooms and then film their sexual frolicking with a prostitute ordered by the G2. The government thus possesses a formidable means of blackmail, particularly if the sexual partner is a minor or of the same sex (even more embarrassing if the target is a traditionally married man).

I do not know how many spies per square foot there are in Cuba, but it is doubtless an impressive figure. One thing is certain: State Security—the mega-organization that is based on the three main pillars of espionage, counterespionage, and personal security, to which I belonged—had octopus-like tentacles that reached everywhere. Every industry, institution, ministry, and school, in even the tiniest village, was infiltrated or controlled by agents. In the countryside as well as in neighborhoods in large cities, their primary task was to collect information on the state of public opinion within a given geographical zone and then synthesize it in reports that were sent daily to their superiors, in a pyramid-like arrangement that ended with the *Líder Máximo*. Thanks to this surveillance, Fidel and Raúl were informed in less than twenty-four hours about the slightest criticism expressed against the regime.

Even the ministers and generals were spied on and tapped. On the vast property of Punto Cero, Fidel's Havanan estate, there is a little house devoted to tapping the public figures who are Fidel's close neighbors. Now that part of the town is almost exclusively inhabited by members of the elite. Situated in the grounds of Fidel's private property but set aside from the main building, this house bears the intriguing nickname of *casa de los misteriosos* (the house of mysterious ones). I had known about this little building for a long time, but simply by reputation, because we guards were not permitted to approach it. One fine day, however, I became certain—completely by chance—that the purpose of the *casa de los misteriosos* was indeed the one we had suspected.

It was around 1990. That day, Fidel and his escort had just arrived at the *Palacio de la Revolución* to begin a working day when the *Comandante* suddenly sent me to his home in Punto Cero to fetch a document he had forgotten.

As I passed the escorts' building, situated a little over fifty yards from Fidel's house, I suddenly remembered I had left a pack of cigarettes in the dormitory and told the chauffeur to stop for a few seconds so that I could go and get them. Inside, I glimpsed two guys fiddling with telephones but, moving hurriedly with my head down, I pretended to be in too much of a hurry to have noticed them. I went out again as quickly as possible with my cigarettes in my hand. As there was no unknown vehicle in the parking lot, I realized they were the lads from the house of mysterious ones, who had walked across from the other side of the grounds. . . . I talked about what I had seen with my wife and three or four close colleagues and then never mentioned it again. Nonetheless, I had discovered that Fidel had even tapped his guards, who were devoted to him body and soul!

It is true that, over the years, Fidel had made the use of tapping so widespread that he had had mikes installed in a good number of the protocol houses (even the one used by his friend

Hugo Chávez had been fitted with them) and monitored the conversations of his ministers, as shown by the double scandal in 2009 of Felipe Pérez Roque and Carlos Lage, then minister for foreign affairs and vice president of the Council of Ministers, respectively.

Tapping is a fundamental of espionage. And in a dictatorship, espionage—also called spying or intelligence—is indispensable. Over the course of history, Fidel accumulated such considerable experience in it that he turned this art into a science. During the guerrilla years, he had organized the system of espionage himself; for a clandestine organization, intelligence is the fundamental weapon that enables its survival. Once in power, he benefited from the precious advice and invaluable technical aid of the Soviet KGB and the East German Stasi. In Cuba, Fidel is the spymaster, possessing cunning, daring, and ability to improvise. Abroad, for example, he alone decided the priority targets: the American administration in Washington, the officials of the United Nations in New York, Cuban exiles living in Florida, not to mention the universities where Castrist sympathizers could be recruited, potential future moles to infiltrate the American administration. It is fundamental to note that Fidel is always projecting ahead into the future, even generations ahead; he can wait for years, even decades, to activate a spy, until the time has come when the spy has acquired a sufficiently high position in the hierarchy of the institution Fidel wants to penetrate. Finally, Fidel personally dealt with the most important secret agents when they were passing through Havana: he would meet them in the evening in a protocol house and talk with them until late into the tropical night.

In 1980, at the time of the so-called Mariel crisis, I had a little glimpse into Fidel's skill in this area. On April 1, 1980, five Cubans forced their way into the embassy of Peru by driving a bus through the gates and demanded political asylum, which they obtained despite Fidel Castro's protests. In reprisal, the latter withdrew Cuban police protection from outside the embassy, as a result of which 750 and then 10,000 Cubans who wanted to leave the island rapidly invaded the diplomatic mission, camping on the premises and refusing to leave. The occupation turned into a humanitarian crisis: the overpopulated Peruvian embassy was not able to provide basic hygienic conditions or feed the occupants decently. Every square inch, inside and outside the building, was occupied by refugees—some had even taken up residence in the branches of the trees in the garden.

I had a front row seat; for three weeks, I saw how Fidel organized everything. At the start of the crisis he acted as a real war leader by deciding to transfer his office to that of the head of counterespionage, then Fabián Escalante Font, which was nearer the Peruvian embassy—in other words, closer to the action. From this command post, he immediately ordered the *Técnica* to install cameras so that he could follow the situation in the diplomatic complex and its surroundings live as it unfolded. Then he sent two medical trucks to park alongside the embassy and authorized those cloistered inside to come out to receive medical treatment. A humanitarian gesture to lend assistance to sick women, men, and children? In reality, half of the doctors in the truck were intelligence officers dressed in white tunics, using the consultations to draw up profiles of the asylum seekers. Meanwhile, I was at the side of the *Comandante*, jotting down his most important deeds and gestures in the *libreta*.

At the same time, Fidel decided to infiltrate the Peruvian embassy by sending in false candidates for exile—once again, they were actually intelligence agents. They pretended to have ailments that necessitated their going to "consult" the supposed doctors, who transmitted Fidel's latest directives to them: as the humanitarian situation was deteriorating and the political tension increased, *El Jefe* asked them to sow conflict among the refugees by provoking crises. In addition, as the lack of food was growing critical, Fidel "generously" delivered supplies . . . but only enough to get the refugees to fight each other over them. Cuban television could therefore calmly film, through the railings, images of fighting and rioting that made it seem as though these people were the dregs of society. That was how Fidel Castro, combining cunning, cynicism, and espionage, managed at least to limit the damage even if he could not turn the situation completely to his advantage.

And the story did not end there. After three weeks of tug-of-war and negotiations with both Lima and Washington, a hundred thousand Cubans were permitted to seek exile in the United States, in the biggest wave of emigration in the history of Castrism since 1959 until the present day. Fidel allowed them to go to the port of the town of Mariel (west of Havana) to embark for Florida on board vessels from the United States, and the Mariel exodus began. It has been said that the *Comandante* took advantage of the situation by emptying the prisons and getting rid of thousands of dangerous prisoners by sending them to the United States. It is completely true: I saw him selecting them personally. I was present when they brought him the lists of prisoners from the prison administrations with the name, the reason for the sentence, and the date of release. Fidel read them and with the stroke of a pen designated which ones could go and which ones would stay—"yes" was for murderers and dangerous criminals, "no" was for those who had attacked the revolution, from near or from afar. In total, more than two thousand criminals found themselves free . . . in the streets of Miami.

Finally, when the asylum seekers were authorized to embark for the United States, Fidel mobilized a hostile crowd on the port of Mariel to give them as humiliating a send-off as possible. Spurred on by policemen and G2 agents in civilian dress, their compatriots insulted the refugees, spitting on and punching them. Of course I thought it was unfair, but what could I do? At the time, I saw it as a simple defensive measure, a legitimate means of protecting the revolution and its noble ideals in the face of "counter-revolutionaries" who had intentionally attacked it by besieging the embassy of Peru. I was young and I swallowed all of Fidel's propaganda without question.

At the time, I had just begun my counterespionage studies at the MININT Higher Institute, for one day a week from 1979 to 1985, and every day in the last months of the course. It was there, on the school benches (but also with spymaster Fidel) that I learned all the techniques taught to Cuban agents sent on missions abroad. Later, these procedures—such as shadowing and countershadowing—came in handy, particularly when I fled Cuba after having served my prison sentence and even though police continued to spy on my slightest movements and activities. The psychology courses, for example, have constantly been useful to me; we learned, among other things, the different methods of extracting information from people during ordinary conversations by activating psychological stimuli such as flattery or by sowing doubt; complimenting people who suffered from lack of recognition in their professional life; or, on the contrary, by casting doubt on the words of people with an over-inflated ego (who were thereby made to give away too much in the conversation). There is no doubt about it: we learned a tremendous amount.

Future diplomats figured among my classmates. Cuban espionage is a network that stretches all over the world and, unlike those of other countries, Cuban diplomats mastered all the espionage techniques perfectly. Before leaving to take up their post they even met with psychologists who gave them insights into their own character, strengths, and weaknesses, so as to correct certain of their psychological traits. They were helped to eliminate tastes, proclivities, or preferences that could constitute flaws the enemy could exploit; their revolutionary motivation was also strengthened with a well-targeted ideological pep talk, a phase that was called mental armoring. As a result, from Paris to Mexico and Berlin to Cairo, every Cuban embassy was a nest of agents. All staff, down to the humblest of receptionists, were initiated in counterespionage, even if their training was not as extensive as that of the "head of post," in other words, the ambassador.

I learned an extraordinary amount from traveling with Fidel and collaborating closely with our representatives abroad. For example, in every embassy it was the cipher officer* who was subject to the closest surveillance because of all the information to which he had access. Forced to live within the diplomatic precinct, he was not allowed to go into the town alone and was always accompanied by one or several colleagues when he went out, in a bid to avoid any defections that would have serious consequences for Cuba.

One of the vital tasks assigned to ambassadors was that of recruiting foreign agents, whether they were simple "influence agents" or full-blown spies. The former were generally university lecturers, politicians, diplomats, journalists, arts and literary figures, or even company heads—in sum, anyone who had a position that gave him or her influence in society and who was favorably disposed in principle to the Cuban Revolution. For Cuba it was a matter of encouraging these people's natural inclination so as to create networks of imperceptible pro-Castrist opinion: "useful idiots," in Lenin's phrase. The second, much rarer, category included those people who consciously worked for the Cuban services after having been recruited by the Intelligence Directorate.

Embassy receptions, cultural events (concerts, film screenings), or professional exhibitions (in the domain of tourism, for example) as well as meetings of cigar lovers all provided fruitful ground for the recruitment of agents. This task was placed under the authority of a recruiting officer, and there was one in every Cuban embassy in the world. It was usually someone cultivated,

*The officer responsible for encrypting communications with Havana.

sociable, and affable, able to talk about every subject and to adapt to every situation. The recruiting officer's first task consisted of sympathizing with people and making them speak in a bid to determine whether this or that person had a pro-Cuban profile and might therefore be recruited. Each potential recruit was the object of psychological profiling and his or her tastes, preferences, weaknesses, sexual orientation, degree of affinity with the Cuban Revolution, and interest in money were all methodically set down in writing. That was the obligatory starting point.

All those who are familiar with the world of recruitment know that there are four levers that can be used to recruit agents: money, ideology, blackmail, and ego. Fidel has always favored the second category, based on the principle that taking on people who were truly motivated and shared his anti-imperialist (that is, anti-American) ideology was the least arduous method and also the safest in the long term. The most famous Cuban moles discovered by the CIA all belonged to that category: people such as Ana Belén Montes, the pro-Castrist mole from the Pentagon arrested in 2001 (and sentenced to twenty-five years in prison) or Walter Kendall Myers, ex-officer in the Department of State arrested in 2009 (and given a life sentence). The notion that they were fighting for the glory of the Cuban Revolution was enough for them.

However, sometimes agents were recruited on a one-off basis by means of blackmail. That is what happened to a French diplomat in a case that I learned about one morning as I was preparing Fidel's mail. I have not yet explained that, other than the physical protection of the *Comandante* and the keeping of the *libreta*, I had each morning to organize all the summary reports sent in by the various ministers and intelligence services. And so one morning in the late 1980s, I caught sight of a counterespionage report concerning a French diplomat serving in Cuba recruited via the blackmail method. The recruitment of a foreign agent is not something that happens every day and was sufficiently interesting for me to want to delve further into the case; I did not have the time right then to read the report in detail because I had to prepare the pile of documents to give to Fidel. I remembered his name, however—and after that did not think much more about it. . . .

However, the story had a follow-up that occurred in Miami; I relate the main details because they are so revealing of how the Cuban security services work. As everyone knows, tens of thousands of exiles live in that southern Florida metropolis, among them a not insignificant number of former Cuban secret service agents who, given my pedigree, naturally made contact with me when I finally managed to escape from Cuba in 2008. One of them, a former intelligence officer who had deserted to the United States in 1995, asked me if I had ever heard of a certain X, as we will call him—a French diplomat recruited in the late 1980s in Havana. His name immediately rang a bell for me, almost twenty years later.

Several days later, the Cuban ex-officer showed me the extract of a nine-page report that he had drawn up for the attention of the American FBI after his desertion, a part of which concerned the diplomat in question. Contrary to what one might imagine, Castrist espionage did not necessarily only target the "big fish" but was also interested itself in middle-ranking officials—who had less prominent positions but were likely to have access to small pieces of information that would then be added to a bigger picture, like a piece in a puzzle. This case shows that Cuban espionage occasionally resorts to the blackmail method even if, as I say, Fidel favors recruitment by ideological sympathy, which is more reliable and longer-lasting.

And so, having found out that this diplomat, Mr. X, was involved with jewelry and art contraband, the *Departamento II* of Cuban counterespionage (in charge of foreign diplomats posted to Cuba) drew up his psychological profile and organized an operation to compromise him by filming him in the act of carrying out an illegal transaction. The operation was successful and the recruitment declared "positive"; the Frenchman was immediately asked to provide information about the interior of his diplomatic building, the alarm system, security measures, and so on, making a search of the premises possible. He was also asked to supply information about the private lives of the other officials, consular or commercial, so as to complete our data and determine whether there were other diplomats with a profile favorable to recruitment.

After detailed study of X's personality, the counterespionage psychologists established that he was very interested in money. It was therefore decided to allow this new agent to pursue his negotiations for works of art, but in exchange for something in return. According to the "instructions of the highest authorities in the country" (in other words, Fidel), the counterespionage service had demanded that the Frenchman "play his part" so that Cuba could obtain financing from French institutions responsible for cooperation and development in third world countries. To this end, the Frenchman had, in the reports he sent to the French ministry of foreign affairs, to present Cuba's political, economic, and social situation in the terms indicated by the Cuban services. X complied and then continued his activities without realizing, at first, that he was always being watched—a surveillance that of course compromised him again, enabling a renewed demand for information.

As far as I know, this gentleman is still a diplomat for his country's foreign affairs.

THE VENEZUELAN OBSESSION

The engines had been switched off and all one could hear were the little waves slapping against the hull of *Aquarama II*. Under the starry sky, the warm air caressed the skin and the full moon lit up the landscape. It was already late—midnight, perhaps. On board Fidel's yacht, a nautical mile from his private island, Cayo Piedra, he and Gabo (Gabriel García Márquez) were engaged in a memorable nocturnal fishing expedition. Fidel had known García Márquez, the Colombian writer and winner of the Nobel Prize in Literature a year his junior, since the early 1960s when Latino journalists from all over South America founded the Cuban press agency Prensa Latina. A correspondent for this agency in the United States for a time, García Márquez had subsequently moved away from Castrism to devote himself to his vocation—literature—before returning to Fidel in the 1970s, fascinated by the man of power and his vision anchored in continental, or "pan-Latino," nationalism.

A third man was on board, a personal guest of the *Comandante*, a South American businessman whose name and nationality I forget. This sea outing was Fidel's idea. How delicious to be fishing in the Caribbean at night while sipping a twelve-year-old whisky! With Fidel, however, an innocent fishing trip could quickly turn into a competition. That evening, luck was on the guest's side. "One down!" the South American businessman exclaimed joyfully as he pulled out his first fish. "And two! And here's the third!" he went on triumphantly, not imagining for a moment that he was upsetting his host. The litany continued: "Four down!" and so on. . . . Two hours later, the guest had at least five fish more at the bottom of his bucket.

Out of the corner of my eye I observed the *Comandante*: he had a sullen air and had not uttered a word for some time. Gabo began to find time hung heavy and he yawned. Late into the night, the author of *One Hundred Years of Solitude* eventually took me to one side and whispered into my ear, "Oh, tell our friend to stop his miraculous fishing, because at this rate we're never going to get back and go to bed. . . ." Gabo knew Fidel well enough to realize he was as bad a loser at fishing as he was at basketball or any other competitive activity—and that he would not give up until he had pulled up at least one more fish than his guest. So I passed on the message to the latter and, one hour later, Fidel had caught up his shortfall and decreed: "Okay, I think we've had good fishing. It's time to go back now!"

Since the 1970s, Gabriel García Márquez divided his time between Mexico, where he had a property, and Cuba, where Fidel had made a protocol house available to him, complete with swimming pool, Mercedes-Benz, chauffeur, cook, and so on, on 146th Street in the Playa neighborhood. During the 1980s, García Márquez spent an enormous amount of time in Cuba, continually cheek by jowl with Fidel, going to visit him at the *palacio*, receiving him in his own house, or else going off with him, on a weekend to the island paradise of Cayo Piedra. One evening in 1984, at around ten p.m., Fidel went to see Gabo in his house. During the conversation, the *Comandante*, who thought of politics constantly, always trying to twist things to his own advantage, suggested to him half-jokingly that he should run in the Colombian presidential election that was to take place in two years' time.

"Listen, Gabo, I think you could legitimately run for Colombian president. . . . You have every chance of winning, you know. . . . You would be an excellent candidate and we in Cuba would support you with every means at our disposal."

I remember that at that moment, Pepín, Fidel's aide-de-camp, took me to one side and said to me, half amused, half incredulous: "Did you hear? The boss is trying to put the idea of becoming president in his head. . . . Let's see where it's all going to take us. . . ."

Not very far, in fact, for Gabo quickly dismissed Fidel's "brilliant" idea. Aware that he was not an electoral animal, the Colombian writer had always, it seems to me, preferred to enjoy the pleasures of life by keeping himself comfortably away from politics rather than launching into an uncertain adventure that did not suit his temperament. If he had chosen otherwise, Fidel would obviously have supported him to the hilt—and with all the political know-how of *El Jefe*, it is not inconceivable that García Márquez, then at the height of his fame, could have won the election in his country. It would then have been very easy for Fidel to advise, influence, and manipulate his friend to get

Colombia into Cuba's orbit for good—in the most democratic way possible.

History decided otherwise, but I recount this anecdote to show to what extent Fidel Castro, with his unbridled creativity, was capable of thinking outside the box in order to redistribute the cards in the great game of politics, at every moment and by all possible means, whether by subversion, elections, or by creating a Trojan horse, which is what Gabo would have been.

Having failed to use his friend to his advantage, it was in the neighboring country of Venezuela that the *Comandante* would win his hand, though much later, by gaining the upper hand over Col. Hugo Chávez, who at the end of the following decade, in 1999, acceded to power in Caracas.

Venezuela had always occupied a special place in Fidel's geostrategic thinking. The *Comandante* had always had Venezuelan gas in his sights, for he knew from the outset that it would be the key to financing his international dream and to standing up to the Americans. It was therefore no coincidence that just three weeks after the triumph of the Cuban Revolution in Havana, on January 23, 1959, he took off for Venezuela on his first international trip. This trip was doubly symbolic: first, because Fidel claimed he took direct inspiration from the *Libertador* Simón Bolívar, the hero of independence from Spain who had already dreamed of realizing the union between all the countries of Spanish America. And second, because Venezuelans identified with the young Fidel Castro, because of a similar past: they, too, had ousted a dictatorship, that of Marcos Pérez

Jiménez, a year earlier on January 23, 1958. As a result, Fidel and his Cuban delegation, including his official companion Celia Sánchez, were given a heroes' welcome by a crowd of men and women, to whom the *Comandante* gave speeches with prophetic overtones. There to seek financial aid from the newly elected Venezuelan president, Rómulo Betancourt, he came up against a flat refusal, which was the beginning of the disagreement between the two leaders. After their meeting, Betancourt declared, "That wasn't a man I met—it was a tropical storm."

The trip to Caracas ended with another significant event, though this one was not of a political nature. Just before taking off in the twin-engine plane that was to fly the delegation to Havana, the head of Fidel's escort, the *barbudo* Paco Cabrera, came back down onto the tarmac to get a weapon he had forgotten. He was caught by a spinning propeller, cutting into his skull and throwing him to the ground in a pool of blood. According to certain accounts, Fidel reacted without compassion to the death of this guard, who had been with him since the Sierra Maestra, declaring simply, "What an imbecile!" I don't know if it is true, but one thing is certain: Fidel was not very grateful to people who devoted their lives to protecting him. The way in which he had me thrown into prison is proof of that, but there are other examples, such as that of my colleague, Capt. Armín Pompa Álvarez, who died in the early 1980s of a sudden illness—we never really found out what—after having been stung by mosquitoes during a tortoise fishing expedition, organized by Fidel, to an island infested with the insects. The *Comandante* had gone to the funeral in the Colón cemetery in Havana, where he had had a wreath of flowers delivered. He had even presented his condolences to the tearful widow and the guard's family, his face expressing such sorrow that his emotion seemed real and sincere. However, as soon as the ceremony finished, he went to enjoy himself with his mistress, the interpreter Juanita Vera, in the meetinghouse of Unit 160. It defied comprehension that *El Jefe* would want to make love just after the burial of someone to whom he was so close and who had been so devoted to him. Some of the members of the escort could not hide their confusion; one of the guards declared, "So, the last thing you should do here is die—if you die, you'll be forgotten in a flash." Indeed, three weeks after his death, nobody ever mentioned Captain Armín again.

To return to Fidel's ambitions in terms of Venezuela, it has to be remembered that from the beginning of the 1960s, the *Líder Máximo*, unable to get along with the president Rómulo Betancourt, had begun actively supporting the guerrilla movement by means of advice, military training in Cuba, and secret consignments of arms to Venezuela. When the dyed-in-the-wool social democrat Betancourt caught wind of this and received proof of it, he launched a tussle that began in 1962 with the expulsion of Cuba from the Organization of American States, the authority that unites all the countries of North and South America. Fidel was isolated on the diplomatic scene—but that still did not make him abandon his fixation on Venezuela.

Starting in 1974, he forged a friendship with the new president, Carlos Andrés Pérez, who reestablished links with Cuba while maintaining friendly links with Washington. As vice president of the Socialist International, the head of state was, like Fidel, opposed to Somoza's dictatorship in Nicaragua. Fidel now had a heavyweight ally in the region who supported him at the United Nations and in other international forums. Thanks to the gas crisis and the escalating price of "black gold," the first term of office of Carlos Andrés Pérez (1974–1979), also known as CAP, corresponded to a period of unprecedented prosperity. It was the time when that country was known as Saudi Venezuela and the Venezuelans as *damedos* (*dame dos*, "give me two of them"—in reference to their purchasing power, greater than all the other countries of the region).

Flushed with the success of his first term of office, CAP came back to power for a second time, from 1989 to 1993. It was my responsibility as scout (or forerunner) to organize the security for Fidel's trip to Caracas for the inauguration ceremony in 1989. However, after several days spent at the Caracas Hilton, the Minister of the Interior José Abrantes suggested to Fidel that the whole of the Cuban delegation move to another hotel that had just opened, the Eurobuilding, which was rather far away but which was, above all, quieter. An atmosphere of chaos reigned at the Hilton, where most of the presidents were staying; the lobby was teeming with journalists who accosted Fidel, presidential advisers sitting around on the sofas, and security officers from every country. On top of that, the elevators were constantly blocked. As a result, Cuban security were not in control of the situation and could not manage to work in peace.

Fidel therefore accepted Abrantes's proposal and sent me ahead as scout to sort out the practical matters involved in the transfer. Once I got there, I found the elevator that my boss was supposed to use two hours later out of order. I immediately improvised a plan B: Fidel would use the goods elevator situated close by. I used it myself, checking its condition with technicians, going over it with a fine-toothed comb to make sure there were no explosives present, and finally placed a Cuban guard in front of the door, another on Fidel's floor, and a third in the basement. In the meantime, the *Comandante* had come into the lobby of the hotel before I had had time to warn either Abrantes or the head of the escort of all these changes.

I went over to Fidel, planting myself in front of him so as to stop him in the middle of the lobby. With a jerk of my chin and without uttering a word, I intimated to him that he was to follow me to the goods elevator—under the disapproving eye of Abrantes, who tried to intervene to contradict me, though in vain. Totally trusting, Fidel followed in my footsteps. In the goods elevator, Abrantes continued shooting daggers at me, his face contorted with irritation: he could not bear that my opinion had carried more weight than his. Once we got to our destination, the two men shut themselves in Fidel's room and then, five minutes later, summoned me to give an explanation for my initiative. I explained it all from beginning to end and Fidel looked at Abrantes in silence, smiling as if to say, "You see, Sánchez is a pro, he knows what he's doing." The minister for the interior didn't address another word to me until we got back to Havana.

Back in Cuba, Fidel announced several days later that we were going back to Venezuela, but this time on an ultra-secret trip to La Orchila, an island of fifteen square miles situated in the turquoise seas about thirty-seven miles north of the capital. This idyllic place housed a military base as well as an air and sea base; access to it was reserved exclusively for Venezuelan presidents, their families and close relatives, military personnel, and a few government officials.

Unusually, we traveled on a single plane, the presidential Ilyushin-62, without being accompanied by the two extra planes that normally followed Fidel's to act as a replacement in case of a breakdown, but also to confuse enemies so that they would not know which plane contained Fidel. Once we arrived, we distributed the traditional presents to our Venezuelan counterparts: cases of rum and boxes of cigars. In return, they offered us baseball caps bearing the inscription LA ORCHILA—which Pepín confiscated almost immediately, in conformity with Fidel's order for us to keep this trip shrouded in secrecy.

Not long afterward, Fidel lost no time in setting out to CAP the "fantastic" idea that he had had in mind for some time. Still obsessed by Venezuelan gas, the *Comandante* explained the advantages to everyone of Venezuela rather than Western Europe supplying gas to Cuba while the Soviet Union could supply hydrocarbons to Western Europe rather than to Cuba. In that way, no supplier—neither Venezuela nor the USSR—would be affected, transport costs would be reduced, and energy security maintained for all concerned. Ingenious and daring, the idea nonetheless seemed unrealistic to Carlos Andrés Pérez, who dismissed it. But the simple fact that it had taken root in Fidel Castro's mind confirmed both his intense interest in Venezuelan gas and his premonitory anticipation at a time when, a few months before the fall of the Berlin wall, Gorbachev's USSR was becoming an increasingly uncertain supplier. It also showed the worldwide dimension of his thinking, as though he felt cramped on his Caribbean island.

In the end, he had to wait another ten years, until the accession to power of Hugo Chávez, to get his hands on some of the Venezuelan black gold. With this new associate, Fidel implemented one of the most sensational alliances in the history of Castrism: the Caracas-Havana partnership. Since 2006, Venezuela has in effect supplied Cuba with discounted gas at a rate of 150,000 barrels a day in return for Cuban doctors being sent into slums and for Cuban "advisers." More than forty years after his first trip to Caracas, Fidel obtained from his disciple Hugo Chávez the aid that he had sought in vain from Rómulo Betancourt. But that was not all. Together, Castro and Chávez, thanks to the political genius of one and the gas of the other, even managed to relaunch internationalism, the nineteenth-century project inspired by Simón Bolívar and the Cuban José Martí (a great anti-imperialist theoretician) that advocated international solidarity by creating the Bolivarian Alliance for the Peoples of Our America, a left-wing organization that principally united Bolivia, Ecuador, and Nicaragua. All this demonstrated one of the most striking features of Castrism: the obsessional perseverance of its head.

Fidel Castro might have waited forty years to get Venezuela where he wanted it, but he succeeded in the end.

FIDEL AND THE
TIN-POT TYRANTS

We had been warned. And, in the airplane, they told us again: beware! That was the advice of the people from Cuban intelligence: "Be careful what you say; the North Koreans put mikes everywhere, listen to everything, and film everything." "Everywhere" did not just mean in the president's office, the ministerial meeting room, or the house of a diplomat for purposes of an investigation, as in Cuba. Everywhere was *absolutely* everywhere: in the elevators, in the hotel corridors, in all the rooms, in the bathrooms, and even in the toilets. On Fidel Castro's first—and last—official visit to the Democratic People's Republic of Korea, in other words North Korea, I was curious to see whether what the Cuban espionage service said was true.

Our Ilyushin, which had set out from Moscow, landed and was now parked opposite the red carpet that had been rolled out onto the tarmac of the airport of Pyongyang. The dictator Kim Il-sung, wearing a beret that made him look like a little old man, stood awaiting his guest next to his son and successor, Kim Jong-il (father of the present leader, Kim Jong-un). Fidel, a red deerstalker on his head, walked down from the gangway and embraced the "Great Leader" vigorously, towering over him; he looked like a Siberian ogre next to the Koreans with his great height, his strange headgear, and his long coat. One could not fail to notice the tumor on Kim Il-sung's neck, as big as a baseball—his paranoid fear prevented him from having it operated on. A young woman approached to give Fidel a bouquet of flowers, then five hundred balloons were released into the sky. There was also a military parade with goose-stepping soldiers. Finally, the two heads of state were able to get into a black, open-top limousine. Escorted by a squadron of thirty motorbikes, we drove toward the capital.

It was grandiose. Along the twenty-five miles between the airport and the capital, tens or hundreds of thousands of Koreans formed a guard of honor, waving Cuban and Korean flags. Portraits of Castro and Kim were placed at regular intervals, every fifty yards. At each bend, ballet dancers dressed in white, yellow, or sky blue appeared like strange apparitions, maneuvering fans, parasols, or ribbons in automated choreographies under the sad, gray Pyongyang sky.

As my vehicle preceded the presidential car by at least a thousand yards or so, I was in a good position to see how the authorities managed to get the people to line up so perfectly; ultra-disciplined, they all stayed behind the white lines stretched across each side of the route. This was not by chance: anyone who went past them, even with just the tips of their toes, received a beating from merciless soldiers positioned every ten yards. I saw that scene repeated along the whole length of the route, making me think of dogs being trained. Something else caught my attention: all the Koreans were dressed identically, so that they resembled tin soldiers.

There were more surprises still to come. The Cubans posted to our embassy told us that when a Korean got up in the morning, his first duty was to clean the section of road outside his house. They also told me about shortages that forced them to get the train to South Korea to stock up the embassy with food and all other supplies.

The objective of this official two-day visit, from March 8 to 10, 1986, was simple. For Fidel, it was a matter of returning a courtesy to the Koreans, who invited him to their Havanan embassy each year to celebrate the declaration of their independence on September 9, 1948, and who never forgot to give him gifts on August 13, his birthday. Of course, it also had something to do with maintaining links between "brother countries," to which end a "friendship and cooperation treaty" was signed between Cuba and North Korea.

Everything was bound by protocol. When we visited the town, the only cars driving on the roads were police vehicles. We admired the twenty-two-yard-high bronze statue dedicated to the Korean leader. Then, Kim Il-sung proudly showed Fidel the model of a dam project currently under way somewhere in the country. In two days, the *Líder Máximo* was decorated three times: with the gold medal of the Democratic People's Republic of Korea, with the Order of the National Flag, and the Order of Soldier's Honor. One evening we attended a ballet at the Grand Theater of Pyongyang; nobody except Fidel, who had an interpreter, understood what it was about—but since the cult of personality was everywhere, one can presume it was about the glory of Kim Il-sung, who all throughout the visit struck me as someone both introverted and feared. He did not even need to give orders to be obeyed: a simple look, and his assistants went running, rivaling each other in servility. However, because of the language barrier, I could not speak to my Korean counterparts to find out more about their country, leaders, and customs—rather, I felt as though I had been plunged into a surreal silent film.

As for the omnipresent mikes that our secret services had talked about, I decided to get to the bottom of the matter. The day after we arrived, I was in the hotel elevator with a Cuban colleague when I declared to him disingenuously, "You know what? I would love to read the works of Kim Il-sung in Spanish. It's probably really interesting. But we can't get them in Cuba. It's a shame, don't you think?" After which we left for the gala dinner given in honor of the *Comandante*. When we got back that evening—surprise! All the members of the Cuban delegation found spread out on their bedspread the complete works of Kim il-sung in Spanish. Clearly, the mikes in the elevator were working well.

That evening, for the first and last time in my life, I saw Fidel drunk. The head of the escort had asked me to mount guard in front of Fidel's presidential suite, telling me that Juanita was due to visit the *Comandante* at some point during the evening. As I have said, the Cuban intelligence service colonel, Juana Vera, was not just Fidel's interpreter at that time but also his mistress. Sure enough, she eventually knocked on the door of the suite and stayed for two or three hours before returning home. Later on that night, the *Comandante*, who always went to bed late, opened his door slightly; I at once sprang up from my chair to ask what he wanted. Having poked his head through the crack, he immediately withdrew it in a gesture of alarm.

"Sánchez," he asked, as if we were in a haunted castle, "who are these two people in front of my door?"

I immediately realized he had been drinking. It looked as though he had downed a large quantity of Chivas Regal whisky, judging from the empty bottles on the coffee table.

"Um, there's nobody here, *Comandante*."

"Yes, there is—there! Who are these people?"

I realized that Fidel was pointing to our reflections opposite, in the huge mirror that covered the whole of the corridor wall!

"Commander, it's nothing—it's just our reflections in the mirror."

"Ah, okay, fine. . . . Listen, I can't sleep, with this wretched hard mattress. . . ."

Usually Fidel took his own large, wooden bed when he traveled abroad; we brought it with us from Havana and reassembled it wherever he stayed the night, making sure we always put his slippers next to it, on the right side. On this occasion, however, for reasons I forget, his bed had stayed behind in Cuba.

"Don't move, *Comandante*, I'll try to find a softer mattress."

"I'm coming with you," he replied.

So Fidel and I duly set off on our nocturnal expedition, he drunk and wearing his sky blue pajamas, in search of another mattress. . . . The simplest solution was to give him my own, so we made for my room, where we loaded the desired object onto our backs. Once again in the corridor, I found myself giving orders to the Commander of the Revolution: "Be careful! Right! Ouch! No, left! Now, vertical, otherwise we won't get through the door!" If the North Koreans film and record everything, there is a sequence of footage worthy of Charlie Chaplin lying dormant somewhere in the secret archives of Pyongyang.

Back in his room, Fidel made me stay with him for an hour to talk (with the proviso that in a "discussion" with him, he was the only one to say anything) and to confide his impressions of the trip to me. "The discipline of the Koreans is impressive," he said admiringly, not realizing that the people were "trained" with the blows of a stick. Had he noticed the suffering of the Koreans? Probably not, since Fidel was eminently self-absorbed and not able to put himself in others' shoes or understand their emotions. Instead, he talked about the giant statue of Kim Il-sung, who had made a strong impression on him, as he had on all the members of the Cuban delegation. Other than that aspect of things, I do not think Fidel Castro particularly admired the Korean system or Kim. For example, he made no reference to the economic model from which he had, in fact, nothing to learn. The *Comandante* certainly valued Kim Il-sung for his feats in battle and his resistance during the Japanese occupation in the 1930s. He respected the way in which he had come to power and, better than anyone, he knew that the North Korean Great Leader had taken solid root at the head of the country. Knowing my ex-boss, however, I am convinced that he thought the excessive cult of personality in North Korea was unreasonable. Of course—and contrary to what his admirers stupidly affirm—the cult of personality around Fidel exists in Cuba, but it is less widespread and takes more subtle, discreet forms: no statues or giant portraits in the streets but rather roadside signs with the "thoughts" of the *Líder Máximo*. Not to mention the photos of him in every house, allowing one to judge people's commitment and adhesion to revolutionary ideas. When all was said and done, Fidel knew perfectly well that he had political and intellectual ascendancy over his Korean counterpart, for it was obvious that beyond his own borders, nobody followed the shady Kim Il-sung. On the other hand, Fidel had extraordinary influence, not just in Latin America but throughout the rest of the world.

Later that year, in September 1986, my path—that is to say, Fidel's—crossed that of another dictator: Muammar al-Gaddafi. It was in Harare, the capital of Zimbabwe, on the occasion of the eighth summit of the Non-Aligned Movement. The atmosphere was electric, primarily because of the divisions within that organization, but also because of the highly explosive regional context: several hundreds of miles from Zimbabwe—which had won independence not long before, in 1980—civil war was raging in Angola, where the Marxist government, supported by thirty thousand Cuban soldiers, was holding out against the attacks of pro-Western rebels supported by the racist regime of South Africa.

I had arrived in Harare three weeks before Fidel, in the company of the whole team of forerunners, the scouts responsible for preparing for the arrival of the *Comandante*. Led by the Minister of the Interior José Abrantes, this *avanzada* (advance team) also included three other guards, a doctor from Fidel's personal medical team, a logistics coordinator (in charge of transport), a *Técnica* specialist, and a member of the protocol team. It was my job to take care of all the issues related to security, to find safe accommodations, to check the itineraries taken by Fidel, and to uncover any flaws in the organization of the Zimbabwean authorities.

Now, I had barely set foot in the capital when I heard a worrying rumor: a South African commando was en route for Zimbabwe to kill Fidel Castro.

Our team was immediately placed on red alert, which meant, for example, that the Cuban MiGs stationed in Angola were mobilized, ready to take off throughout the duration of the summit. Another immediate consequence was that Havana decided to reinforce the escort to exceptional numbers during Fidel's visit: along with almost all his usual close guard, thirty or so men, the "special troops"—elite marksmen and explosives experts—were also sent, another hundred or so soldiers. The trip to Harare has remained in the annals of the escort; never before had so many soldiers been mobilized for a mission abroad.

In Harare, that neat and tidy capital that was one of the jewels of British colonial empire in Africa, my first decision consisted of going over our diplomatic representation in great detail. And there, in the ambassador's office, bingo! Hidden between two beams in the false ceiling, I discovered a microphone—which I immediately opened, before sending it to Havana for analysis (I later realized that the equipment had been placed there by our own services, either to listen to the ambassador or to check my own competence). As a result, the idea that Fidel should sleep in our embassy was immediately dismissed: it was much too risky.

With the briefcase of cash I had been given, containing $250,000, I went off in search of a secure place for the *Comandante* to stay. I found a bungalow that fitted the bill—today it serves as the residence of the Cuban ambassador to Zimbabwe. I bought it and had it entirely renovated by workers sent specially from Cuba; they repaired the roof, repainted all the walls, strengthened the perimeter fencing, and dug an air raid shelter ten yards underground, in case the South Africans had the bad idea of bombing the house of the *Líder Máximo*. Following the instructions of the head of the *Técnica*, they also carried out sound insulation work so that nobody would be able to spy on Fidel's conversations from the exterior with the help of those "shotgun microphones" that can go through walls.

I also bought two other houses—later resold—in the vicinity in which to house the minister of the interior and the diplomat Carlos Rafael Rodríguez. In addition, our workers built in the garden of one of these houses two prefabricated buildings in which soldiers could be accommodated in bunks. Finally, the logistical coordinator left on a mission to Zambia to buy the vehicles we lacked: a Mercedes for Fidel and four Toyota Cressidas for the escort. Total budget of the operation for the five days' stay of the Cuban leader: over two million dollars.

Eventually all the preparations were finished and we were ready for the start of the eighth conference of the Non-Aligned Movement, in the presence of Robert Mugabe, Ali Khamenei, Rajiv Gandhi, Daniel Ortega, Gaddafi, and dozens of other leaders of African, Arab, and Asian delegations.

My first observation was that those responsible for protocol in the host country had organized things badly. While the heads of state were initially allowed to go as far as the entrance to the Sheraton Hotel with their personal guards, the latter were later stopped fifty yards away, creating incredible chaos: a fight broke out between the Zimbabwean security men and the notorious "amazons of Gaddafi," the exclusively female guard of the Libyan leader, who had also had his green (the color of Islam) armored limousine brought there by special plane, as well as his tent and two camels. Thus ensued a surreal, grotesque spectacle, for the Libyan "amazons" have a combat technique unique to them in which they whirl around 360 degrees and then end their spin by delivering slaps to the face of their adversaries with the help of centrifugal force.

In another surprise, the parking area assigned to our vehicle cortege was between those of the delegations from Iran and Iraq—countries that had been at war for six years! As a result, when the guards and the chauffeurs of the two countries spotted each other, they exchanged copious insults and spat in each other's faces. We had to use oceans of tact to sweet-talk the Iranians and the Arabs, dividing our contingent into two groups so we could create friendly relations with the two camps at the same time, making sure we swapped positions after each half day.

One of the flaws in the organization suited us: from the beginning, we had noticed that the Sheraton Hotel, where the conference was taking place, was not equipped with metal detectors. We took advantage of that to bring in—in flagrant violation of the rules—a Browning 9mm pistol hidden in a briefcase carried by Fidel's head of escort, the only one authorized to accompany the *Comandante* to the inside of the plenary session hall. Nobody ever knew that Fidel Castro had a firearm within reach.

I still think it was a good idea: had not Indira Gandhi, to whom Fidel paid homage during his speech, been assassinated at point-blank range two years earlier?

Colonel Gaddafi (he and Fidel were the stars of the summit) gave a virulent speech full of saber-rattling against the entire planet, including the Non-Aligned Movement, which he accused of hypocrisy because of its lukewarm positions against the United States. The uncontrollable Bedouin demanded that everyone follow him in his crusade against Washington, whose air force had bombed Libya five months earlier in April 1986. He demanded a vote with a show of hands, but no diplomat was prepared to follow the injunctions of such a loose cannon. The incensed Gaddafi, who along the way had also criticized the USSR, left in high dudgeon, swearing he would never return and taking refuge in his Bedouin tent, which had been erected in a beautiful, sunny garden.

Fidel, whose political experience was beyond question, had always viewed the Non-Aligned Movement with the greatest seriousness, for it was, in fact, one of the main platforms from which he could address the world. For him, it was crucial to maintain both its unity and its credibility.

The *Comandante* therefore decided to go and see Gaddafi at home to try to get him into line and to urge him to go back on his decision and return to the plenary sessions. The Libyan colonel ushered us into his garden and then, after greeting Fidel, planted himself in front of me just a foot from my face, staring at me with his defiant gaze for fifteen long seconds as though he wanted to chase me away. To show him what Cuban men are made of, I did not let myself be stared down and looked back without blinking, gritting my teeth. Staring straight into some-

one's eyes without blinking for fifteen seconds is already difficult enough, in normal circumstances—but faced with such a
lunatic, it was virtually interminable. I had the impression it
went on two hours! Finally, just as I was about to unlock my
gaze from his, he stopped his pantomime.

After that, Fidel went into the tent with his Arabic interpreter; at that moment, I saw a guy passing who looked like a
spitting image of Gaddafi. A veritable double! I couldn't believe
it. . . . True, we also used a double for Fidel Castro, but he had
to be made up to give the illusion of being Fidel—and even then
you needed to be far away. This, on the other hand, was an au-
thentic double!

Fidel talked for forty minutes, explaining to the Guide of the
Jamahiriya* just how necessary his presence was to the good
outcome of the summit. At the end of it, the Libyan agreed
to return to the Sheraton, but only to listen to the speech of
his Cuban counterpart. Once again, Fidel had got what he
wanted. . . . That same afternoon, the desert colonel reappeared
to hear the Cuban declare, "As long as apartheid continues in
South Africa, Cuba will keep its troops in Angola." Then Gaddafi left again in his Lincoln with his Amazons to go back to his
camels and his tent. As I watched him moving away, I said to
myself he was the greatest basket case I had ever encountered in
my life.

Fidel did not hold him in great esteem, either. I think that
Gaddafi had disappointed him enormously. At one time, the
Comandante had thought the Libyan colonel would become a

---

*In 1977, Colonel Gaddafi changed the name of the country to the Great
Socialist People's Libyan Arab Jamahiriya.

revolutionary leader capable of taking part of the Arab world along with him—but he quickly realized that despite his vast financial assets from gas, the man was incapable of having a coherent conversation. In front of us, Fidel said of him, "He's an eccentric who loves exhibitionism." Which was a polite way of saying that he was completely off the wall, impulsive, unpredictable, and unaware—the opposite of the dictator, Fidel Castro, in short. Many things can be said of Fidel, but not that he was intellectually mediocre like those tin-pot tyrants named Muammar al-Gaddafi and Kim Il-sung.

A KING'S RANSOM

Is Fidel Castro loaded? Does he possess a hidden fortune? Does he have a secret bank account in a tax haven bank? Is he rolling in gold? I have often been asked these questions. In 2006, the American magazine *Forbes* published an article devoted to the fortunes of kings, queens, and dictators all over the world. It placed Fidel's fortune among the top ten, alongside those of Elizabeth II, Prince Albert of Monaco, and the dictator of Equatorial Guinea, Teodoro Obiang. The figure of $900 million was advanced based on an extrapolation: the magazine attributed to Fidel Castro a part of the turnover of the companies he created and controlled (Corporación Cimex, El Centro de Convenciones, and Medicuba) and into which he placed family members who held the purse strings for him. Relying on the testimonies of numerous senior Cuban officials who had defected, the magazine affirmed that Fidel syphoned off and used a considerable part of the national wealth according to his whim. It is not untrue. And even if the methodology used by *Forbes* was not scientific, they were more or less in the right ballpark.

The article by the American publication enraged the

Comandante, who replied several days later to these "infamous calumnies." He claimed that he possessed nothing other than his nine hundred pesos of monthly salary—in other words, thirty-eight dollars. Highly comic when you knew, as I did, the reality of his daily lifestyle and when you had seen, year after year, the leaders of state companies taking instructions from and delivering accounts to the *Líder Máximo* (who decided everything), either directly or via his two assistants Pepín Naranjo and Chomy, the secretary of the Council of State (his private secretary, in other words, since Fidel presided over that institution).

Nobody will ever be in a position to give a precise evaluation of Fidel's fortune. But to get close to the truth, one has first to understand the Cuban reality that Fidel Castrol reigns over his island of eleven million inhabitants like an absolute monarch. In Cuba, he was the only person able to decide what to do with everything—take it for his own, sell it, or give it away. He alone, with the stroke of a pen, could authorize the creation (or the closure) of a state company, on the island or abroad. Gathered together as conglomerates, all the national companies are run like private businesses and placed under the control of three main institutions: MINFAR, headed by his brother Raúl until 2008; MININT, closely monitored by Fidel; or the Council of State, presided by him. It was Fidel who appointed, and fired, the business heads. In reality, this mode of functioning made Fidel the super-CEO of "Cuba holding," of which he had also drawn up the organization. How many times had I heard him in his office giving economic directives to Pepín, to Chomy, or else to Abrantes, the minister of the interior, concerning the sale of particular assets or the creation of a front company in Panama to get around the American embargo!

Cuba was Fidel's "thing." He was its master, in the manner of a nineteenth-century landowner. It was as though he had transformed and enlarged his father's property to make Cuba into a single hacienda of eleven million people. He did what he wanted with the national workforce. For example, medical schools trained doctors not so that they could freely practice their profession, but rather to become missionaries, sent under orders to the slums of Africa, Venezuela, or Brazil, according to the internationalist politics conceived, decided, and imposed by the head of state. Now, on missions abroad these good Samaritans were given only a small fraction of the salary their host country would normally pay them, for the lion's share was given to the Cuban government, acting as a service provider. In the same way, French, Spanish, or Italian hotels that hired Cuban staff on the island did not pay their employees themselves, as is the case in any free society: instead, they paid the salaries to the Cuban state, which invoiced this labor at a high price (and in cash) before transferring a tiny proportion to the workers concerned in virtually valueless Cuban pesos. This modern variant on slavery is reminiscent of the relationship of dependence that existed in the nineteenth-century plantations toward the all-powerful master. Moreover, it was in complete contradiction to the principles of the UN's International Labour Organization, which stipulates in writing that "every worker has the right to receive a salary without intervention of an intermediary."

To free himself from all control, Fidel—who was above the law—had long ago created, in the 1960s, the notorious *reserva del Comandante*, a private account made up of special funds syphoned off from national economic activity. Designed for the exclusive use of the *Comandante*, it escaped all checks and was a virtually sacred and *intocable* (untouchable) resource that Fidel used as he saw fit. Fidel explained that the needs of the Revolution, that is to say the threat of imperialist aggression, made this unorthodox means of financial management necessary. In reality, the reserve served the private interests of Fidel Castro as much as the public ones. It was the pocket money that allowed him to live like a prince without ever thinking of the cost—and it also permitted him to behave like a great feudal overlord when he went to the countryside to "his" lands, across "his" island. Fidel could dip into his coffers to build a dispensary, a school, or a road, or to assign cars to a certain municipality (the *reserva* also included a fleet of vehicles) without going through a ministry or any organization. All the benefactor had to do was turn to his aide-de-camp and tell him an amount for a certain project to become reality . . . and for Fidel to immediately have the air of a fairy godfather—or a man of the people.

However, the relationship he had with money was not that of nouveaux riches like the Italian Silvio Berlusconi or the former Argentinian president Carlos Menem, who were so enamored of luxury, consumption, and instant gratification. True, the austere Fidel Castro did not neglect his own comfort, possessing as he did (albeit secretly) a thirty-some-yard yacht, for example. But he did not feel the need to replace it with the latest, flashier model. For him, wealth was above all an instrument of power, political survival, and personal protection. In this regard, knowing his caution-loving character and his mentality of an old Spanish peasant, it is unthinkable that he would not have made arrangements to protect his back—as do all dictators—in the eventuality that he and his family were forced to flee Cuba and settle abroad, for example in Galicia (Spain) on his father's native land. Moreover, one day his wife Dalia said to me, in passing: *"No te preocupes, Sánchez, el futuro de la familia está asegurado."* ("Don't worry, Sánchez, the family's future is assured.")

Considered an asset of the Revolution, the *reserva* was not held by those in power to be something taboo; it was mentioned openly and directly in front of or by Fidel. It was not a state secret—unlike the actual size of the *reserva*. Since its creation in the 1960s, it was constantly replenished as the *Comandante* drew from it. When Cuba was dependent on the subsidies from the USSR, one often heard Fidel telling Chomy, his private secretary, to take a sum of x million dollars (since the currency of Fidel's account was the dollar) from those funds to put into the reserve. In the same way, the *Líder Máximo* could do what he wanted with Soviet gas—give some to Nicaragua or sell some on the black market to generate cash. When Hugo Chávez agreed to sell Venezuelan black gold to Cuba at a discount, I am certain that these discretionary kinds of arrangements continued.

Various sources fed this special fund, starting with the companies placed under the guardianship of the Council of State (under Fidel's leadership), as indicated in *Forbes* magazine in 2006. Among these were the Corporación Cimex (banks, property construction, car rental, and so on), Cubalese (wound up in 2009, this company supplied foreign embassies and companies with services such as the "rental" of Cuban staff or accommodations), or else the *Palacio de Convenciones*, created in 1979 to house the sixth summit of the Non-Aligned Movement and headed by the loyal Abraham Maciques. One day in the mid-1980s, when the latter was welcoming Fidel to the convention center, I saw him give us an overnight bag filled with a million dollars in cash. As always, it was the aide-de-camp Pepín Naranjo who was assigned to carry the booty and allocate it to the reserve. Another day, also in the mid-1980s, it was the Minister of the Interior José Abrantes who came into Fidel's office with a suitcase full of bills, uttering the sacred phrase, "Commander, this is for the Revolution!" Fidel simply replied, "Very good," and turned to Pepín to tell him to put it in the *reserva*.

I know that the director of the national bank, Héctor Rodríguez Llompart, was Fidel's "financial adviser," but I do not know what financial channels were involved or whether foreign bank accounts existed (in my view, they did). One thing is sure, however: Fidel never lacked cash, as demonstrated by my experience in Harare, for example, when I was given a suitcase with $250,000 in cash to prepare for the arrival of the Cuban head of state.

One of the funniest episodes I ever witnessed was the following: once, I heard Fidel say to Pepín and Chomy that part of the funds of the *reserva* would be used to loan money to the national bank, governed by Llompart. Now, the pair of them, Llompart and Fidel, fixed the interest rate at 10 percent. In other words, the *Comandante* was going to lend money that did not belong to him to the country that he governed, via the bank that used interest rates that he fixed, pocketing the 10 percent profit along the way!

Fidel used anything that came to hand to feed the reserve. On occasion he could behave like the owner of a small business. His flotilla on the Caleta del Rosario was made to contribute: his private marine included his yacht *Aquarama II* and other smaller vessels, plus two fishing boats named *Purrial de Vicana I* and *II*, of which one of the captains was called Emilio. After their expeditions to sea, their catches were sent to freezing units at the port of Havana and at Unit 160. These fish were not meant for the consumption of the Castro family, who did not eat frozen fish, but were sold at one of the biggest food markets in Havana, the Super Mercado situated in the Miramar quarter on the corner of Third Avenue and Seventh Street.

Little streams making great rivers, a turkey production unit and a sheep-breeding farm were used to the same end of increasing the reserve. To this could be added the business transacted in Lunada during the Angola war on the *kandonga*, the celebrated Angolan black market on which Cubans were very active for fifteen years. This, too, swelled the funds in the Commander's reserve.

At the time of the publication of the article in *Forbes*, the historian Eusebio Leal—who was very close to Fidel—stepped up to the plate to defend the reputation of the *Comandante*. As proof of the disinterestedness of the *Líder Máximo*, he revealed that in the 1990s the latter had asked him to distribute 11,687 gifts he had received to museums and cultural centers, including paintings, jewelry, ivory objects, and fine carpets from 133 countries. It might be true, but it proves nothing. Because for my part, I saw contraband diamonds in Fidel's office that had come from Angola and been sent by Patricio de la Guardia and Arnaldo Ochoa, respectively head of the MININT mission and head of the Cuban military mission in this war-torn African country. They were small diamonds placed in a Cohiba cigar box. Chomy and Pepín passed them from hand to hand in front of Fidel, his personal doctor Eugenio Selman, and me. I can still remember their dialogue.

"Okay, Pepín, you know what you need to do with them. Sell them on the international market. . . ."

"Yes, *Comandante*," replied the aide-de-camp, who had suddenly transformed into a gemology expert. "But you know the value of these stones is doubtless not very high, because they're small. . . . Well, they must be worth something, anyway, because their size will be appreciated in costume and fine jewelry making."

As far as business was concerned, Fidel sometimes had the mentality of a Caribbean pirate. Operating outside the law, navigating in informality and dealing in contraband posed him no problems at all since circumstances demanded it and his position as resistance fighter against the American embargo authorized everything. Moreover, contrary to what he claimed, he had always known about all the illegal activities (including drug trafficking in the 1980s) imagined and carried out by his brother Tony and Arnaldo Ochoa within the *Departamento MC* (MC

Department),* in their endeavor to find cash by any means whatsoever so as to keep the Revolution afloat. In the same way, Fidel knew about the parallel activities of the Minister of the Interior Abrantes, who manufactured counterfeit Levi's jeans in secret workshops (in which Cuban prisoners worked) and trafficked adulterated Chivas Regal whisky to sell on the black market in Panama. All this with the same end in mind: feeding the Commander in Chief's reserve.

I knew about all these commercial operations because Fidel and his entourage talked about them in front of me for seventeen successive years and because Pepín and Chomy, with whom I collaborated closely on a daily basis, regularly gave explanations about them to the Commander in Chief, without taking account of my presence because I effectively belonged to his most intimate circle.

Be that as it may, Fidel's finest coup was perhaps when, in 1980, he ordered the temporary reactivation of the gold mine of La Dolita situated on the Isla de la Juventud, the large island in the shape of a comma situated south of the Cuban coast. After having exhausted its resources, the Spanish had closed it down permanently during colonial times. However, learning that gold was experiencing a boom on the world markets, Fidel took it into his head to check whether, by any chance, modern equipment would enable any residual deposits that may have been overlooked to be extracted from La Dolita. His intuition was excellent: around 130 to 150 pounds of gold were collected and melted into ingots. I saw them with my own eyes when they were transported to the *palacio* to be shown to Fidel. Pepín asked

*More on that in chapter 15.

me to help him schlep them into a wheelbarrow, and that was how I was able to estimate the weight: a single man could not have lifted it all at one go. I did not bother to ask him what this treasure would be used for or where it was going: I already knew the answer. . . .

Although Fidel Castro's personal wealth cannot be measured, his assets can be estimated. In a country in which there is no real estate market, it is difficult to put a price on the immense property of Punto Cero (with its swimming pool, tree-filled grounds, and greenhouses) or the paradise island of Cayo Piedra. Nonetheless, these exceptional properties still have an intrinsic value that can be compared with their equivalents on the luxury market, very sought after in the Caribbean Sea, the Bahamas, Grenada, or Antigua. Using this measure, the private island of Cayo Piedra is worth at least between two and ten million dollars.

Fidel's assets are not limited to these two main residences. There are dozens of others; to restrict myself to a rigorous, objective, and minimal estimate, I will detail only the twenty or so houses that are for the exclusive use of the *Comandante* and that I know about because I have set foot in them and seen them with my own eyes, without taking account of the other pieds-à-terre that could be likened more to official accommodations.

Let us review this property portfolio, region by region, from the west to the east of the island. In the province of Pinar del Río, in the extreme western edge of Cuba, he owns three properties: the American House (with open-air swimming pool); the farm of La Tranquilidad in the locality of Mil Cumbres (very little used by Fidel; I went there only twice); and La Deseada, a hunting lodge that I knew well, situated in a swampy zone where he shot duck in winter.

In Havana, other than the estate of Punto Cero, the *Comandante* has six landing places: the House of Cojímar, his first home after the Triumph of the Revolution in 1959; the house on 160th Street in the fairly upmarket district of Playa; a third house reserved for his amorous encounters, the House of Carbonell, situated in the precinct of Unit 160; an adorable little 1950s-style house in Santa María del Mar, facing the sea and next to the Trópico hotel (in the municipality of east Havana); and, finally, the two houses equipped with air raid shelters for the Castro family in case of war: the House of Punta Brava (where Dalia lived in 1961 before she moved in with Fidel) and the House of Gallego, very close to Unit 160.

In the province of Matanzas, he owns two vacation homes on the north and south coasts: in the north, a house situated in the heart of the holiday resort of Varadero that was particularly valued by his and Dalia's sons because it leads directly onto the beach, and in the south, La Caleta del Rosario (in the Bay of Pigs), where a marina serves as the home port for the yacht *Aquarama II* and the rest of Fidel's private flotilla. Further to the east, in the province of Ciego de Ávila, another house has direct access onto a beach of fine sand: the one on the Isle of Turiguano, near the tourist hot spot of Cayo Coco, appreciated by divers the world over, on the northern coast of Cuba.

In the province of Camagüey, still further east, is the small hacienda of San Cayetano, which, even though Fidel did not ride horseback, possesses an outside manege (known as a "schooling yard" in the riding world). Another house in Camagüey, named

Tabayito, is hidden inside a complex that includes other properties given to members of the elite. Finally, I know of another property called Guardalavaca in the province of Holguín and two residences in Santiago de Cuba, the large town situated in the eastern part of the island: a house in Manduley Street (with two floors and a bowling green) and another, with a swimming pool, inside a complex belonging to the minister of the interior.

I am not sure that even the president of the United States has such a well-stocked property portfolio. But whatever the case, Fidel will swear, staring into your eyes and challenging you to believe him, that he earns just nine hundred pesos a month.

AT DEATH'S DOOR

There had been an initial warning. In 1983, Fidel had had serious health problems that reoccurred in 1992. So when he fell really ill in 2006 and was forced to hand over the reins of power to Raúl, I was one of the few people in the world—along with his Cuban doctors and his immediate entourage—to make the connection with his earlier medical history.

In March 1983, when we had been back about a month from New Delhi, India, where Fidel had attended the seventh Non-Aligned Movement summit, life was following its normal course: the *Comandante* went every day to his office to deal with the business at hand. The month of April even began with a happy (although secret) event, about which I learned only years later: the birth of Abel, the illegitimate son of Fidel and Juanita Vera, his interpreter. Judging by photos recently sent me by well-informed friends, this baby is today in his thirties, with Latin lover looks.

Two weeks later, on the evening of April 20, we were

accompanying Fidel back to his residence of Punto Cero at past midnight. As usual, Dalia greeted him on the doorstep, kissing him and taking his Kalashnikov from his hands before placing it in their bedroom on the first floor. Then the *Comandante* retired to his apartments while we his escort went home—that is, to the dormitory situated in the building about fifty yards from the main house.

Around two a.m., the bell that alerted us every time Fidel was about to leave rang out. We leaped out of our beds and ran out to the cars, convinced that an urgent meeting, an international event, or a secret rendezvous meant he had to return to town. And, indeed, the head of the escort Domingo Mainet informed us that we were returning to the *palacio*: ten minutes later, our convoy of three Mercedes was streaming through the darkness of the sleeping capital.

When we got to the basement car garage of the palace, Fidel got out of the vehicle and I immediately noticed something abnormal: under his military uniform, he was wearing a blue pajama top! What was more, when he turned around to go toward the elevator, I saw a stain on his rear end. At the time, I imagined he must have sat down on something wet—but in the elevator, I also noticed his pallor. I decided he must be suffering from a simple digestion problem, not imagining how worrying the situation really was. But Domingo Mainet did not press the button for the third floor (where his office was) but rather sent us up directly to the fourth, where Fidel's private clinic was to be found.

It was a miniature hospital that contained just three bedrooms: Fidel's, with a bathroom and terrace overlooking Havana, a second for the bodyguards (principally the two "blood donors" who always slept there in case *El Jefe* was hospitalized), and a third for the medical staff on duty. This secret clinic also comprised an X-ray room, a pharmacy, a medical laboratory, and all the modern medical equipment one can imagine— including an expensive SOMATOM CT scanner made by German manufacturer Siemens. There was also the dental office where Professor Salvador, his dentist, had carried out all the Commander's implants at the end of the 1980s to replace his original teeth. A gym for rehabilitation exercises, a kitchen, and a dining room completed the scene. All that for the exclusive use of one person: Fidel. Unlike the other leaders of the Revolution, *El Jefe* did not use the *Centro de Investigaciones Médico Quirúrgicas* (CIMEQ), even though it was the pride of Cuban medicine. He possessed his own infrastructure.

That night, when we reached the fourth floor of the *palacio*, Fidel's medical team was already there in full force. There was the surgeon Eugenio Selman, his personal doctor; Dr. Raúl Dorticós, one of the most eminent Cuban doctors, who enjoyed an international reputation; Dr. Ariel, the anesthesiologist; and Dr. Cabrera, responsible for Fidel's blood bags and for transfusions. Not to mention Wilder Fernández, his personal nurse, plus two female nurses. The *Comandante* was immediately taken in hand by this assembly of specialists.

The following morning, as the latter were all coming out into the corridor to confer, I learned from their conversation that their illustrious patient was suffering from a cancerous ulcer in the intestine. I do not know what treatment they administered, but I do know that Fidel stayed in that clinic for eleven days and that afterward he convalesced for three months in his Havanan residence of Punto Cero. Thus, from April 20 to July 17,

Fidel Castro did not appear in public and did not give a single speech.

It was on that occasion that the strategy of disinformation consisting of putting Fidel Castro's "double" on display at the back of the presidential Mercedes was first used; the vehicle drove through Havana so as to dispel any rumors about the absence of the *Comandante*. From time to time Fidel's personal hairdresser made up Silvino Álvarez, the Commander in Chief's double, and altered his appearance by decking him out with a false beard. Then we would leave in convoy from the Palace of the Revolution to pass ostentatiously in front of the Western embassies. At regular intervals, when we crossed a group of people in the street, the false Fidel installed in the real one's place in the right-hand side of the backseat would lower his window and greet people from afar. During those months of convalescence, the whole of the escort kept his routine: every day we would perform Fidel's usual trip between home and office so that nothing seemed out of the ordinary. Nobody realized that anything was amiss; for all concerned, Fidel was indeed in Havana, absorbed in his work as "father of the nation."

From the time of that first health alert, particular attention was paid to Fidel's diet. His doctors having prescribed a strict regimen based on white meat and fresh vegetables, agricultural greenhouses were put up in the garden of his residence at Punto Cero and he virtually gave up red meat. The *Comandante* also got into the habit of drinking a freshly squeezed orange juice, nice and cold and served without fail—wherever he was and 365 days a year—at exactly four p.m. However, no decree against alcohol was set down and Fidel continued regularly drinking whisky, though less than before. This, as well as his abstinence in terms of cigars (he had stopped smoking in 1980), allowed him to recover his health. Fidel reappeared in public on July 17 and gave a speech in the botanical garden of Lenin Park in Havana for Children's Day. Everything went back to normal, but I have to admit that from that day forward I saw Fidel a little differently; sometimes I even caught myself, rather shamefacedly, looking at his posterior.

The second attack came nine years later in 1992, after Fidel Castro's memorable journey to Spain. That year, the *Líder Máximo* had a thousand good reasons to go to the land of his ancestors: to take part in the Ibero-American Summit in Madrid on July 23 and 24, to attend the inauguration of the summer Olympic games in Barcelona on July 25, to celebrate the Cuban national holiday in Seville on July 26, to visit the Seville Expo in the same town on July 27, and, finally, go on a pilgrimage to Láncara, his father's native village in Galicia, sixty miles or so from Santiago de Compostela. I remember that Fidel's visit was greeted by a sarcastic article in the great Spanish daily *El País*, which gave an ironically exaggerated description of the number of security men in place around the Commander of the Revolution. The author talked of "fifty armed men landing at Barajas airport at an hour kept secret until the last minute, on board two Ilyushin airplanes in the colors of Cubana de Aviación, one of which serves as a decoy."

I myself had arrived in the Spanish capital several days earlier, at the head of the team of forerunners. At the Ritz Hotel, one of the most beautiful luxury hotels in Madrid, I had put the time to good use by fraternizing with the manager, giving him three bottles of Havana Club rum and a box of Lanceros No. 1, the cigars manufactured by Cohiba that were so beloved by Che: such attentiveness is always useful in case one later needs to ask a favor or a service in the aim of improving the protection of the head of state. I also had Fidel's bed, delivered in pieces from Havana, assembled, and I inspected the room. For the second time in my career, I discovered a mike—after the one I discovered in the false ceiling of our embassy in Zimbabwe—hidden by secret agents in a window frame of the presidential suite. We never found out who hid it there. Finally, I had a secret passage created via the dressing room so that Fidel's suite had direct access to the room of his interpreter, Colonel Juanita; the son she had had with *El Jefe* was then nine years old.

Shortly after the two Ilyushins had landed and we had checked in to the Ritz Hotel, we learned that Orestes Lorenzo was in Madrid—a name that must be remembered, for his story was absolutely incredible. At the time, I didn't see things that way, but today I have to say that I have limitless admiration for him. A year and a half later, on March 20, 1991, this Cuban air force pilot had banked, aimed for the lights of Florida, and defected while in command of his MiG-23. He landed a few minutes later on the air base of Key West. Needless to say, he made all the headlines. This fearless officer demanded freedom for his thirty-four-year-old wife, Victoria, and their two boys of eleven and six—in other words, for them to be able to leave Cuba to join him in his new life. Fidel, of course, rejected the demand, swearing that they would stay in Cuba for the rest of their lives and that the "traitor" would never see his family again. Orestes Lorenzo had then begun a terrible shuttling, going as far as New York, Geneva, and the UN Human Rights Commission to raise media awareness. All in vain. He even managed to speak to Mikhail Gorbachev and George H. W. Bush, without any greater success.

For the moment, this kindly dad with his naïve, baby-faced looks, was in Madrid. He had chained himself to the railings in the Retiro park and had begun a hunger strike in front of posters and photos of his family under which the caption CASTRO'S HOSTAGES had been written. The media had devoted several articles to him. Now, at a certain moment during our brief stay in the capital, Fidel—leaving or coming back to the Ritz Hotel—decided he wanted to drive past the Retiro to see the extent of the scandal for himself: "So let's go and see for ourselves what *este loco* [this madman] is doing." Without Orestes Lorenzo having the least idea, we drove past him, just a few feet away. Fidel, with all the contempt of which he was capable, threw out, *"Este ridículo no va a lograr nada."* ("This ridiculous man will not get anywhere.") And yet, the following December 19, the "madman" accomplished one of the most beautiful and quixotic feats I have ever heard of. Like something out of a fairy tale, he went to get his family at the controls of an old, hired twin-engine 1960s Cessna, landing in daylight on a section of motorway in the north of Cuba where his wife and children were waiting for him, as per the instructions he had managed to relay to them thanks to two fake Mexican tourists. After picking up his family, right under the noses of Cuban radar surveillance, the epic voyage ended in glory after a low-flying skim across the sea: the hero brought his old crate to rest in Florida where, after a hundred minutes of extreme tension, he could at last kiss his beloved wife and darling children.

Many years later, when I, too, had gone to live on American soil, I met Orestes at his large house in Florida, where he lived with his family. Blissfully happy, he is today a wealthy head of a business. When I told him how, twenty years earlier, Fidel had passed a few feet away from him in Madrid during his hunger strike, we both fell silent for a moment as though overcome by our overlapping destinies.

After Madrid, Fidel, the monarch of Cuba, had gone to be with another king, Juan Carlos, on the occasion of the Olympic games in Barcelona. Among the personalities in the official box one could make out Nelson Mandela, François Mitterrand, Felipe González of Spain, the Catalan Jordi Pujol, the Argentinian Carlos Menem, and the U.S. vice president Dan Quayle. Fidel Castro had always taken the Olympic games very seriously, particularly the performances of the Cuban athletes who were, according to him, the expression of the greatness of the Revolution and of his country's development. While the USSR had disintegrated a few months earlier that year, Fidel had proof that Cuba remained a great nation: at the end of the competition, our athletes were fourth in the medals table, behind the United States, Germany, and China but ahead of Spain, South Korea, Hungary, and France.

Finally, after a stopover in Seville, the visit to the self-governing region of Galicia was the high point of the trip. On the land of his ancestors, the former minister under Franco,

Manuel Fraga, now president of the Galician assembly, welcomed him like both a king and a brother. It was three days of celebration and emotion. Fidel visited his father's house in Láncara, where he met three distant cousins, after which Manuel Fraga organized a dominos tournament. The two politicians even played a game in the open air, sitting on the back of a truck. Fidel, the sore loser, must have won fairly quickly, or I would have remembered: we would have been there waiting for his victory until four in the morning. . . .

At a certain moment, a little girl of twelve or so, clearly from a humble background, appeared beside me. She was crying and looking at the *Comandante*. "What's the matter?" I asked her. She explained that she, along with all her family, were fervent admirers of Fidel. She had not thought twice about walking for three days, a bundle on her shoulders and sleeping out under the stars, to see the great man. So I said to her, "Leave your bag here and come with me." I took her to Fidel, who, like me, asked her, *"Qué te pasa?"* Then Fidel kissed her. Overwhelmed, trembling with emotion, she then said to me, "You've done such a huge thing for me."

I have not forgotten that girl. I would really like this book to reach her and for her to remember the human moment we shared.

Several moments later, the crowds all around us began serving aguardiente (a Spanish brandy) and cooking in the street, with the hope of offering these things to Fidel and getting him to taste them. A line formed, for each of them wanted to honor the guest of the day with an empanada (fried dumpling filled with meat and vegetables) or a traditional local product. The intention was laudable, but my task consisted of preventing the

Comandante from eating anything that had not been tested by our security services. So I tried to usher the "cooks" away as politely as possible, as I tasted each food. "Oh, I think it's a little bit too salty for his taste," I would say to one. "Put it there, I'll give it to him later," I said to another. Despite everything, the *Comandante* tasted a few rather fatty dishes and finished his Spanish journey as he had begun it: with a feast that ruined his diet.

I don't know whether these departures from routine were behind the episode that followed, but no sooner had he arrived back in Havana than Fidel fell seriously ill for the second time in his life, in circumstances similar to the first. In early September 1992, while we were in the Havanan residence of Punto Cero, the Commander in Chief's leaving bell rang out at an unusual hour for the night owl he was: before daybreak! When I arrived at the *palacio* car garage, I noticed that Fidel—exactly like nine years earlier—was wearing only a military fatigues shirt on top of his blue pajamas and that his rear end was stained with blood. On the fourth floor, the whole of the clinic's medical staff rapidly moved into action, but I soon realized that the situation was worse than in 1983. His doctors were more worried and Fidel was paler. At a certain moment, I saw him—for the first time in my life—lying unconscious on a stretcher.

Worried, I asked for an explanation from his nurse Wilder Fernández, who was one of the members of the escort. He told me that the transfusions were not working: "Fidel's body is not accepting the blood." Tears in his eyes, he added desperately, "Sánchez, Fidel is at death's door. We have told the head of the escort to warn Raúl so that he can decide what should be done in the coming hours. He should get here at any moment."

In 1983, nobody had been informed about Fidel's eleven-day hospitalization. Not even Raúl. But, this time, things were different. When the defense minister arrived on the fourth floor, the doctors immediately told him of the gravity of the situation. The decision was made to tell Dalia and her children, but not Fidelito or Jorge Ángel.

In the ensuing minutes, Raúl decided the procedure to be followed to alert the family and the highest political institutions in the country should the unthinkable happen: first, close colleagues would be told, then the members of the PPC politburo, then the members of the Council of State, then the chief of staff of the armed services, the members of the Central Committee of the PCC, and finally the people. The announcement would be spread over several days. The people would first be told that Fidel had been hospitalized, then that his condition had gone from "serious" to "critical," and finally that the Commander in Chief had left us: all by means of a PCC politburo communiqué broadcast on television, radio, and in the *Granma* newspaper.

I do not know how because I am not a doctor, but Fidel managed to bounce back. I heard a rumor that with the help of the escort's compatible blood donors, they had proceeded to give direct transfusions, vein to vein! If it was true—and it seems completely plausible because Fidel could have taken the inspiration for that from one of his historical texts, an old medical treatise or suchlike, to demand that such an experiment be tried—it was pure madness. Indeed, according to the doctors to whom I have spoken since I came to the United States, such a technique does not offer any advantages over a classic transfusion.

Whatever the case, his convalescence would last fifty-five days. Once again, Fidel's hairdresser and makeup artist stuck a false beard on the double of the *Comandante*, Silvino Álvarez, who played his best character study, installed at the back of the presidential Mercedes.

In the end, after nearly two months' absence from public life, Fidel reappeared at the *Palacio de Convenciones* on October 29, to give a speech to Cuban members of parliament. None of them were aware that just a few weeks earlier, their leader had been at death's door.

FIDEL, ANGOLA, AND
THE ART OF WAR

War, at last! Over the course of his long life, Fidel Castro has advised, trained, and supported dozens of armed groups, inspiring hundreds of thousands, or maybe millions, of anti-imperialist fighters all over the world. In Latin America, not a single country escaped his influence. And in Africa—where Che Guevara went in person to fight in 1964—no less than seventeen revolutionary movements have benefited from his expertise. But, in the end, all these subversive actions were occasional, limited in number and duration, and ultimately very modest in terms of the real planetary ambitions of the *Comandante*. They were "only" guerrillas. . . .

In Angola, Fidel Castro escalated his involvement with troops on the ground, tanks and other armored vehicles, batteries of artillery, helicopters, and fighter planes. For seventeen years, from 1975 to 1992, he accomplished the feat of sending to a front more than six thousand miles away from the Cuban coast a total contingent of two to three hundred thousand fighters and civilians. It is unprecedented: until now, no country of comparable size had carried out a military project so far away, for so long, with so many men. Cuban soldiers in Angola contributed to the weakening of the racist regime of South Africa by inflicting on it a bloody military and political defeat.

This incredible story—curiously little known outside of Cuba—began in Lisbon on April 25, 1974, when the Carnation Revolution brought down the Salazarist dictatorship that had held power in Portugal since the 1930s.

As soon as it was in power, the new government decided to abandon its colonial empire. In addition to Mozambique, Guinea Bissau, Cape Verde, Macao, and Timor, its "jewel in the crown" was Angola, rich in gas and minerals. In Angola, the three independence movements that had thus far confronted the colonial power separately immediately started fighting among themselves. The Popular Movement for the Liberation of Angola (known by its Portuguese abbreviation MPLA) headed by the Marxist leader Agostinho Neto was supported by the Soviet bloc. The two other movements, the National Front for the Liberation of Angola (FNLA) led by the independence fighter Holden Roberto and UNITA under the leadership of Jonas Savimbi, received the support of the West.

In order to calm the heightened tensions which threatened to drag the country into civil war, in January 1975 the Portuguese preemptively announced the date of future independence: the following November 11. The countdown started for each of the movements to prepare for war. Everybody understood that whoever controlled Luanda, the capital, the day the

Portuguese left would automatically become the country's new masters.

Agostinho Neto—who had met Che Guevara ten years earlier in the Congo—naturally called on Fidel Castro to help. The latter, in a flash of genius, immediately devised and organized the notorious and insanely daring Operation Carlota. This consisted of quickly establishing air and maritime bridges between Havana and Luanda in order to transport thousands of "internationalists" and equipment that would enable Neto's MPLA to seize Luanda before the fateful day. In the autumn of 1975, thousands of soldiers crossed the ocean aboard cruise ships and the four-engine Britannia planes of Cubana de Aviación, to reach the shores of southern Africa in the greatest secrecy. The operation was facilitated by the fact that the Cuban contingent included numerous blacks and mixed-race men who blended easily into the background.

World opinion was shocked when it was discovered that thousands of Cubans had arrived in Luanda. Not just the Americans but also the Soviets! Fidel had not thought it necessary to warn the Kremlin about his great maneuvers; faced with the fait accompli, the Soviet leaders were flabbergasted, and with good reason: it was the first time, since the colonial period had begun at the start of the century, that an entire army had arrived on the African continent from overseas.

The Commander in Chief's plan worked perfectly. On November 10, 1975, after a week of fighting, Agostinho Nero's MPLA won a decisive battle with the support of Cuban troops that enabled them to besiege Luanda. On November 11, the new leader of the country declared independence. In the middle of the cold war, Angola toppled into the Soviet bloc, its new Marxist government receiving the reinforcement of Russian military advisers and war equipment, allowing it to control most of the country. In Havana, the myth of Cuban invincibility, originating with the Bay of Pigs, was confirmed.

I had not yet joined Fidel's escort at the time. At the age of twenty-six, I was studying at the specialist college of MININT, with the aim of becoming a security officer responsible for VIPs. However, as my deepest desire was to die for the Revolution, I went to talk to an officer to beg to be sent to Angola to take part in the glorious saga. To my great surprise, he rebuffed me sharply, asking who I took myself for. He explained that it was not for me to decide my future but for the Revolution to choose what mission suited me best. Later, I realized that two years before being appointed as one of Fidel's bodyguards, I had already been preselected for the role.

In 1976, divine surprise: the American Senate, not wanting to be dragged into an "African Vietnam," voted for the Clark Amendment, which forbade the United States from exporting arms or intervening militarily in Angola. In March 1977, Fidel embarked on his first triumphal visit to Angolan soil, where the situation was more or less under control. After the natural death of Agostinho Neto in 1979, he was replaced by José Eduardo dos Santos (still in power today). However, things got more complicated in the 1980s. To start with, the American invasion of Grenada, in which 638 Cubans were taken prisoner, dealt a serious blow to the myth of Cuban invincibility. Then, in Angola, the South Africans relaunched a military offensive, in the southeast of the country. However, Fidel constantly sent human reinforcements while the Russians continued to supply tanks, planes, helicopters, and missiles without concern for expense. Notwithstanding all this, the losses on the ground began to accumulate and ten years after the start of the conflict, Cuban mothers feared only one thing: that an officer from MINFAR would knock on their door one morning, holding a bouquet of flowers, as was the custom, to tell them their son had died in combat. In total, more than twenty-five hundred Cubans lost their lives in the Angolan conflict.

Meanwhile, the difference of opinion between the Cubans and the Russians became more obvious. According to Fidel, Soviet war theory was unsuited to the African battlefield. To make things worse, the Russians were unable to adapt to the local mentality. While the natural affinity between the Angolans and the Cubans was obvious, the Soviets seemed like aliens from outer space. First serious disagreement: in July 1985, the Soviet military commander insisted on launching a great offensive, Operation Congreso II, against the area of Mavinga, strategically situated in the southeast of Angola, about six hundred miles from the capital. Fidel was opposed to it because he thought the circumstances unfavorable—and what happened next proved him right. After having attained the objective, the Cuban-Angolan forces were compelled to withdraw quickly, because the Russians had not correctly secured the supply column. A battle for nothing . . .

In the war room of MINFAR in Havana one day with Fidel—which was where he followed all the fighting—I heard him once again repeating to Raúl, "I knew that was going to happen. I told them, the Russians, they had to secure the rear and the supply. . . . Now it's too late. . . . They should have thought of it before!" After which the *Comandante* gave the order to his brother—who had always been the liaison agent between Havana and Moscow—to make known his complete unhappiness with what had gone on "to the highest authorities in the Kremlin." Which he did.

The following year, between May and August 1986, the Soviets made the same mistake. They launched their second great offensive, which, for the same reasons, ended in lamentable failure: the South Africans and Jonas Savimbi's UNITA sabotaged the bridges that spanned the rivers, cutting off the retreat of the Cuban-Angolan forces. Once again, Fidel made his displeasure known to Mikhail Gorbachev—whom, to his concern, he saw also forging diplomatic ties with the United States. That did not bode well for Cuba.

The following month, in September 1986, Fidel attended the summit of the Non-Aligned Movement in Zimbabwe, as did I and Colonel Gaddafi. Fidel then decided to make a stopover in Angola, where forty thousand Cubans, soldiers and civilians, were stationed, including Raúl's own son, the young Alejandro Castro, who is today a colonel. It was the second time Fidel had set foot in Angola, after the trip in 1977.

Fidel stayed in the country for three days. On the second evening, he went to visit our troops on the front line. His escort was minimal: three bodyguards, including myself; the head of the escort, Domingo Mainet; and Dr. Selman. We took off in three helicopters at dusk and, like in a film, flew at low height toward the combat zone. After landing in the middle of the bush, I realized we were just several hundred yards away from the South Africans. The enemy was so close that you could see the lights of their camp—if they had known that Fidel was within reach. . . .

There, the *Comandante* addressed our soldiers, galvanizing them with words, assessing their morale, discussing their daily routine, and trying to understand the military situation. It made one think of Napoleon talking to his soldiers. "What region in Cuba do you come from? From Oriente province? Ah, very good. . . ." "How long have you been in Angola?" "The supplies, are they alright?" I remember that when we got back to Luanda that evening, Fidel's morale was sky high, keyed up by the trip.

After the failure of their two great offensives, the Soviets finally gave up command, leaving the tactical and strategic initiative to Fidel Castro. A fact that is so extraordinary it must be emphasized: throughout the whole of the war, Fidel directed military operations from Havana, from the other side of the world. One had to see him at it to believe it, the strategist in his MINFAR war room, surrounded by geological survey maps and models of the battlefields! Past master of the art of war (he had read Sun Tzu), he was Napoleon and Rommel rolled into one.

Via the written word or telephone, he dictated his instructions to his generals, which gave rise to bulletins such as this:

> The defensive perimeter east of the river must be reduced. Withdraw 59th and 26th squadrons to the fortified positions nearer the river. These two squadrons should cover the whole of the southwestern sector, so that the 8th can devote itself to food provisions. At the moment they are too exposed to attacks that could come from the zone the 21st squadron was previously defending. Given the situation, such a risk is unacceptable and should be immediately corrected.

Almost two decades later, in the 2000s, the former general and former South African minister of defense Magnus Malan, who had fought him at Cuito Cuanavale, was incredulous: "I don't understand how he managed to do it. Commanding operations from 10,000 kilometers [about 6,200 miles] away is theoretically impossible. . . . No, I'll never understand," he avowed in a spirit of fair play and what amounted to an unintentional homage to his former enemy.*

The legendary battle of Cuito Cuanavale was the ultimate clash between Cuba and South Africa. It lasted six months, from September 1987 to March 1988, and went down in history as the biggest military battle in Africa since the Second World War. This African Stalingrad with tanks, helicopters, fighter planes, and batteries of missiles ended with an impasse. Nobody had won and each side claimed victory—but the South Africans had

---

*See the documentary film *Cuba, an African Odyssey* (Jihan El Tahri, 2007).

to admit that they would never militarily overthrow the Marxist government of Luanda. They therefore accepted negotiations for peace on these terms: Fidel would bring his army back to Cuba, on condition that the South African Defence Force left Namibia and granted total independence to that former German colony, placed under South African protection since 1945, which served as a buffer state to Angola. And so Namibian independence was declared. At the same period, international pressure led to the racist regime in Pretoria making other concessions: the liberation of Nelson Mandela and then the abolition of apartheid. Three years later, Nelson Mandela declared that Cuito Cuanavale "destroyed the myth of the invincibility of the white oppressor. [It] was a victory for all Africa."

Fidel gained even more prestige through that extraordinary adventure. It would, however, be unfair not to speak about the crucial role of Arnaldo Ochoa in Angola. Considered the best Cuban general, he had taken part in all, or almost all, the events of the Castrist saga. For my generation, this hawk-nosed soldier with his irresistible charm was the very model of an accomplished guerrilla fighter. A member of the resistance in the Sierra Maestra at the time of the fight against Batista, he found himself in the Congo with Che Guevara in 1964, then in Venezuela in 1966 so as to organize a guerrilla *foco*. A vital cog in Operation Carlota in Angola in 1975, he also led the expeditionary Cuban corps in Ethiopia during the Ethio-Somali War (1977–1978) before becoming in 1984–1986—again at Fidel's express wish—the special adviser of the Nicaraguan defense minister Humberto Ortega to help that country in its bid to withstand the attacks of the Washington-financed Contras.

Fidel named this genius of the Revolution, the most decorated soldier in the country, "hero of the Republic of Cuba," the only holder of that title. In 1987, when the Cuban army found itself in a delicate position mainly through Soviet errors, Ochoa became head of the Cuban military mission in Angola. Once there, however, this skilled strategist—who was also Raúl Castro's best friend—thought himself in a better position than Fidel to judge the reality on the ground. One day, for example, Ochoa suggested a weeklong break to allow the combatants to recuperate while the *Comandante*, for his part, wanted to return to battle without delay. The general got it into his head to formulate alternative propositions to the tactical choices decreed by *El Jefe*.

In the *palacio* or in the MINFAR war room, I heard Fidel grumble to Raúl: "Ochoa is showing signs of incompetence" (implying mental incompetence), "Ochoa is out of touch with reality," or else "Ochoa's feet are not on the ground." In January 1988, when the battle of Cuito Cuanavale was in full flow, the general was summoned back to Havana, where Fidel ordered him to withdraw all squadrons except one from the eastern bank of the Cuito. Back in Angola, however, Ochoa did not implement this strategy, which he believed to be wrong, and made other, probably better, choices. Several weeks later, Ochoa was recalled to Luanda and then to Havana.

Deep down, I was worried for him—I had long known that nobody, not even the hero of the Republic of Cuba, could contradict Fidel. To do so was, sooner or later, to risk disgrace. Little did I imagine, however, that the countdown to his death had already started.

Less than a year later, Arnaldo Ochoa was shot by a firing squad. By order of Fidel.

THE OCHOA AFFAIR

The end of 1988. A day like any other was coming to a close in Havana. In a few minutes, my life would be overturned.

Fidel had spent his afternoon reading and working in his office when he stuck his head through the door to the anteroom, where I was, to warn me that Abrantes was about to arrive. Gen. José Abrantes, in his fifties, had been minister of the interior since 1985 after having been, notably, the Commander in Chief's head of security for twenty years. Utterly loyal, he was one of the people who saw *El Jefe* daily. He also belonged to the circle of people closest to the supreme power, along with Raúl Castro and those whom readers already know but whose positions I will reiterate here: José Miguel Miyar Barruecos, aka Chomy, Fidel's personal secretary; his personal doctor Eugenio Selman; the diplomat Carlos Rafael Rodríguez; the spymaster Manuel Piñeiro, aka Redbeard; and his two friends—the writer Gabriel García Márquez, known as "Gabo," and the geographer Antonio Núñez Jiménez. Another characteristic made Abrantes stand out: other than Raúl, he was one of the rare people able to enter Fidel's office without going through the main door of the *Palacio de la Revolución* but rather via the basement car garage at the rear, then the elevator that led directly to the third floor.

That day, around five p.m., after parking in the garage, José Abrantes came into Fidel's anteroom. I announced his arrival: *"¡Comandante, aquí está el ministro!"* ("Commander, the minister is here!"); nobody, not even his brother Raúl, went into Fidel's office without being presented first. I closed the double door, then went to sit in my office (next to the anteroom) where the closed-circuit TV screens monitoring the garage, the elevator, and the corridors were found, as well as the cupboard housing the three locks that turned on the recording mikes hidden in a false ceiling in Fidel's office. A moment later, the *Comandante* came back, opened the door again, and gave me this instruction: *"Sánchez, ¡no grabes!"* ("Sánchez, don't record!")

While the two men were talking privately, I attended to my work, reading that day's *Granma*, tidying papers, jotting down Fidel's latest activities in the *libreta*. The interview seemed to go on forever . . . one hour went by, then two. The strange thing was that Fidel did not ask me to bring him a *whiskycito* (a little whisky) or to offer a *cortadito* (a strong espresso) to his interlocutor, who usually drank it in abundance. Never before had the minister of the interior stayed so long in the office of the *Líder Máximo*. And so, as much out of curiosity as to kill the time, I put on the listening headphones and turned key no. 1 to hear what was being said on the other side of the wall.

And then I eavesdropped on a conversation I should never have heard.

Their conversation centered on a Cuban *lanchero* (someone who smuggles drugs by boat) living in the United States, apparently conducting business with the government. And what business! Very simply, a huge drug trafficking transaction was being carried out at the highest echelons of the state.

Abrantes asked for Fidel's authorization to bring this trafficker temporarily to Cuba, as he wanted to have a week's vacation in his native land, accompanied by his parents, in Santa María del Mar—a beach situated about twelve miles east of Havana where the water is turquoise and the sand as fine as flour. For this trip, explained Abrantes, the *lanchero* would pay seventy-five thousand dollars—which, at a time of economic recession, wouldn't go amiss. . . . Fidel was all for it. But he expressed a concern: how could they ensure that the parents of the *lanchero* would keep the secret and not go and blab everywhere that they had spent a week near Havana with their son, who was supposed to live in the United States? The minister had the solution: all they had to do was make them believe their son was a Cuban intelligence officer who had infiltrated the United States and whose life would be gravely endangered if they did not keep his visit to Cuba absolutely secret. "Very well . . . ," concluded Fidel, who gave his agreement. Finally, Abrantes suggested to the *Comandante* that Tony de la Guardia, an old hand at special missions as well as a hero of struggles for independence in the developing world, look after the logistics of the trip. There, too, the *Comandante* had no objection.

It was as if the sky had fallen in on me. Stunned, incredulous, paralyzed, I wished I had misheard or that I was dreaming, but alas it was true. In just a few seconds, my whole world and all my ideals had come crashing down. I realized that the man for whom I had long sacrificed my life, the *Líder* whom I worshipped like a god and who counted more in my eyes than my own family, was caught up in cocaine trafficking to such an extent that he was directing illegal operations like a real godfather. In a state of distress, I put the headphones back in their place and turned the key to switch off mike no. 1, suddenly feeling a sense of immense solitude.

Abrantes finally left the office and, as he crossed the threshold, I let nothing of my dismay slip. But from that moment on, I no longer saw Fidel Castro in the same way. However, I decided to keep this terrible state secret to myself and not talk of it to anyone, not even my wife. Try as I might to remain professional and to chase this revelation from my mind, the disappointment would not leave. My life was irredeemably changed—and it would be even more so less than a year later, when Fidel sacrificed the devoted Abrantes by sending him to prison in order to show the world that he himself knew nothing about this drug trafficking that would have ruined his reputation.

Meanwhile, the *Comandante*, with his talent for dissimulation, went back to work as if nothing was amiss. One has to understand his logic. For him, drug trafficking was above all a weapon of revolutionary struggle more than a means of making money.

His reasoning was as follows: if the Yanks were stupid enough to use drugs that came from Colombia, not only was that not his problem—as long as his involvement was not discovered, that is—but, in addition, it served his revolutionary objectives in the sense that it corrupted and destabilized American society. Icing on the cake: it was a means of bringing in cash to finance subversion. And so, as cocaine trafficking increased in Latin America, the line between guerrilla war and trafficking drugs gradually blurred. What was true in Colombia was just as true in Cuba. For my part, I never managed to accept this twisted reasoning, an absolute contradiction of my revolutionary ethics.

The year 1989 began with a celebration of the thirtieth anniversary of the Triumph of the Revolution. For world communism, however, it was a dangerous year. In China, demonstrators prepared to defy the tanks on Tiananmen Square while in Europe, the Berlin wall was about to come down. As for the island of Cuba, now deprived of Soviet subsidies, it would undergo an unprecedented existential crisis: in July, at the end of a Stalinesque trial, the heroic general Arnaldo Ochoa was shot with three others, all judged guilty of having "tainted the Revolution" and "betrayed Fidel" because of drug trafficking that, allegedly, the Commander in Chief knew nothing about. The Ochoa Affair caused a real national trauma and took with it the last illusions of Castrism: in Cuba, life is divided into before and after 1989.

To understand the affair, one has to go back a little, to the time of the creation of the MC Department in 1986, when economic aid from Moscow was starting to dry up. Placed under the authority of MININT, in other words of Minister José

Abrantes, and headed by Col. Tony de la Guardia, the *Departamento MC* had the precise aim of generating dollars with the aid of front companies based principally in Panama, Mexico, and Nicaragua—hence the joke that the meaningless acronym MC, which had no particular meaning and merely corresponded to a stupid, malevolent military alphabet naming system, actually stood for *Moneda Convertible* (Convertible Currency).

Heir of the Z Department, created at the start of the 1980s, the MC Department made use of anything that came to hand and traded in everything: tobacco, lobsters, and cigars smuggled into the United States, clothes and electric goods exported to Africa, artwork and antiques peddled in Spain, not to mention the diamonds and ivory brought from Africa and sold in Latin America or elsewhere. Some of the business was legal, some not, but the existence of the department itself was in no way secret. On the contrary, the official daily *Granma* had one day explained its mission in these terms: "Its purpose is to fight against the economic blockade—or embargo—of the United States that has been in operation since 1962 so as to have the means to procure products such as medical equipment, medication, computers, and so on."

What was mysterious, on the other hand, was its functioning, its financial channels, and its accounting. Run without transparency, disorganized, and constantly having to improvise, the MC Department had only one obligation: to get paid in hard currency by third parties, principally Panama, which had always been the first rear base of illicit Cuban commercial activities under the reign of Fidel Castro. It was inevitable that in those years and in that region, the path of the "bandits" of Departments Z/MC would cross those of Colombian drug traffickers, also in search of easy money. It was therefore not altogether a coincidence that the Department MC soon acquired another nickname, the "Marijuana and Cocaine Department"!

The Americans first became suspicious of Cuba in this regard back in the 1980s, due to the testimonies of deserters from the various Cuban espionage services; senior Panamanian government officials working closely with President Manuel Noriega;* and drug traffickers arrested in Florida, some of whom asserted that the Cuban government was linked to Pablo Escobar and his Medellín cartel. In the mid-1980s, articles published in the American press talked of the increase in drug trafficking in Cuba, which served as a transit route for the Colombian white powder, and the possibility that the drug traffickers were linked to the highest levels of Cuban power.

Sensing that a scandal was brewing and probably alerted by the intelligence agents infiltrated in the United States, the *Líder Máximo* decided to take action to nip any possible suspicion about him in the bud. To clear his name, Fidel used the official daily paper *Granma* to inform its readers that an inquiry had been opened in April. Then, like a seasoned chess player, he suddenly changed the direction of the game by carrying out what might be likened to a castling move. In a good position to know who the Cuban officials involved in drug trafficking were, on June 12 he arranged for the arrest of the twins Tony and Patricio de la Guardia of the MC Department; Gen. Arnaldo Ochoa, recently re-

---

*Found guilty in the United States in 1992 of drug trafficking and money laundering.

turned from Angola; and nine other senior MININT officers and two from MINFAR. A second wave of arrests, several weeks later, included Minister of the Interior José Abrantes and, in the latter's entourage, two generals and four colonels.

Three weeks later, the double trial of General Ochoa began. First, on June 25, the accused testified alone, in his uniform, before a "military honor court" on the fourth floor of MINFAR, where he was demoted to the rank of private in the presence of the whole general staff of forty-seven generals. Then, on June 30, the accused was presented to the "special military court," accompanied by thirteen codefendants, all wearing civilian dress, this time on the ground floor of the building in the *Sala Universal*, where MINFAR's screening room was transformed into a courtroom for the occasion. The entirety of the proceedings were christened *Causa no. 1/1989*; the trial against José Abrantes, which followed soon afterward, was called *Causa no. 2/1989*. The hasty trial against Ochoa lasted four days and will remain forever imprinted on Cubans' collective memory as one of the greatest injustices of the endless reign of Fidel Castro Ruz.

At the time, however, the government congratulated itself in the official press and on the radio for having brought this case to justice, sending out the message that the whole world was watching in amazement and that only a true, strong, unshakable, and deep Revolution was capable of such unusual and extraordinary proof of courage and morality. The Machiavellian Fidel, while declaring himself "appalled" by what he pretended to have discovered, even claimed that "the most honest imaginable political and judicial process" was under way.

Obviously, the reality was completely different. Comfortably installed in Raúl's office on the fourth floor of MINFAR, Fidel Castro and his brother followed the live proceedings of *Causa no. 1* and *Causa no. 2* on the closed-circuit TV screens. Both trials were filmed—which is why one can today see large sections of them on YouTube—and broadcast to every Cuban home, though not live: the government wanted to be able to censor anything that might prove embarrassing.

Fidel even had the means to alert the president of the court discreetly, via a warning light, whenever he thought a session should be interrupted. I saw all that with my own eyes as I was there, either in front of the open door of Raúl's office or inside the room. Whenever the court went into recess, Raúl gave me the following order: "Tell the head of the escort that the trial *compañeros* will be coming up at any moment." Indeed, less than five minutes later, the president of the court, the public prosecutor, and the jury members would swarm out onto the fourth floor of the ministry to take their instructions from Fidel, who, as usual, organized and ordered everything, absolutely everything. Later, the *Comandante* twice acknowledged in public that at the time he had been in contact with the members of the court, but anxious to keep the powers separate, he had refrained from influencing them! When one knows Fidel's mode of functioning, such a declaration does not stand up for a single second but is, rather, evidence of the blackest humor.

During *Causa no. 1* and *Causa no. 2* the prosecutors easily demonstrated the accused's involvement in drug trafficking—which had, indeed, been proven. True, I might have been shocked by the fact that Ochoa, that hero of the Cuban Revolution, had agreed to take part in drug trafficking. But what could he do when the head of state himself was behind this trafficking, just as he presided over the other smuggling operations—tobacco, electrical goods, ivory, and so on? According to his logic, of course, it was all for the good of the Revolution!

At one point, the prosecution dwelled specifically on the issue of a hangar situated at an airport in Varadero where drugs and other contraband material were stocked en route for the United States.

That immediately rang a bell. I remembered having accompanied Fidel, Abrantes, Tony de la Guardia, and several other officers from Department MC to this hangar two years earlier. Having left the *palacio* in a convoy of three cars a good hour earlier, we had arrived at this building located on the right side of the Pan-American route. I had stayed outside while Abrantes and Tony de la Guardia had shown Fidel a supposed stock of bottles of rum and cigars destined for export. Then, having spent just a quarter of an hour there, we had turned around and gone back to the presidential palace.

At that moment in the trial I realized that, two years earlier, Fidel had not gone to visit a stock of rum and cigars—indeed, why would a chief of state waste three hours going to see something so banal and uninteresting?—but rather a stock of white powder waiting to be sent to Florida. For, as was his custom, the Commander in Chief, wary of his subordinates and cautious in the extreme, wanted to check everything himself, down to the smallest details, to reassure himself that the best arrangements had been made to hide the contraband merchandise.

All that explains the harshness of the verdicts of *Causas no. 1* and *no. 2*. At the end of these parodies of justice, General Ochoa, his aide-de-camp Capt. Jorge Martínez (both members of MIN-FAR), Col. Tony de la Guardia, and his subordinate Maj. Amado Padrón (both from MININT) were condemned to death on July 4, 1989, for having organized the transport of six tons of cocaine from the Medellín cartel to the United States, receiving $3.4 million in exchange. Three weeks later, José Abrantes received a sentence of twenty years of imprisonment and the other defendants lesser sentences of imprisonment. The greatest purge ever organized within the ministry then ensued, with almost every senior MININT officer being fired and re-placed.

There is not the shadow of a doubt that Fidel, and nobody else, made the decision to send Ochoa to the firing squad and Abrantes to prison for twenty years—where after just two years of detention in 1991 he would suffer a fatal heart attack, despite his perfect state of health, in circumstances that were, to say the least, suspicious. By getting rid of these two, the *Líder Máximo* eliminated two men who knew too much, people with whom he had discussed the ultra-sensitive topic of drug trafficking. With Ochoa and Abrantes dead, the chain of command was broken and along with it, every natural link likely to connect him to that shady business.

One might express surprise that during these trials, broadcast on television, officers as courageous as the four defendants under the shadow of the death sentence did not at any moment rebel and scream the truth to the world. That would be to underestimate Fidel's Machiavellianism and the way in which the Cuban system manipulates people. It was obvious that the accused had secretly been given the message that given the services they had rendered in the past, the Revolution would show its gratitude to them: it would not abandon their children and even if the court was asking for the ultimate sentence, it would be well-intentioned toward them and toward their family. . . . Which virtually amounted to promising these men that they would be spared, not executed—as long as they admitted their mistakes and declared that, yes, they deserved the death penalty. Which they did . . . because men in their position could not do anything else.

However, on July 9—that is, five days after their sentence—Fidel summoned the Council of State in order to "lock down" the Ochoa trial, thereby involving all the leaders of the highest government authorities, composed of twenty-nine members, civilian and military, ministers, members of the Communist Party, presidents of mass organizations, and so on. They were to ratify the court's decision or, on the contrary, reprieve the accused and commute the death penalty. Each of them had to give an individual pronouncement; they all confirmed the sentence. Vilma Espín, turning her back on the friendship she and her husband, Raúl Castro, had had with Ochoa and his wife, uttered the terrible phrase: "Let the sentence be confirmed and carried out!" On Thursday, July 13, one month, almost to the day, after their arrest, around two in the morning, the four condemned men were executed by firing squad.

There followed the most painful episode of my career. Fidel had asked that the execution of Ochoa and the three other condemned men be filmed. And so, two days later, on a Saturday, a chauffeur arrived at the residence in Punto Cero, where I was, to deliver a brown envelope containing a Betamax cassette video. The head of the escort José Delgado (who had replaced Domingo Mainet two years earlier) said to me, "Take that to Dalia, she is waiting for you: it's a film for *El Jefe*." I immediately took the envelope to the *Compañera*, not imagining for a moment that it could be the video of Ochoa's death and even less that Fidel, like Dracula, would want to watch such a bloodthirsty "show." Thirty minutes went by and Dalia came back holding the cassette: "The *Jefe* told me that *los compañeros* should watch this video," she said to me, giving me what was effectively an order. I therefore relayed her message to the head of the escort who, in his turn, gathered everyone together, fifteen or so people including the chauffeurs and Fidel's personal doctor, Eugenio Selman. Then somebody put the cassette in the VCR.

The video had no sound, which made the scenes we began to watch even more unreal. First, we saw vehicles arriving in a quarry at night, lit by projectors: later I found out it was the airfield at Baracoa, reserved for government leaders, west of Havana, where several years earlier I had twice watched a cargo of clandestine arms being loaded on board a plane, en route for Nicaragua, in the presence of Fidel and Raúl.

I have often been asked how Ochoa faced death. The answer is clear and unambiguous: with exceptional dignity. As he got out of the car, he walked straight. When one of his torturers proposed to put a band over his eyes, he shook his head in a sign of refusal. And when he was facing the firing squad, he looked death square in the face. Despite the absence of sound, the whole excerpt shows his courage. To his executioners, who cannot be seen in the footage, he said something that one could not hear but which one could guess. His chest pushed out and his chin raised, he probably shouted something like "Go on, you don't frighten me!" An instant later, he crumpled beneath the bullets of seven gunmen.

The four men were executed in several minutes. They obviously did not all have Ochoa's proud courage. However, Tony de la Guardia, who also had a remarkable career behind him (after having been member of the escort of President Allende in Chile, he had taken part in the Angola campaign, in the taking of Somoza's bunker in Nicaragua, and in hundreds of secret missions), was undeniably courageous. Less so than Ochoa, but courageous all the same. One could see his suffering and his resignation—but at no moment in the last minutes of his life did he crumple.

The sight of my two other colleagues was harder to bear. On the walk between the vehicles and the firing squad, Captain Martínez and Major Padrón collapsed several times, the guards each time having to pick them up. One could see that they were crying and begging. Urine stains could be seen on their trousers. It was pathetic and very hard to watch; one had to have a strong stomach. A heavy silence fell over the room and nobody dared speak. I would have preferred not to relate this episode—and I have absolutely no desire to make the least judgment of those underlings who, in essence, were taking the flak for Fidel. The obligation to tell the truth requires me to do so, however. Everyone needs to know what the *Comandante* was capable of to keep his power: not just of killing but also of humiliating and reducing to nothing men who had served him devotedly.

After Ochoa's death, Raúl Castro plunged into the worst bout of alcoholism of his life. Not only had he been unable to save his friend's skin but, in addition, he had had to publicly validate the execution of this "hero of the Republic of Cuba," just as the other members of the Council of State and the military general staff had been obliged to do. Unable to resolve the conflict of having taken part in the execution of his friend, he turned to vodka, which had long been his favorite drink.

There was doubtless another factor involved: having watched the elimination of his counterpart Abrantes (sentenced to twenty years in prison), Raúl could logically fear that he, too, would be hounded from his position of defense minister. If Abrantes, who was Tony's boss in the hierarchy, had been punished, was it not logical that he himself, Ochoa's boss, would suffer the same fate?

The government number two was dead drunk so often that the ministers and the generals could not have failed to see it. His wife, Vilma, was worried and confided in the head of Raúl's escort, Colonel Fonseca, explaining the situation to him. Vilma feared that Raúl's depression would lead to suicidal impulses. Fonseca spoke about it to his counterpart, José Delgado, the new head of Fidel's escort—my boss, in other words. And the *Comandante* decided to go and lecture his younger brother.

One Sunday morning we set off for La Rinconada, the house of Raúl and Vilma situated less than a mile away from that of Fidel and Dalia. We went in by the back door of the garden, where Raúl greeted us wearing a white *guayábera*, the traditional Cuban shirt, and canvas trousers. Then the minister of defense made off toward a wooden *karbay* on the grounds, in a little clearing surrounded by vegetation. When we had got to this shelter, typical of Native Caribbean culture, Fidel gestured to me not to follow him farther, so while the two Castros sat down on a bench, I went to wait slightly to one side—but from where I was, I could hear all of their conversation. They, on the other hand, did not see me because I was hidden by shrubs. That was when I heard Fidel admonishing his brother, launching into a long, moralistic tirade.

"How can you descend so low? You're giving the worst possible example to your family and your escort," began the *Comandante*. "If what's worrying you is that what happened to Abrantes will happen to you, let me tell you that Abrantes *no es mi hermano* [is not my brother]! You and I have been united since we were children, for better and for worse. So, no, you are not going to experience Abrantes's fate, unless . . . you persist with this deplorable behavior. Listen, I'm talking to you as a brother. Swear to me that you will come out of this lamentable state and I promise you nothing will happen to you. I will even give a speech reminding people that you are a leader with integrity and I will explain that you have suffered a lot because of Ochoa's crime, which disappointed you enormously. And if there are people who think you are mixed up in all that business, they are nothing but *hijos de puta*!"

And, sure enough, shortly afterward Fidel spoke out in praise of Raúl, applauding his integrity and his devotion to the Revolution. Raúl, for his part, carried on drinking vodka, but in far more reasonable quantities.

As for me, I was like thousands of soldiers: I forced myself to stifle the doubts that the Ochoa Affair had created in me.

PRISON AND . . . FREEDOM!

For me, the 1990s began with a series of successes, in direct contrast to the country's general situation. Deserted by the Soviet Union, whose dissolution was officially pronounced on December 8, 1991, and isolated on the international scene, Cuba was effectively collapsing into the worst economic crisis of its existence. In an attempted response, Fidel decreed the Special Period in Time of Peace, which consisted principally of developing tourism and allowing individuals to open *paladares* (home restaurants) so as to earn the money vital for saving the Revolution. But it was not enough, as the *balseros* crisis would prove: in 1994, thirty thousand Cubans abandoned their "native ships" to escape on board *balsas* (makeshift rafts) en route for Miami, at the risk of feeding the sharks that patrolled in the Straits of Florida.

As for me, I was more than ever devoted to serving Fidel. Promoted to head of *la avanzada*, I was now responsible for preparing for all his trips within the country or abroad—like, for example, the trip to attend the inauguration of President

Fernando Collor de Mello in Brasília, Brazil, in 1990; to the Ibero-American summit in Guadalajara, Mexico, in July 1991; or else to Spain the following summer. What is more, I was considered the best shot in Cuba since I had won the national twenty-five-meter (just over twenty-seven yards) pistol shooting competition, which had further boosted my status within the escort and beyond. In short, focused on my work, I had chosen to forget the Ochoa Affair, which, through an immense purge on every level, had profoundly destabilized the MININT, now directed by Gen. Abelardo Colomé Ibarra, also known as Furry. Solely focused on my professional success, I also managed to disregard the deteriorating atmosphere within the escort, no longer the same since that idiot José Delgado had replaced Domingo Mainet as head.

However, the wind turned suddenly during 1994. To start with, my daughter, Aliette, married a Venezuelan and went to live with him in Caracas. Then, my younger brother, who was working as a chef at the Council of State and who had therefore served Fidel at table several times, decided to try his chance on a *balsa* and became another exile to Florida, where he settled after his perilous journey.

Two members of my family abroad: that was enough to turn me into a suspect. The head of the escort, Colonel Delgado, summoned me to ask if I knew that my brother had intended to leave Cuba. I replied no—which was not true. Delgado then informed me that with a *balsero* brother and a daughter outside the country, I could not keep my job: in fact, I understood that Fidel himself had personally fired me from the escort. Initially, however, there was a possibility of my staying within MININT, as my knowledge and experience were sufficiently valuable for the ministry to continue to use them.

It was painful. I had spent twenty-six years in service of the *Comandante*, since 1968, seventeen of them within his escort, and it was difficult to turn the page all at once, just like that. That was when the head of the escort made his proposition: "Listen," he said to me, "take two weeks' vacation to think about a posting within MININT that could suit you and come back to see me." But as I thought about it all on the way home, I began to say to myself that it was perhaps time for me to leave the profession. I was forty-five, I had achieved a sort of professional peak and traveled all over the world. In short, I knew I would not go any higher. So why not retire? In the military, one can take retirement very early.

When I got home, I told my wife my intentions and I wrote to the Cuban social security to make a pension claim. Two weeks later, I wrote my resignation letter, which initially seemed to have been accepted. Soon, however, Gen. Humberto Francis Pardo, boss of Personal Security—the department in charge of the protection of all dignitaries—summoned me to tell me that my leaving was out of the question: "You're not going anywhere and certainly not retiring!" Sure of my rights, my total loyalty to the Revolution, and the excellence of the service I had given, I stood up to him by demanding to go through a *conducto reglamentario* (an appeal system allowing one to go over someone's head to their superior) so as to speak directly to Furry, the minister of the interior. I did not have the slightest intention of criticizing the system but wanted only to explain to him my desire to return to civilian life.

———

Two days later, two lieutenant colonels came knocking at my door to announce that General Francis wanted to see me in his office again. So I immediately got in my car and drove to answer his summons. When I got there, General Francis in person gave me the order to get into another vehicle, which was going to take me "somewhere" where we could talk quietly. No sooner had I got into the white Lada than two guards sat one each side of me on the backseat. Then Colonel Laudelio, from Military Counterintelligence (a department in charge of surveillance of all Cuban military), got into the front and told me we were going to the detention center in Havana. Things were not looking good. . . . Known as Cien y Aldabó, after the names of the streets where it was located, this center is the most terrible and the most feared in Cuba: it is there that the police interrogate detainees under civil law, by beating and torturing them, and inflicting every kind of mistreatment.

From the nervous demeanor of my two guardians, I immediately realized I was in an extremely difficult situation. But I did not imagine that the problem was me. I thought that a member of my family or a friend had committed a crime. However, once we got there, Laudelio threw at me, "Okay, Sánchez, you're an intelligent guy, you don't need three hours of explanation: you are here as a prisoner!"

With that, I exploded. "What am I accused of?"

"Control yourself. We'll explain all that to you tomorrow."

"But why am I here?" I insisted.

They took off my belt, removed my shoelaces, and threw me

in a cell for twenty-four hours, without warning my wife, who was worried sick when I did not come back.

The following day, they "explained" to me that I was a "traitor to the homeland" and that corroborating evidence proved that I was preparing to leave Cuba. Which was completely untrue: such an idea had never even crossed my mind.

Then, the interrogations began. That was when I discovered that, contrary to what Fidel Castro had always declared, they practice torture in Cuba—as in all the Latin American dictatorships that preceded ours, Chile, Argentina, Uruguay, and so on.

Carried out by Military Counterintelligence men wearing heavy overcoats, the interrogation took place in a little room in which the air-conditioning was running full blast while I, like all the prisoners of Cien y Aldabó, was wearing only a sleeveless T-shirt. The cold seared my chest and face; when I asked my persecutors if it was possible to lower the air-conditioning, they replied in mocking tones that they were really sorry, but they didn't have access to the controls, which were outside the room. Then they left me alone for three or four hours, until my nails and lips were blue.

They spent a week trying to get me to confess that I was a counter-revolutionary, doubtless thinking that I would finally crack and sign a statement. But I was so shocked by what had happened to me that I signed nothing. One of the interrogators said to me, "You must know that you are here by order of Fidel?" And after a week he told me that the prison authorities were now awaiting the orders of the *Comandante* to know whether I could be freed or not. I was there by the express wish of the man whom I had served for quarter of a century!

At that moment, I would have liked to have been able to speak directly to my former boss, because I knew it would have been easy to show him I was an innocent victim of a setup and that he was on the wrong track. And that he had probably been misled about me by the malice of certain members of the escort. I had not forgotten that our boss José Delgado was secretly jealous of me—for the good and simple reason that he was himself talentless. In addition, my responsibility as physical trainer of the group gave me considerable power within it since it was I who selected those who would go on foreign trips.

Whatever the case, I never got to see Fidel—which shows, yet again, that he treats human beings like so much detritus the moment they are no longer useful to him. I knew that, but like many people in that situation, I thought that given all I had done for him, I would be spared.

I was then placed in isolation in an unspeakably squalid cell in which I did not see the light of day for two months. In Cien y Aldabó, the cockroach-infested cells are designed to stink of urine and excrement; there is nothing but a hole in which to relieve oneself while the water tap, giving the equivalent of two glasses of water a day, was just four inches away from this disgusting latrine. So as to break my inner biological clock, breakfast was served at two p.m. and the main meal (revolting, cold, and inadequate) at eight in the morning. In addition, it was stiflingly hot and the contrast with the interrogation room was unbearable. To complete this sordid picture, my warders brought me a visibly infected mattress made of rice straw, and after several days my skin had broken out into a spectacular rash, with pus-filled spots all over the lower half of my body, including my testicles.

Fortunately, a CIMEQ doctor, a certain Alfredo who had been imprisoned for leaving Cuba illegally, worked in the prison infirmary and managed to treat me. After two months, however, I was physically broken and emotionally destroyed, having lost almost 65 pounds, going from 183 to 119 pounds. Unable to take any more, I finally asked to speak to someone in authority and the next day was taken to see a colonel (I never knew his name) who said he knew who I was. "I've been wanting to meet you for a long time!" he declared. To which I bitterly replied that he knew where to find me. Then I presented him with an ultimatum.

"If you haven't got me out of that rat hole by tomorrow, I am going to begin a hunger strike and I'll have the first person who comes into my cell. . . ."

The colonel was visibly upset. He took my threat seriously. Apparently, the message went as far as Fidel for, the following day, twelve armed men were sent to come and get me and take me to the prison of La Condesa, in the town of Güines, eighteen miles south of Havana.

Being transferred to Güines represented slight progress, even if "white torture" (that left no marks) was also common practice. There, I was imprisoned with twenty-two others, many of them dangerous criminals, in what is called in Cuba a *galera*, since its conditions do indeed resemble those of a galley ship.

Güines had its own microclimate, which meant that at night, the temperature fell markedly below the average of other Cuban towns. In winter the warders took us out into the courtyard at three in the morning and made us undress. We had to stand there, naked, facing our jailers, who humiliated us: "Are you cold? That's strange . . . we're not!" Then those sadists burst into laughter while we prisoners shivered in the night. These kinds of practices and other, far worse, affronts were habitual in prisons on the island, and had been for decades. But that never stopped Fidel and Raúl Castro from declaring to the world that torture did not exist in Cuba, that their government was too civilized for that. . . .

In Güines, my jailers continued to threaten me: "If you deny having carried out counter-revolutionary activities and mixing with deviants, if you don't sign the statement we give you, you will never get out of here. . . ."

Gritting my teeth and looking them in the eyes, I replied, "If that's my destiny . . ."

Finally, about a month after my transfer, eight men who were armed to the teeth took me before the military court of Playa, a municipality in Havana. During my hearing, behind closed doors, all my rights were flouted: the president did not listen when my lawyer spoke, the prosecution witnesses were allowed to speak to each other in the adjoining room, and so on. In a supreme outrage, I saw certain of my former colleagues lining up to accuse me of counter-revolutionary deviance. However, thanks to what I knew of penal law and also because my work record was completely clean, I nonetheless managed to make a case with convincing arguments in my own defense, reminding the judges that I should not be appearing before them, and even less be in prison, because my only fault was to have asked to retire—which, I knew, did not constitute any form of crime.

The prosecutor asked for eight years of imprisonment. Several days later, my wife came to tell me the verdict: two and a half years in prison. She was relieved, for it was much less than the eight she was expecting—but I was shocked and disgusted. I appealed the sentence. The following month, the military court in the municipality of Diez de Octubre, Havana, reduced my sentence on appeal to two years' imprisonment.

In La Condesa, I received a visit from the former head of the escort Domingo Mainet, who, at the end of the 1980s, had been appointed inspector of prisons in the province of Havana. Now each of us were, literally and metaphorically, on either side of a barrier. Mainet asked me how things were going and I replied, "Very badly. And you know perfectly well I shouldn't be here because you know me very well." Afterward, he asked if I thought I was in prison through Fidel's personal wish—obviously, I refrained from telling the truth, for I knew the Cuban system and that attacking the *Comandante* would only have made things worse for me. So I contented myself with replying, "He was probably misled by your successor as head of escort, José Delgado, and by the people of Military Counterintelligence." And I added, "Now, if you haven't got anything else to say to me, I'd like to return to my cell."

Another time, it was General Francis, the supreme head of Personal Security, who came to see me. When I went into the office of the prison governor—who had never before been visited by such an important general—a buffet had been laid out.

Francis began by saying to me that I would soon be seen by the minister of the interior, Abelardo Colomé Ibarra . . . which never happened. Then he invited me to eat. I refused point-blank, explaining that it wasn't the kind of meal we usually ate and that, as he certainly knew, there was no valid reason for me to be rotting in prison. The general, a little shamefaced, lowered his head and gulped, and I put an end to the conversation by asking, as I had done with Domingo Mainet, to return to my cell. Once again, I refrained from all criticism of Fidel, so as not to compromise my chances of being released.

I am also certain that attempts were made on my life during my time behind bars—in the same way that, doubtless, they had got rid of the former minister of the interior, José Abrantes, who was sentenced to twenty years' imprisonment in August 1989 and who died of a "heart attack" in January 1991. When I contracted acute otitis, the prison doctor prescribed me medicine that, far from making me feel better, had the effect of making my ailment worse every day. Fortunately, during a visiting session, a doctor who was there to see a relative took interest in my case. He discovered that the medicine I was taking was going to lead straight to a stroke. Indignant, he complained to the prison governor, accusing him of trying to kill me. Then, by threatening to denounce him to the authorities, this doctor got permission to treat me himself, once a week, in the visiting room. Thanks to this guardian angel, who advised me to stop going to the prison infirmary, I immediately stopped the initial treatment and was saved. Without him, this book would not exist.

Indeed, it was actually in La Condesa that I decided to write this book. One day, when I was sunbathing in the prison courtyard, I looked at the blue sky and swore to myself that, as the *Comandante* had not had the slightest scruples about locking me up here or making my family suffer from this injustice despite all I had sacrificed to protect him, I would reveal Fidel Castro's real nature to the world. The idea for this book was thus born one sunny day in 1995, almost twenty years ago, when I was wearing the gray uniform of an ordinary prisoner several miles from the fine sand where nonchalant tourists from all over the world came to drink mojitos and dance the salsa, not concerning themselves for a moment with the fate of the victims of the Castro brothers.

Finally, two years after my arrest—not a day more or less—I was released. I was terribly weakened. Although I had put on a bit of weight since my guardian angel doctor had begun looking after me, I still weighed forty-four pounds less than at the time of my arrest.

Out of prison, I went to Personal Security to put my situation in order. And there I met with a surprise: reading the documents they gave me, I saw that my right to a retirement pension had been recognized at least two years earlier, in other words, before my arrest! Which meant that, from an official point of view, I was already a civilian and not a soldier at the time of my trial. And that the whole procedure was therefore unlawful since as a civilian I could not appear before a military court. . . . But I swallowed my rage. At least I had got out. . . .

I did not know that the police harassment was not finished.

I was immediately placed under close surveillance by G2, and agents from State Security were posted in front of my house twenty-four hours a day, following me wherever I went, whether driving to see my mother or just walking to the end of the road to get a bit of fresh air.

I didn't do much the first year. Now expelled from the Cuban Communist Party, it was difficult, even impossible, for me to get a job. Living off my retirement pension of three hundred pesos (about sixteen dollars)—because I had received the pension payment that had been approved before my arrest, which again shows the absurdity of my trial—I spent much time in the house doing nothing, with my wife, catching up on the time that had been stolen from me in prison.

Wherever I went and whoever I spoke to, I refrained from criticizing Fidel Castro or from formulating the least opinion about the political or social situation in Cuba. As a result, the intelligence services had no way of knowing my state of mind toward the Revolution. After a year, two officers came to offer me a job. Knowing the Castrist system like the back of my hand, I knew that this was in order to put me under closer surveillance, for State Security has informers and agents in every factory in the country as well as in schools, government offices, hotels, restaurants, markets, and so on. And so I became first the manager of an operations center for trucks transporting wheat and flour, then administrative manager and night manager for Café TV, a downtown cabaret, and finally an executive in a surveillance unit belonging to the minister of public works.

Having studied counterespionage, I put into practice all the disinformation techniques I had learned in college or on the ground. Far from criticizing Fidel, I pretended to worry about his security: "The Commander in Chief should be careful when he goes to such and such a country because the enemies of the Revolution are everywhere there," I would slip into a conversation with my colleagues, knowing that my words would be repeated. I also took part in all the revolutionary activities, whether it was attending neighborhood meetings or going to mass demonstrations ordered by the *Comandante*.

At the same time, however, I was discreetly finding out about clandestine emigration networks, which had proliferated in Cuba since 1990. I found out that the services of people smugglers cost at least ten thousand dollars and so I began selling various objects—trinkets, electrical goods, and such—so as to get part of the sum together to be able one day to get on a speedboat that would take me to freedom. My father and my uncle, already settled in the United States, sent me money via clandestine channels and via my daughter, who had left Venezuela for Florida and came to see us in Cuba every two or three years. In addition, I began getting documents (photos, qualification certificates, medals, and so on) out of the country so that, when the time came, I would be able to show without fear of contradiction that I had really worked as Fidel's bodyguard for seventeen years.

Released from prison in 1996, it took me twelve years to succeed in leaving the island, in 2008, after ten unsuccessful attempts to escape. Each time, there was a problem: the boat of the people smugglers was not at the appointed place; a coastguard was patrolling in the area; or, quite simply, I sensed I was being followed. Of course, I systematically applied the techniques of countershadowing I had learned at the MININT college so as to lose the G2 agents. I would lose myself in the crowd at a very busy place; turn off suddenly into a public bathroom to change my hat and T-shirt; and then, after several minutes, retrace my steps after having turned at the corner of a street to make sure I was alone. But all this song and dance was exhausting and I wondered if I would ever manage to get out of the country.

In 2008, my luck changed. My wife had obtained authorization to go and see her sister in the United States. She was supposed to stay in Florida a month unless I finally managed to escape. A week after she had left, I received a message via the smugglers' network that a "passage" to Mexico was planned over the next few days. This time, the rendezvous was fixed for the province of Pinar del Río, the most westerly of the island. I had a bad premonition as two of my previous attempts had failed in Pinar del Río—once, the border guards had even fired warning shots into the night. I had got away, though the experience had left me terrified. In addition, I had the mistaken impression that "my" smugglers, to whom I had paid twelve thousand dollars, were in the pay of State Security. If that were the case and they "ratted" on me to the authorities, I knew that I would return behind bars for a long time, a very long time. . . . In short, I felt the net tightening around me. Recently, G2 police had come to question my neighbors to find out why I traveled to the other side of the country, for example to Santiago de Cuba, where I had no family.

Despite everything, I decided to run the risk. My contact had told me that the rendezvous was arranged near Los Palacios, sixty miles west of Havana. By an irony of history, I therefore found myself, on the due date, stuck in a swampy zone just 650 yards from a house that I knew very well because I had been there dozens of times with Fidel: La Deseada, the wooden chalet where he stayed when he went duck hunting. I stayed in the mangrove for two days, not moving and not eating, waiting for the people smugglers to arrive. I was beginning to lose all hope when, finally, the boat loomed up in the darkness, all its lights extinguished.

Forty-five of us fugitives boarded the boat, but the captain told us that he had received the order to take only thirty people. He therefore suggested that fifteen volunteers leave the vessel; of course, nobody was willing. After fruitless negotiations, he decided to turn on the engines around three in the morning with all his cargo! Now, with the weight of the passengers, the boat was floating so low in the water that a propeller knocked against something and broke. Fortunately, three engines remained and that was how we went out into international territorial waters. Halfway to Yucatán (Mexico), another boat came to meet us and, in mid-ocean, a section of the passengers boarded onto it. The two vessels then continued their route.

As night was falling the following day, we finally arrived off the coast of Cancún, the Mexican vacation resort town situated around 150 miles from the extreme west of Cuba. The smugglers waited until dark to off-load us onto a beach where a truck was waiting for us, which took us to a house inland.

For a week, the smugglers took us out in groups of four or five to accompany us discreetly to the airport where we were to get onto flights for Nuevo Laredo, a town near the frontier with Texas, nine hundred miles from Cancún. I was one of the last to leave. Before departing, the smugglers gave me some advice:

"Speak as little as possible, so as not to be recognized by your accent."* Then they wished us good luck.

In Nuevo Laredo, the plan was simple: assume a nonchalant air and cross the border on foot, along with the tide of border inhabitants who cross the Rio Bravo bridge each day to go and work on the other side, thereby avoiding border checks. Afterward, it would be easy: once Cubans place a single toe on American soil they—unlike all other Latin Americans—have since 1996 benefited from the Cuban Adjustment Act, which grants them automatic political asylum.

Just before crossing the bridge frontier of Nuevo Laredo, our little group of five people had a moment of panic: what if, so close to the goal, we were arrested by the border guards? I breathed deeply, collected myself, and said to my comrades, none of whom knew that I was a soldier, "Follow me, I'll go in front!" I explained to them that if the Mexican frontier guards approached us, we had to run for the United States because the Latin American officials would never be so unwise as to shoot in the direction of Americans. We started out, the three hundred yards or so that separated us from the United States seeming to us interminable. However, once we reached the last Mexican customs official, spontaneously and without reflecting I tapped him on the shoulder, smiled, and said to him joyously, "Have a nice day!" The instant after, I was in the United States, along with my fellow passengers.

---

*Any Latin American can easily distinguish between Cuban and Mexican accents, very different from each other.

To the first policeman I encountered, a tall black man, I uttered the two magic words that acted as open sesame: *"¡Asilo político!"* But he did not understand Spanish. So I turned to one of his colleagues, a Colombian by origin, who immediately realized we were Cubans. Seeing from our exhausted faces that we had not eaten in a long time, this Colombian gave us sodas as well as a meal from Kentucky Fried Chicken, which we devoured on the spot. That was my first introduction to American cuisine: nothing extraordinary, but it was still ten times better than the usual Cuban fare! Then we were taken, separately, to immigration officers who all spoke Spanish.

Like all Cubans who turn up in the United States, the official asked me the obligatory question: "Have you, closely or from afar, collaborated with the government of Cuba?"

"Yes," I replied.

"What did you do?"

"Bodyguard of *Comandante en Jefe* Fidel Castro for seventeen years!"

My interlocutor stopped speaking, looked at me over his glasses, and then asked me if I was serious. When I confirmed that I was, his jaw dropped. It has to be said that until now, I remain the only member of Fidel's escort to have defected. The official gave me a huge smile, got up, and said, "Don't move, I'm coming back." He then disappeared for an hour, coming back with a huge file that he placed on the desk. Written on a white label on the top could be read: JUAN REINALDO SÁN-CHEZ. It was *my* file, which he had had sent to him by the FBI! I remember that the officer spent the next hour filling in my application for asylum while asking me the most anecdotal, amusing questions. For example, he wanted at all costs to know how Fidel managed to eat with such a long, bushy beard! Finally he wanted to know whether I would agree to a debriefing interview with an FBI agent, to which I replied, "You bet! With great pleasure!"

I then telephoned my uncle, whom I had always thought of as my dad. On the other end of the line, in his house in Miami, I heard him shouting and dancing for joy: "Really? You've done it? I love you, my son! Come quickly, we want to see you *ahora* [right away]!" We all felt like we were living the happy ending in a film. He bought a plane ticket for me and, eight hours later, I landed in Miami, to be met by the finest of welcoming committees: my whole family! Well, almost. My mother was still in Cuba and my son, too—but both later managed to leave the island, in 2012. The others were mad with joy: my wife, my daughter, my son-in-law, my grandchildren, and my uncle/dad!

When we got to my daughter's, where a fine meal and new clothes awaited me (I had left Cuba with nothing other than what I was wearing), I began by slipping into a hot bath, shaving, and making myself presentable to celebrate that unhoped-for event: my freedom. For the first time in years, I could relax, finally letting go of the feeling of oppression I had from being permanently followed by State Security agents. The sword of Damocles, which had been hanging over me for so long, had disappeared.

For a Cuban, meeting up with family is the most wonderful experience there is. Never again would I have to go through that separation that causes suffering to so many families. We sat down to eat *camarones al ajillo*, a typically Cuban dish of shrimp in garlic, with rice and black beans, and we spent the evening laughing and kissing each other.

The following day, after not much sleep, I visited the neighborhood of Little Havana and realized that the architecture in no way resembled that of Havana, even if hundreds of thousands of Cuban exiles played dominos there in the public parks, drinking *café cubano* all day long and re-creating that warm atmosphere characteristic of my people.

After a year, I was able to find work as an independent consultant in security and also as a political analyst of Cuba. I am convinced that nothing will improve on the island as long as the Castro brothers are in power. From afar, I see my former boss Fidel slipping into old age and sickness. He is gradually fading away, less and less capable of reigning over people or events. . . . I know how much he must suffer when he looks in a mirror to see himself diminished in that way. I know him.

When I think of him, I feel no hatred, resentment, or grudge. Those are negative sentiments that would prevent me from living. I have always been optimistic, convinced that tomorrow will be better than today. If I resent anyone, it is more his henchmen who dragged me before the court, the prosecutor, the judges, the Military Counterintelligence officers, certain former colleagues who gave false testimonies, and other informants. They are the ones who implement the dirty work and who keep the system going.

I simply made a mistake. I committed the error of having devoted the first part of my life to protecting a man whose fight for the freedom of his country and revolutionary ideals I had admired before seeing him become gripped by the fever of absolute power and contempt for the people. More than his limitless ingratitude toward those who had served him, I reproach him for his betrayal—for he has betrayed the hopes of millions of Cubans. Until the end of my days, two questions will turn in my mind: why do revolutions always go wrong and why do their heroes systematically transform into tyrants who are even worse than the dictators they overthrew?

INDEX

Abrantes, José, 72, 85, 176–77, 186, 194, 198, 201, 233, 242
  arrest, trial, and conviction of, 235, 238
  drug trafficking with Fidel's consent, 228–31, 237
  suspicious death in prison, 238, 254
Africa, U.S. policy in, 129, 220
"African adventure," 98
agents, recruitment of, 165–69
Agrotex, 145
air force, Cuban, 2, 74
Alexander the Great, Fidel's children named for, 52
Algeria, 60, 69, 98
Allende, Beatriz, 103–4
Allende, Salvador, 98, 102–4
Almeida Bosque, Juan, 34, 35
Álvarez, Silvino, 74–75, 208, 216
American House (Fidel property), 202
Andropov, Yuri, 133
Angola, 130n, 218
  Fidel's visit to, 222–23
  independence movements in, 218
Angolan Civil War (1975–1992), 39, 53, 130, 186, 199, 219–22
  Cuban involvement in, 217–27
  Cuban loss of life in, 221

  Fidel's long-distance directing of, 223–25
anti-Americanism, 154
Apaletegui, Miguel Angel ("Apala"), 110
apartheid, 225
Aquarama II (Fidel's yacht), 1–7, 11, 14–15, 88, 170–71, 196, 199
Arafat, Yasser, 94, 133
Arce, Bayardo, 116–17, 119, 120n.
Argentina, 21, 98, 130
Arias, Óscar, 127, 155–56
Ariel, Dr., 207
arms trafficking, 126–27
Arronte Martínez, Andrés, 74
Arrugaeta, José Miguel, 110
Artunduaga, Arjaid, 108
assassinations, 86–87
August 13 (Fidel Castro's birthday), 67–68
avanzada (forerunners of trips abroad), 82–83, 186–88, 209–10, 245–46

balseros (rafters escaping from Cuba), 245
Baracoa military airfield, 125–26
barbudos (Sierra Maestra veterans), 3
basketball, Fidel's love of, 30–31

Basque separatism, 94, 109–12
Bastidas, Adina, 101
Bateman, Jaime, 107–8
Batista, Fulgencio, 22, 22n
  regime, 3, 22–23, 45
Bay of Pigs, 4, 5–7
  Fidel property near, 10
Bay of Pigs invasion, 6
Belén Montes, Ana, 166
Berlin wall, fall of (1989), 130
Berlusconi, Silvio, 196
Besteiro, René, 63–65
Betancourt, Rómulo, 174, 175
Birán (Fidel's birthplace), 69
Bishop, Maurice, 121, 124
blackmail
  and recruitment of agents, 166–69
  over sexual matters, 158
Black Panthers, 95, 109
bodyguards
  blood donors for Fidel, 74, 206–7,
    214–15
  Cuba's heavy use of, compared to
    Sweden, 137–38
  See also escort
Bolívar, Simón, 105, 173, 179
  sword of, stolen by M19, 106–8
Bolivarian Alliance for the Peoples of
  Our America, 179
Bolivia, 99
Borge, Tomás, 116–17, 119, 120n
Borja, Rodrigo, 154
Boumediene, Houari, 60, 69
Bourgoin, Gérard, 12
Brazil, 101–2, 130
Brezhnev, Leonid, 3, 46, 76
  Fidel attends funeral of, 130–34
Britain, secret service of, 87
Bush, George H. W., 129, 211
Bush, George W., 153

Caballero, Pablo, 11, 73
Cabral, Amílcar, 98

Cabrera, Dr., 207
Cabrera, Paco (bodyguard), 174
Camagüey, Fidel property in, 203–4
Cancún, Mexico, 259
Carnation Revolution, 218
Carrera, General, 126
cars used by Fidel, 76–78
  weaponry, clothing, food, etc.
    carried on, 77–78
Castellanos Benítez, Jesús, 73
Castro, Abel (illegitimate son by
  Juana Vera), 205
Castro, Agustina (sister), 141–42
Castro, Alejandro (son) ("El
  Brother"), 52, 54–55
Castro, Alex (son) ("El Buenachón,
  El Gordito"), 52, 54
Castro, Alexis (son), 52, 54
Castro, Ángel (father), 140, 141, 143
Castro, Angelita (sister), 141–42
Castro, Angelito (son), 52, 56–57, 59
Castro, Antonio (son) ("Tony"), 52,
  55–56, 59
Castro, Enma (sister), 141–42
Castro, Fidel
  (1953) assault on Moncada
    barracks, 22, 48
  (1953) imprisoned by Batista, 48
  (1959) appearance on US
    television, 45–46
  (1959) entry into Havana, 23–24
  (1983, 1992) health crises, 205–16
  anecdotes about. See Castro, Fidel,
    anecdotes
  assassination attempts on, 2, 52,
    88–91, 186
  author's inside knowledge of, 40–41
  birthday celebrations (August 13),
    68–69
  blood group A negative, 74, 206–7,
    214–15
  called El Comandante, 5
  called El Jefe (the chief), 4
  children of, 5, 44–63

circle of people closest to, 228
competitiveness of (a sore loser), 171
contradicting him, unsafe, 226–27
conversational style, 69–71, 185
day-by-day documentation of activities of, 85
deceptive movements of, 75–76
the decision-maker, 194–202
double for ("fake"), 74–75, 208, 216
drinking habit of, 60, 114
drunk (only once), 183–85
and espionage, personal involvement with, 160–63
extraconjugal visits, 33
family, security of, 90
family life, a secret, 11
food, meals, diet, 58–60, 208
food, testing for threats, 90–91, 213–14
friends and confidantes of, 13, 28, 68, 154–55
full name Fidel Alejandro Castro Ruz, 2
godfather of (Hibbert), 70
gratitude not shown by, 174–75
as guardian of Simón Bolívar's sword, 107–8
guerrilla leadership of, 92, 105–9, 112–13, 118, 217
with guests aboard his yacht, 5–7
health problems, 31, 205–16
inaccessible to family members, 140–41
luxurious lifestyle of, 40
Machiavellianism of, 239
marriages and mistresses of, 42–44, 52
a night owl, 116
and the Ochoa trial, 236
old age and sickness of, 263
paternal feeling lacking in, 48, 49, 60, 67

personal life of, unknown to the Cuban people, 41, 43–44
personal security team of. See escort
personal wealth and property of, 9–10, 193–95, 202–4
physical prowess, 14
profane language of, 129
psychological profile, 39–40, 42
salary (900 pesos a month), 194
schooling, 69–71
self-absorbed, not empathetic, treating people like dirt, 185, 250
shooting skill of, 96
siblings of, 141–43
sports participation, 30–31
tricks, cheating, and lies of, 69–71, 110
trips abroad, 81–83, 130–36, 173–74, 176–78, 180–92, 205, 209, 246
underwater fishing and diving by, 14–16
vacations of (unknown to Cuban public), 10
walkabouts, security during, 121
as war general, 223–25
weapons carried by, 77–78
worldwide followers of, 91–92, 97
Castro, Fidel, anecdotes
chicken eggs of, stolen by staff, 61
mattress quest in Pyongyang, 184–85
mocking the accidental death of a bodyguard, 174
swift visit to Ireland for Irish coffee, 130–31
two months' rent in advance, 71
two notebooks at school, 69–71
Castro, Fidel (2) (son) ("Fidelito"), 11, 44–47, 61, 147
trained in the USSR, 46
Castro, Fidel (3) (son of Fidelito Castro), 46

Castro, Jorge Ángel (illegitimate son), 47–48, 147
Castro, José Raúl (son of Fidelito Castro), 46
Castro, Juanita (sister), 51, 141–43
Castro, Lina (mother), 141
Castro, Mirta (daughter of Fidelito Castro), 46
Castro, Ramón (brother), 139–41
Castro, Raúl (brother), 141–42
  children of, 44, 148–51
  close relationship to Fidel, 11, 28, 68, 143–46, 228
  conversations with Fidel, 226, 236
  and the Cuban Revolution, 22, 24
  defense minister, 25, 90, 126, 194
  drinking habit of, 114, 146, 242–44
  drug trafficking involvement, 200
  economic role of, 145
  family feeling of, 46, 52–53, 147–49
  government role, 47
  guerrilla leadership of, 144–45
  harsh toward traitors and enemies, 143
  historical role of, 144–45
  liaison with USSR, 222
  organized and methodical, 144
  personality of, 146–47
  power ceded to (2006), 43
  reprimanded by Fidel, 243–44
  security of, 27, 34
  supposedly illegitimate son by Lina, and nicknamed "El Chino," 142–43
  told of Fidel's health crisis, 215
  wife of (Vilma Espín), 43
Castro, Raúl Guillermo ("Raulito," El Cangrejo) (grandson of Raúl), 149
Castro Espín, Alejandro (son of Raúl) ("El Loquito, El Tuerto"), 148, 150–51, 222
Castro Espín, Deborah (daughter of Raúl), 148, 149

Castro Espín, Mariela (daughter of Raúl), 104, 148, 149–50
Castro Espín, Nilsita (daughter of Raúl), 148, 151
Castro family, 67, 197, 209, 212–13
cattle breeding by Fidel, 29–30, 32
cayo (key, or sandy island), 7
Cayo Blanco del Sur island (renamed Ernst Thälmann Island), 12
Cayo Largo del Sur, 62
Cayo Piedra, 4, 7–16, 61–63
  description of, 7–9
  existence of, unknown to Cuban public, 10–11
  as Fidel property, 202
  preparations for meeting an attack on, 88–89
  underwater life around, 13–14, 84–85
  visitors to, 11–13, 170–71
Central America, as theater of the cold war, 125–27
Central American and Caribbean games, 30
Centro de Convenciones, 193
Centro de Investigaciones Médico Quirúrgicas (CIMEQ), 207
Chamorro, Violeta, 128
chauffeurs, Fidel's, 73
Chávez, Hugo, 101, 160, 173, 179
Che. See Guevara, Ernesto "Che"
Chernenko, Konstantin, 134
Chibás, Eduardo, 21–22
Chile, 102–5
  guerrilla fighters in, 94
Chomy. See Miyar Barruecos, José Miguel
CIA
  attempts on Fidel, 2, 91
  Bay of Pigs invasion, 6
  respect for Cuban secret services, 87
Ciego de Avila, Fidel property in, 203
Cienfuegos, Camilo, 8, 24
Cienfuegos, Osmany, 8

Cien y Aldabó detention center, Havana, 248–51
cigar lovers, targeting of, 165
Cimex, 145, 193, 197
cipher officers, 165
Ciudadela (Citadel) training camp, 81
civil identity database, Cuban, 48
Clark Amendment, 220
coast guards, 74
cold war, 38–39, 88, 125–27, 130n
Collor de Mello, Fernando, 84, 246
Colombia, 106–8, 172–73
    drugs from, 232–34
    guerrilla fighters in, 94
Colomé Ibarra, Abelardo ("Furry"), 98, 246, 254
Comecon (Council for Mutual Economic Assistance), 133–34
communism, worldwide troubles of (1989), 232
Communist party in Cuba. See Cuban Communist Party; Popular Socialist Party
Congo, 98, 225
contraband and counterfeit goods, 200–201
Contras (Nicaragua), 125, 129, 225–26
Council of Ministers, 152–53
Council of State, 194, 197, 239
counterespionage, 163–69, 256–57
    training in, 38
Cousteau, Jacques-Yves, 13
Cuba
    diplomatic corps, espionage role of, 164–69
    economy. See economy, Cuban
    expelled from OAS, 175
    myth of invincibility, 220–21
    national holiday (July 26), 68
    pre-Castro period, 20–23
    rural life, pre-Castro, 21
Cubalese, 197
Cubanacan, 145

Cuban Adjustment Act (U.S.), 260
Cuban Atomic Energy Commission (CEAC), 46
Cuban Communist Party (PCC), 46, 144
Cuban missile crisis (1962), 89
Cuban Revolution (1959)
    Batista overthrow, 3
    celebration of Triumph of the Revolution, 232
    dates significant to, 67–68
    exporting of, 119–25
    gratitude of, not shown to Ochoa defendants, 239
    historical figures of, 13, 148
Cubans
    declining life style of, 16
    music and dance, Fidel's lack of interest in, 20, 42
    Spanish accent of, 260n
Cuito Cuanavale, Battle of (1987–1988), 130, 224–25, 226
cult of personality, 185–86

Dalia. See Soto del Valle, Dalia
Debray, Régis, 97
de Gaulle, Charles, 34, 88
de la Guardia, Patricio, 103, 200
    arrest of, 234–35
de la Guardia, Tony, 103, 200, 230, 233, 237
    arrest, trial, and execution of, 234, 238, 241
Delgado Castro, José, 50, 87, 240, 243, 246, 250
Departamento América, 100–101
Departamento Chequeo, 156
Departamento II of Cuban counterespionage, 168
Departamento MC. See MC Department
Department of Urban Struggle, 109
diamonds, 200

Díaz, Orestes, 58, 73
Díaz-Balart, Lincoln and Mario, 45
Díaz-Balart, Mirta (Fidel's first wife), 42, 44–45, 48, 147
diplomatic corps, Cuban, and recruitment of agents, 164–69
disinformation, 74–76
Dobao, Roberto, 139, 141
documentation service, Cuban government, 85
dolphins, 1, 4, 9
Dominican Republic, 97
Dorticós, Raúl, 207
dos Santos, José Eduardo, 220
drug trafficking
    official authorization of, 17–18, 200, 228–32, 237
    official investigation, arrests, and trials, 234–40
Duvalier, François, 97–98

Echarte Urbieta, José Ignacio, 110
economy, Cuban
    Basque involvement, 112
    pre-Castro, 21
    Raúl and, 145
    subsidies from Soviet bloc, dried up, 16, 232, 245
Ecuador, 154–55
Eisenhower, Dwight, 6
Ejército Guerrillero del Pueblo, 98
ELN (Ejército de Liberación Nacional), 94, 98, 106
El Once building, Vedado, Havana, 27–30
    stable for cattle in, 29–30
El Salvador, 118, 125
    guerrilla fighters in, 94
embargo, American, 112, 200, 233
emigres, networks of, 257
Enríquez, Miguel, 102–4
Escalante Font, Fabián, 161
Escobar, Pablo, 234

escort (escolta) (Fidel's personal bodyguards), 27, 67–92
    author's position and responsibilities in, 79–86
    duties of, 1–2, 8, 11, 146–47
    Fidel's affinity for, more than for his real family, 67–68
    Fidel's personal interest and say in, 80
    forced to watch the Ochoa execution video, 240–42
    history of, 71–78
    organization of, 72–74
    power given to, 145–46
    professional excellence of, 87
    size of, 187
    tapping of, by Fidel, 159
    training of, 73, 79, 80–81
    travel in four vehicles, 73
escuela de especialistas (specialist school for security training), 34
Espín, Vilma (Raul's wife), 43, 147, 242–43
    acting as Fidel's first lady, 148
    confirms Ochoa's sentence, 239
espionage, 160–63
    foreign, and recruitment of agents, 100–105
Esquipulas II agreement, 127
Esteban Hernández primary school, 53
ETA (Euskadi Ta Askatasuna), 94, 109–12
Etarras (Basque terrorists), 109–12
Ethio-Somali War, 225
exiles and asylum seekers, Cuban, 45, 245
    at Mariel crisis, 161–63
    in Miami, 45, 51, 163, 167, 262–63
explosives, training in, 110
eyes
    hands more dangerous than, 79
    staring into, 190–91

Falklands war (1982), 130
fallout shelters for Fidel and military staff, 89–90
Fangio, Juan Manuel, 23
FARC (Fuerzas Armadas Revolucionarias de Colombia), 94, 98, 106, 110
Fatah, 94
Febres Cordero, León, 155
Federation of Cuban Women, 43, 148
Fernández, Alina (illegitimate daughter), 11, 49–51
  defection to Spain and Miami, 50
  modeling career, 49–50
Fernández, Orlando, 48–49
Fernández, Wilder, 73, 214–15
Figueroa Peraza, Angel, 73
film watching by Fidel, 32–33
Finalé, El Viejo (the Old One), 7, 14
firearms
  shooting posture taught by author, 79–80
  smuggled, 130–31, 189
fishing, Fidel's love of, 171
FLN (Front de Libération Nationale), 98
FMLN (Frente Farabundo Martí para la Liberación Nacional), 94
foco (focalism), 97, 99
Fonseca, Colonel, 242–43
food rationing, 57
Forbes magazine, 193–94, 199
foreign visitors, surveillance of, 157–58
forerunners. See avanzada
Fox, Vicente, 153–54
FPMR (Frente Patriótico Manuel Rodríguez), 94, 104, 150
Fraga, Manuel, 213
France
  a blackmailed diplomat of, 166–69
  secret service of, 87
Francis Pardo, Humberto, 82, 83, 247–48, 253–54
Frank País front, 143

Frank País Orthopedic Hospital, 56
FSLN (Frente Sandinista de Liberación Nacional), 94, 115–17

Gaddafi, Muammar al-, 186, 188, 190–92
GAESA (Grupo de Administración Empresarial S.A.), 145, 149
Gairy, Eric, 124
Galán, Luis Carlos, 88
Galicia, Castro family roots in, 197, 209, 212–13
Gallegos, Gabriel, 1
Gamonal, Alfredo, 72
Gandhi, Indira, 88, 133, 190
Gandhi, Rajiv, 188
García Márquez, Gabriel ("Gabo"), 12–13, 68, 85, 120, 154–55, 170–73, 228
gas, 178–79
Gaviota S.A., 145
Geocuba, 145
Gerena, Victor Manuel, 109
German Democratic Republic (GDR), 12
gifts received by Fidel, 69, 199–200
Gladys (flight attendant), 43
glasnost, 134
gold, 201–2
González, Felipe, 110, 121, 212
Google Earth, 10
Gorbachev, Mikhail, 85, 134–35, 211, 222
Gorostidi Artola, Jokin, 111
Granma (newspaper), 234
Granma (yacht), 22
Grau, Ramón, 22
Grenada, 121
  Cuban Revolution exported to, 124
  U.S. invasion of, 129, 220–21
Group of Personal Friends (Chile), 103
grupo operativo, 33–34
Guardalavaca (Fidel property), 204

Guayasamín, Oswaldo, 154–55
guerrilla fighters
 mixed up with drug trade, 232
 Sierra Madre days, 71–72, 75, 143, 225
 training of, 93–97
 See also individual countries
Guevara, Ernesto "Che," 22, 97, 98, 99, 144, 219, 225
Gutiérrez Fischmann, Juan ("El Chele"), 104–5, 150
Guyana, 35
Guzmán, Abimael, 95
Guzmán, Jaime, 105, 150

Habash, George, 94
Haiti, 97–98
Handal, Schafik, 118
Harare, 186
Havana
 Fidel property in, 203
 pre-Castro, 20
helicopter, Fidel's, 10
Hibbert, Luis Hippolite, 70
Holguín, Fidel property in, 204
homosexual rights, 149
Honecker, Erich, 12
House of Carbonell (Fidel property), 33, 203
House of Cojímar (Fidel property), 203
House of Gallego (Fidel property), 90, 203
House of Punta Brava (Fidel property), 203
house on 160th Street, Playa, Havana (Fidel property), 203
hunting and fishing, Fidel's, 10
Hussein, Saddam, 60, 69, 76, 133

Ibero-American Summit, 209, 246
India, trip to, 205
infidelity, Cuban national sport, 42

information, psychology of extracting, 164
informers, everywhere in Cuba, 256
internationalism, Cuban, 179
International Labour Organization, 195
Interpol, 104
IRA (Irish Republican Army), 94
Iran, 189
Iraq, 60, 69, 189
Ireland, 131
Isla de Pinos (Isla de la Juventud), penitentiary on, 48
Israel, secret service of, 87

Jamaica, 121
January 1 (Triumph of the Revolution), 67
Jaruzelski, Wojciech, 133
jefe de carro, 80
John Paul II, 88
Jorge (bodyguard), 63–65
Jotake rocket launcher, 110
Juan Carlos, King of Spain, 212
July 26 (Moncada barracks attack, 1953), 68
July 26 Movement (M26), 22–23

Kalashnikov rifles, 77
Kennedy, John F., 6, 89*n*
 assassination, 34, 87
Kennedy, Robert F., assassination, 87
Kentucky Fried Chicken, 261
KGB, 132, 160
Khamenei, Ali, 188
Khrushchev, Nikita, 89*n*, 133
Kim Il-sung, 180–86
 works of, in Spanish, 183

La Abuela (mother-in-law, Dalia's mother), 63–65

Laborde, Maria, 47
La Cabaña, 157
La Caleta del Rosario (Fidel property near the Bay of Pigs), 4, 10, 59, 203
La Condesa prison, Güines, 251–55
La Deseada (Fidel property), 10, 203, 259
La Dolita gold mine, 201–2
Lage, Carlos, 5n
lanchero (drug smuggler), 230
Lansky, Meyer, 36
La Orchila, Venezuela, 177–78
La Rinconada property, 147–48
Latin America
  guerrilla movements in, 94, 97, 105–8
  U.S. and, 125, 129, 153–54
La Tranquilidad (Fidel property), 202
Laudelio, Colonel, 248
Leal, Eusebio, 199
Lenin High School, Havana, 55
Leyva Castro, Ricardo, 72
libreta of Fidel's daily actions, 84–85
Libya, 191n
literacy campaign, 52
Llompart, Héctor Rodríguez, 198
López Michelsen, Alfonso, 12
Lorenzo, Orestes, 210–12
Luanda, 218–20
Luciano, Lucky, 21
Lula da Silva, Luiz Inácio, 101–2

Macheteros, 109
Maciques, Abraham, 198
Mainet, Domingo, 64–65, 72, 73, 77, 79, 87, 126, 131, 206, 223, 240, 253
Malan, Magnus, 224
Mandela, Nelson, 212, 225
Manley, Michael, 34, 121
Marcos "assistant commander" (Mexico), 95

Mariel, Cuba, 162–63
Mariel crisis and exodus (1980), 161–63
Martí, José, 179
Martínez, Jorge, 238, 241
Marxism, 38–39, 117
Matanzas, Fidel property in, 203
Matos, Huber, 24
Mayda (author's wife), 35–36
MC Department, 200–201, 232–35
mechanics, car, 76
Medellín cartel, 234, 238
Medical-Surgical Research Center, Havana, 91
Medicuba, 193
Menem, Carlos, 196, 212
Mexico
  Castro brothers' exile in, 22
  and the United States, 153–54
Miami
  Cuban exiles in, 45, 51, 163, 167, 262–63
  exiled dictators in, 119
microphones, hidden, 83, 187, 210
Middle East, 109
MI5 (British), 87
Military Counterintelligence, 249
Ministry of Cuban Revolutionary Armed Forces (MINFAR), 89–90, 150, 194, 235
Ministry of the Interior (MININT), 26, 150, 194, 232, 246–47
  Higher Institute, 38, 163–64
  purge of (1989), 238
Mitterrand, François, 212
Miyar Barruecos, José Miguel ("Chomy") (Fidel's private secretary), 102, 136, 194, 197, 198, 200, 201, 228
M19 movement, 94, 106–8
moles, 166
Moncada barracks assault, Santiago de Cuba, 22, 68, 143
Mons del Llana, Nicolas (cook), 58

Moreno Copul, Pedro (cook), 58
Mossad, 87
Movement of the Revolutionary Left, 102
MRTA (Movimiento Revolucionario Túpac Amaru), 94
Mugabe, Robert, 188
music
  Cuban, 20
  Fidel's lack of interest in, 42
Myers, Walter Kendall, 166

Namibia, 225
Naranjo, José ("Pepín"), 5, 33, 49, 51, 52, 61, 62, 68, 73, 115, 131, 136, 172, 178, 194, 198, 200, 201
national bank, 198
National Front for the Liberation of Angola (FNLA), 218
National Union for the Total Independence of Angola (UNITA), 129–30, 130n
Navarro Wolff, Antonio, 108
Neto, Agostinho, 218–20
Nicaragua, 68, 114–28
  army, 121–23
  Contras in, 225–26
  Cuban Revolution exported to, 119–25
  elections in (1990), 127–28
  guerrilla fighters in, 94
  Sandinista victory in (1979), 113
Non-Aligned Movement summits
  6th, 76, 198
  7th, 205
  8th, 186–92, 222
Noriega, Manuel, 110, 234
North Africa, 109
North Korea, trip to, 180–86
nuclear war, threat of (Cuban missile crisis), 89
Nuevo Laredo, Mexico, 259–60

Núñez Jiménez, Antonio, 13, 68, 228
Núñez Téllez, Carlos, 116–17, 120n

Ochoa, Arnaldo
  in Angola, 39, 225–27
  arrest, trial, and conviction of, 148, 235–39
  contraband handled by, 200
  death by firing squad, 17–18, 241
  drug trafficking involvement, 200
  military genius of, 225–26
  in Nicaragua, 125–26
Ochoa Affair, 232–44
  video of executions, 240–42
oil, 178–79
Olivares, Augusto ("El Perro"), 103–4
Olympic games
  Barcelona, 1992, 212
  Moscow, 1980, 130
Operation Carlota, 219
Organization of American States, Cuba expelled from (1962), 175
Ortega, Daniel, 95, 113, 116, 119, 120n, 127, 188
Ortega, Humberto, 68, 95, 113, 116–17, 119, 120n, 226
Orthodox Party, 21

Padrón, Amado, 238, 241
"pajama plan," 47
Palacio de Convenciones, 198
Palacio de la Revolución, 85, 89, 95, 206–7
  private medical clinic in, 206–7
Palestine Liberation Organization (PLO), 98, 109
Palestinian cause, 94–95, 109
Palme, Olof, 34
  assassination of, 135–38
Panama, 233, 234
Pascal Allende, Andrés, 102–4
Pedro Marrero stadium, Havana, 30

pelicans, 4

Pepín. *See* Naranjo, José

perestroika, 134

Pérez, Bienvenido ("Captain Chicho"), 72

Pérez, Carlos Andrés ("CAP"), 121, 175–76, 178

Pérez, Eloy, 36–37

Pérez Jiménez, Marcos, 173–74

Personal Security service (*seguridad personal*), 26–27, 32–35

  Department no. 1 (security of Fidel), 26. *See also* escort

  Department no. 2 (security of Raúl), 26–27

  Department no. 3 (security of ministers), 27, 72

  three rings of Department no. 1 (*anillos*), 27, 72–74

  See also Unit 160

personal security specialists, training of, 38

Peru

  embassy of, in Havana, and Mariel crisis, 161–62

  guerrilla fighters in, 94

Pham Van Dong, 34

photography, official, 10–11

Pilar (interpreter) ("Pili"), 43

Pinar del Río, 100

  Fidel property in, 202–3

Piñeiro, Manuel ("Barbarroja"), 68, 100–103, 107, 120, 127–28, 228

Pinochet, Augusto, 88, 103–5

  assassination attempt, 150

Pioniera I and *II* (speedboats), 2, 8

plantation rule, in Fidel's Cuba, 195

Playa Girón, 6

Playa Larga, 6

Polisario Front, 95

political asylum

  granted by Fidel, 109, 110

  granted by U.S., 260–62

Pompa Alvarez, Armín, 174–75

Popular Front for the Liberation of Palestine, 94–95

Popular Movement for the Liberation of Angola (MPLA), 218–20

Popular Socialist Party (PSP) (Communist), 72

Portugal, colonial empire of, 218

Prensa Latina, 170

Prior, Carlos, 22

protocol houses, 111, 116, 159

public opinion, monitoring of, 158

Puerto Rico, 109

Pujol, Jordi, 212

Punta Brava, 90

  Dalia's secret home in, 52

Punto Cero (Fidel property in Havana), 10, 56–61, 90, 202

  casa de los misteriosos on, 158–59

  daily life, 59–61

  food raised on, 57, 59–60, 61, 91, 208

  house and furnishings, 57–58

Punto Cero de Guanabo training camp, 93–97, 104, 110

  curriculum of, 99–100

  secrecy of, 95

Puntos de Entrenamiento de Tropas Irregulares (Training Centers for Irregular Troops), 100

Purrial de Vicana I and *II* (fishing boats), 199

Pyongyang, 180

Quayle, Dan, 212

Ramírez Sánchez, Ilich (Carlos the Jackal), 95

Reagan, Ronald, 88, 124, 129

recording, Fidel's practice of, 152–89

  archiving of recordings, 153

  equipment used, 152

  purpose of recordings, 153

recording (*continued*)
    recording of Fidel's visitors,
        85–86, 116
    "Sánchez, ¡no grabes!" ("Sánchez,
        don't record!"), 152, 229
reserva del Comandante, 196–202
Revolution in the Revolution (Debray),
    97
Revuelta, Natalia ("Naty"), 42, 48–49
Reyes Betancourt, Ambrosio, 74
Roberto, Holden, 218
Rodríguez, Carlos Rafael, 136–37,
    188, 228
Rodríguez Araque, Alí, 101
Rodríguez López-Callejas, Luis
    Alberto, 149
Rodríguez Vargas, Pedro, 72
Romero, Jorge Luis, 24–25
Ronda Marrero, Alejandro, 95, 104
Roosevelt, Franklin D., 115
Ruiz Hernández, Henry
    ("Modesto"), 116–17, 119, 120*n*

Sahara, 95
Salvador, Dr. (dentist), 207
San Cayetano (Fidel property), 203–4
Sánchez, Aliette, 246
Sánchez, Celia (*la madrina*), 27–28,
    31–32, 42, 52, 148, 174
Sánchez, Juan Reinaldo (author)
    (1949) upbringing, 19–25
    (1967) grandmother and uncle
        leave for United States, 25
    (1968) meets and marries Mayda,
        35–36
    (1971) in Unit 160 for four years,
        32–33
    (1974) security training, 34–35
    (1976) chosen for Fidel's personal
        escort, 36–38, 79, 220
    (1994) retirement claim, 247
    (1994) loses his job in the escort,
        246–47

    (1994) arrested and detained,
        248–55
    (1994) appears before military
        court, and sentenced, 252–53
    (1996) released, 255
    (2008) escape to U.S., 36, 257–60
    children of, 36
    eavesdropping by, 230
    excellent record of, as Fidel's
        bodyguard, 16–17
    family of, 86, 262
    FBI file of, 261–62
    firearms skill, 19–20
    first encounters Fidel, 28–29
    good at sports, 24
    the idea for this book, 255
    loss of confidence in Fidel, 132,
        134, 231
    manual work experience, 25
    military training of, 25–26
    not a drinker, joke regarding, 137
    once unshakeable belief in the
        Cuban Revolution, 86, 263–64
    position in Fidel's escort, 79–86
    promotions and medals, 83–84
    retirement pension, 255
    retirement request, imprisoned
        for, 18
    training routine, 81
Sandinistas, 68, 113, 115–28
    guerrilla movement, 115–18
    loss of power (1980 onward),
        124–28
Sandino, Augusto, 114
San Martín, José de, 105
Santa Clara air base, 2
Santa María del Mar, Havana, Fidel
    property in, 203
Santiago de Cuba, 69
    Fidel property in, 204
Savimbi, Jonas, 130*n*, 218
secrecy, Fidel's, reasons for, 43
secret services abroad, 100–105
security training, 34–35

Selman, Eugenio, 5, 73, 107, 131, 200, 207, 223, 228, 240
Sendero Luminoso, 94
Sermar, 145
Servicio Automotriz S.A, 145
shadowing and countershadowing, 163–64, 258
Shakur, Assata, 109
Shannon Airport, Ireland, Fidel's stop for Irish coffee in, 130–31
Sierra Maestra, 3, 22, 27
  guerrilla days, 71–72, 75, 143, 225
slavery, modern variant on, in Cuba, 195
Smirnova, Natalia, 46, 62
Socarras and Álvarez (car mechanics), 76
socialism, Soviet model of, 134
Socialist International, 175
socialist youth movement (Cuba), 72
Somoza, Anastasio "Tacho," 88, 113–15
Somoza, Tacho II, 115
  assassination of, 119
Soto del Valle, Dalia (wife)
  activities of, 53, 80
  called "La Compañera," 61
  cheating on Fidel, 63–66
  children of, 51–57
  daily life, 8, 10, 11, 15
  and the family, 197
  Fidel's cheating on, 42
  home of, in Punto Cero, 58, 60–61
  marriage to Fidel, 28, 78
  and Ochoa, 240
  personality of, 60–61
  secrecy of, 5, 33, 43–44
  security of, 90
  told of Fidel's health crisis, 215
South Africa
  in Angolan war, 218, 223–25
  loss in Angola, consequences, 225
Soviet bloc, 133
Soviet Union. See USSR

Spain, 110–11, 121
  trips to, 209, 246
Special Period in Time of Peace (1992), 16, 245
special troops, attached to the escort, 187
Special Works Program, 25
spies and agents
  external, 160
  internal, 158
Stasi, 160
State Security Department (G2), 72, 158, 256
Stroessner, Alfredo, 119
Sweden, 135–38

Tabayito (Fidel property), 204
tapping, 158–60
Técnica (technical department of the secret police), 82, 156–58
  also known as State Security, G2, or Department K, 156
  functions KC, KT, KJ, and KR of, 156–57
  in Mariel crisis, 161–62
Tecnotex, 145
Thälmann, Ernst, 12
Thatcher, Margaret, 131
Titolo, Paolo, 149
torture and abuse, in prisons, 249, 251
Tricontinental Conference (Trico), 98
trips abroad by Fidel, 81–83, 130–36, 173–74, 176–78, 180–92, 205, 209, 246
  advance parties of, 82–83, 245
tropas (shock troops), 109–10
Trujillo, Rafael Leónidas, 97
Turcios Lima, Luis Augusto, 98
Turiguano, Isle of, Fidel property on, 203
Turner, Ted, 12
turtles, 9

Ubre Blanca (cow), 30
Unit 160 of the Personal Security
    service, 32–33, 55, 58, 68–69,
    157
UNITA, 218, 222
United Fruit Company, 21
United States
    and Africa, 129, 220
    attempts on Fidel, 52
    Black Panthers in, 95, 109
    drug problem in, abetted by Fidel,
        232, 234
    Fidel's feelings about, 129
    imperialism of, defeated at Bay of
        Pigs, 6
    Interest Section in Havana, 157
    and Latin America, 125, 129,
        153–54
    relations with Cuba, 157
    secret service of, 87
urban combat, training for, 81
Urtiaga Martínez, José Angel,
    110
Uruguay, 130
USSR
    alliance with Cuba, 6, 46, 133
    and Angola, 219–20, 221–22
    collapse and dissolution of (1991),
        16, 245
    Fidel's visits to, 130–35
    gas, 178
    poverty of, 134
    secret service of, 87

subsidies to Cuba, 232, 245
war doctrine, not suited to Angola,
    221–22

Valdés, Ramiro, 34, 131
Valle de Picadura dairy farm, 139
Varadero
    airport, smuggling from, 237–38
    Fidel property in, 203
Venezuela, 21, 101, 121, 173–79
    gas and oil, 178–79
    guerrilla movement, 94, 175, 225
Vera, Juana (interpreter) ("Juanita"),
    43, 131, 175, 183, 205, 210
Vesco, Robert, 62–63
Vietnam, 98
Vietnam War, 135
Villalobos, Joaquín, 118
Vilma. See Espín, Vilma
Vizcaino, René, 73

Walters, Barbara, 12
Wheelock, Jaime, 116–17, 119, 120n
Williams, Eric, 34

Zapata, Orlando, 102
Z Department (later MC
    Department), 233
Zimbabwe, 186
Zorada (maid), 58

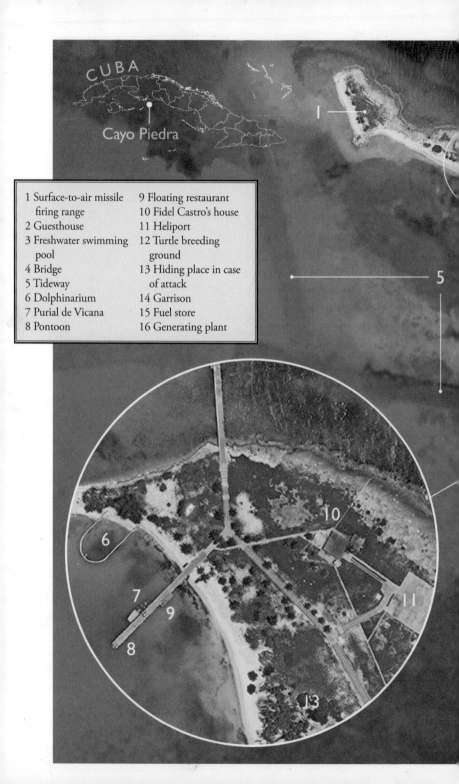

CUBA

Cayo Piedra

1 Surface-to-air missile firing range	9 Floating restaurant
2 Guesthouse	10 Fidel Castro's house
3 Freshwater swimming pool	11 Heliport
4 Bridge	12 Turtle breeding ground
5 Tideway	13 Hiding place in case of attack
6 Dolphinarium	14 Garrison
7 Purial de Vicana	15 Fuel store
8 Pontoon	16 Generating plant